# The Big E

## A Saga of Success...
## and Stolen Promise

To Nora —
With gratitude for your
friendship,. support and
encouragement during
"the best of times" and
"the worst of times."

Paul

**Paul A. Willax**
**Retired Chairman of the Board**
**and Chief Executive Officer of**
**Empire of America FSB**

# The Big E

## A Saga of Success...
## and Stolen Promise

The rise and unnecessary fall of Empire of America,
a community bank that served
savers, borrowers, and investors
for one hundred and thirty-six years

**Paul A. Willax**

Retired Chairman of the Board
and Chief Executive Officer of
Empire of America FSB

Published by
Brass Tacks Publishing
Electromedia Technologies LLC
Naples, Florida

# The Big E
## A Saga of Success and Stolen Promise

## Brass Tacks Publishing
An imprint of
## Electromedia Technologies LLC
Naples, Florida

For information
E-mail: *Willax@BrainFoodToGo.com*
Web site: *www.BrainFoodToGo.com*

**ISBN: 978-0-9815692-3-9**

Printed in the United States of America

## COVERS

**Front cover:** The original 1890 rendering of the proposed Erie County Savings Bank Building on Shelton Square that accompanied the bank's application for a building permit from the City of Buffalo, New York.

**Back cover:** Photograph of the bank's Main Place Office Tower in Buffalo, New York, which was opened in April, 1969.

# DEDICATION

This book was written to honor the customers, team members, Trustees, Directors, and shareholders of Empire of America who, over the course of nine generations, energized an institution dedicated to serving the financial needs of people in every walk of life.

It is dedicated to Oscar Willax, Harlan Swift, Austin Murphy, Bill Schreiber, and Dan Brown, the bankers who played such important roles in my personal and professional lives.

It was written especially to honor the memory of Harlan Swift, the man who made it possible for me to partake in the exciting adventures of the Erie County Savings Bank and Empire of America FSB. Harlan was a leader in our community and in the savings industry. But, more importantly, to me, he was a gentleman, a mentor, a motivator, and a teacher. He was a moral man who set the standard for all Empire team members throughout his tenure. His legacy was a continuing spirit that empowered every Big E team member to strive and succeed during "the best of times" and "the worst of times."

Of course, Os, my dad, richly deserves a special tribute, also. He taught me the values of integrity, hard work, loyalty, perseverance, kindness to others, and humility. He was a role model to be revered both at home and at his "other home" of fifty years, The Marine Trust Co. – Jefferson-Utica Branch. I wish he could have lived longer so I could have learned more.

The tale herein is also told for the benefit of my daughter, Jennifer, and my son, Jonathan, who deserve to know what Dad did when he "went to work."

# Also by Paul Willax

## Books

LotzaLists for Business Owners
LotzaLists for Business Managers
LotzaLists for Bank Branch Managers
Brass Tacks Tips for Business Owners
LotzaLists for Your Campus to Career Crossover
LotzaTips for Creating a Brass Tacks Business Plan
LotzaTips for Creating a Brass Tacks Strategic Plan
LotzaTips for Leaders in Business
The Business Ownership Audit
Going *with* the Gold
Monster in the Wilderness  (Editor/contributor)
Meeting the Challenge to a Free Society  (Co-editor/contributor)
An Economic Analysis of Buffalo Area Industry
The Use of Economic Indicators in Dynamic Business Planning
The Practical Research Handbook  (Co-editor/contributor)
The Asset Securitization Handbook  (Contributor)

## eBooks

LotzaTips for Creating a Brass Tacks Strategic Plan
LotzaLists for Your Campus to Career CrossOver
LotzaTips for Leaders in Business
LotzaTips for Managing Your To Do Lists

## Monographs

Syllabus for College Level Courses in Data Processing; Student Guide to Graduate Study in Business Administration; The Role of Radio and Television in the Business Community; Introduction to Forecasting; Management Simulation (Co-author); New York State – Its Public Machinery and Its Economic  Engine; An Economic Analysis of New York State - Its Metropolitan Areas; A Survivor's Guide to Coping with the Future; The Four Ps of Marketing; Home Video/Audio – A New Marketing Channel; *Boss Bashing* – A Tool for Executive Self-Evaluation; *MatchPoints* – An Exercise for Entrepreneurial Couples.

## To learn more about these books visit
### *www.BrainFoodToGo.com*

# TABLE OF CONTENTS

# INTRODUCTION

*It was the best of times, it was the worst of times, it was the age of wisdom, it was the age of foolishness, it was the epoch of belief, it was the epoch of incredulity, it was the season of Light, it was the season of Darkness, it was the spring of hope, it was the winter of despair, we had everything before us, we had nothing before us, we were all going direct to Heaven, we were all going direct the other way.*
Charles Dickens

This book presents a chronicle of the events that contributed to the growth, success, and unfortunate demise of the Erie County Savings Bank, a venerable financial institution which was established in Buffalo, New York in 1854. During the following one hundred and thirty-six years, the bank served multitudes of savers, borrowers, and investors in almost every state of the nation. In 1977, the bank's name was modified to Erie Savings Bank, and in 1982 it was changed to Empire of America FSB. It has also borne a memorable nickname – the *Big E* – which was, for many, the bank's most endearing identity.

A mere memorial plaque would not adequately reflect the bank's extraordinary accomplishments. Your chronicler, who served as Chairman of the Board and Chief Executive Officer of the Big E, believes that a true appreciation of the value that the bank contributed to society is best attained by reviewing the strivings, struggles, and successes which enabled it to provide worthwhile benefits to countless people and communities across the country.

Accordingly, one objective of this book is to provide an account of the exciting rise of Empire of America.

Hard work and a passion to please enabled the bank to become one of America's largest and most innovative providers of financial services. Its strategy of growth, product development, and diversification enabled it to deliver – until 1990 – new and better ways by which families, individuals, businesses, and communities could enrich their financial futures. Ultimately, it became one of the ten largest savings banks in the nation.

From its origins, the Erie County Savings Bank pledged to "do things of import," an oath it honored for 136 years. Each successive year found it offering even greater promise for the future... until another kind of promise was broken. As a consequence, the bank's great hopes and dreams for those it touched were ultimately denied.

Therefore, another objective of this book is to present a narrative of events that shaped the unfortunate fall of this revered institution. The following pages document a demise that was caused, in large part, by governments that dabbled destructively and uncaringly in an inherently free marketplace in order to advance problematic social and political agendas.

Most importantly, however, this book offers the story of a band of dedicated bankers who eschewed a government bailout in favor of a "sweat equity" workout. The work ethic and dedication of its team members enabled the bank to meet and master huge challenges. Their incredible performance during the bank's final decades is probably best characterized by the exhortation *"never give up!"* Their cups were always half-full; there would always be one more day to savor energy from another sip.

This book has been published, *first and foremost,* to ensure that the Big E's employee and shareholder alumni have a documented account of the amazing things they accomplished. While the unfortunate outcome of our efforts was disheartening, our journey was exhilarating and astonishingly productive.

### Success and stolen promise

The subtitle of this book alludes to "success" and "stolen promise." To be sure, many successes are proudly described in the following pages. The intimation of snatched promise, however, deserves some prefatory explanation.

The entire Empire "family" – customers, team members, shareholders, directors, vendors, and the denizens of the communities it served across America – hung in there until the bitter end. They did so because of *"promise."*

"What promise?" you ask.

Actually, there were two kinds of promise and each, while related to the other, is defined differently.

The first "promise" consisted of Empire of America's vision for the future, a place where the financial needs and dreams of "people of modest means" (as cited in its original application for a banking charter) could be abundantly satisfied.

Dictionaries describe this kind of promise as: "an indication of a successful prospect or future; a basis for expectation; the quality of potential excellence; the traits of someone who will probably do great things; having a lot of potential." The French elegantly express it as *"donner de belles espérances."*

Such promise was artfully illustrated by British author James Allen who opined in the 19th century, *"Your vision is the promise of what you shall one day be."*

Lamentably, the Big E's promise was extinguished – *stolen* – by circumstances beyond its control despite valiant efforts to preserve it. Importantly, those conditions were neither inevitable nor inexorable. Governmental legislators, policymakers, and regulators did much to create those circumstances and little to effectively resolve them.

The most detrimental intrusions of public policy-makers and regulators were dedicated to perpetuating – against all economic practicality – the historical, extremely delimited role of savings institutions (also referred to herein as "thrifts") as the providers of residential housing finance. Forces in the public sector – and within the industry – wanted thrifts to preserve and perpetuate the days of yore when they were small institutions that concentrated almost exclusively on serving local mortgage needs.

For over one hundred years, this was a realistic role for thrifts. During that period, the nation's economic infrastructure enabled thrifts to operate like businesses while they, simultaneously, accommodated society's needs for housing finance. Their staid "intermediation" business model was able to provide revenues sufficient to support their operational activities.

However, as time passed, savers' habits changed and direct competition from other financial service providers began to siphon customers and revenues from savings institutions. As a result, the industry could no longer sustain housing finance as its exclusive mission. It needed new customer service capacities, lending powers, capital acquisition techniques, and scope in order to accommodate emerging market realities while also continuing its traditional functions. But legislators and regulators, under pressure from various segments of the financial services industry, failed to provide the tools necessary to enable thrifts to restructure and reinvigorate themselves. Highly-trumpeted public policies for industry reform were, in reality, flawed and came to nothing. They demonstrated, once again, that it is well-nigh impossible for public agencies to successfully manipulate the fortunes of private institutions in a free market.

Decades of ill-founded meddling by the government to preserve functional and competitive patterns of the past spawned laws, regulations, and policies that ultimately conspired to extinguish Empire's great *promise* for the future.

The second kind of "promise" alluded to in this book was contractual in nature. In Empire's case, the fulfillment of this type of promise was essential to the realization of the first type.

In this context, a promise is: "a declaration, written or verbal, which gives to the person to whom it is made a right to expect or to claim the performance or forbearance of a specified act; to afford reason to expect; to cause hope; to give assurance by a binding declaration; to give ground to expect good."

In the early 1980s, Empire was given promises – in exchange for significant services rendered – that, if honored by the government, would have ensured the bank's survival and success. In relatively short order, however, these contractual promises were unilaterally annulled – *stolen* – by the promisor. What had originally suited the promisor's (i.e. the federal government's) critical needs was no longer compatible with the promisor's fears. It worried that its innovative collaboration with Empire might entail too much effort, risk, and reputational peril in the long-run. Consequently, with a single piece of legislation – which a subsequent adjudication determined was not legal – the federal government vitiated covenants with Empire that were absolutely essential to the bank's survival and to the realization of its hard-earned promise for the future. With the stroke of a Presidential pen, the rules of the "game" were changed.

An observation made centuries earlier by Italian diplomat and author Niccolo Machiavelli summed it up: *"The promise given was a necessity of the past: the word broken is a necessity of the present."*

Hence, in Empire's saga, a promise stolen resulted in stolen promise.

President Ronald Reagan characterized the situation a bit more spiritedly in 1982: *"If you go to bed with the government, expect more than a good night's sleep."*

While this book provides an overview of the origins and development of Empire of America, a principal focus is on the events that led to its untimely and unnecessary demise in 1990. Cicero, the Roman philosopher, once observed that there is more to be learned from the causes of events than from events themselves. Accordingly, this tome examines in detail the *causes* of Empire's disheartening demise.

Appropriately, the overarching theme of this chronicle is the bank's courageous responses to the enormous opportunities and challenges that confronted it during its incredible era of success and stolen promise.

**An invitation**

Given the paucity of available records from the last years of the bank's operation, coupled with your author's personal desire to employ a wide perspective in which to interpret events, it has taken twenty-five years to compile this book. Procrastination contributed a bit to the delay, too. In addition, I wanted sufficient time to pass so that the biasing angers and irritations of events that had haunted me for years could subside and give way to constructive reminiscence. Further, I didn't feel the need to gain rapid reputational redemption. I wanted to spend adequate time assembling the facts surrounding Empire's demise so that our understandably aggrieved shareholders would have access to an informative history... not just a contemporary refutation.

Needless to say, despite my effort to rustle-up and remember facts and figures from almost a quarter-century of association with Empire, there likely are some errors, misinterpretations, and omissions in my recounting. When you find them, please let me know. In compiling this tome – and during my years with Empire – I always endeavored to adhere to my mother's admonition, *"Paul, just do your best."* This book is the best I could do... *so far.* Your input could make it better.

As I wrote this chronicle, I never felt I had enough personal stories and reminiscences from other people who "saw that; did that" during the Empire era. Therefore, I hope you will accept this undertaking as a "work in progress" and feel free to contribute your recollections to its eventual "completion."

They, along with any suggestions you have for enhancing the accuracy, relevancy, completeness, or readability of this book, can be sent to me at *Willax@BrainFoodToGo.com.* Such input would be invaluable in the compilation of another edition.

Of course, readers will make their own judgments about the goals, strategies, and tactics employed by Empire during its struggles. So, I invite you to tender your sentiments, especially as they pertain to what the bank might have done differently during its struggles. Such comments could be fruitfully employed in future writings, particularly if this book is eventually recast as a "case study" for educational use.

In the words of Samuel Johnson, "A writer only begins a book. A reader finishes it."

Who knows how many revised editions it will take to make this book the kind of homage that the Big E family deserves?

*Chapter One*

# THE FIRST HUNDRED YEARS

## The foundations

To facilitate a true appreciation of the genesis of Empire of America and the principles that guided its growth and success, this Chapter will review the historical milieu from which savings institutions, as we know them today, emerged. (NOTE: In this book, the terms "savings bank," "savings and loan association," "S&L," "thrift institution," "thrift," and "savings institution" are used interchangeably.)

Because of the savings industry's traditional role in home financing, these pages will also provide some insight into the evolution of homeownership in the United States.

The work of Dr. David Mason, a business historian with banking experience, contributed greatly to the historical overview in this Chapter. In his book, <u>From Building and Loans to Bailouts</u>, he reflects knowledgeably on the origins of the thrift industry. Since there are very few reliable sources for this kind of background information, his work provides an invaluable window to an important part of American history.

According to Mason, the savings industry traces its origins to the British building society movement that emerged in the late eighteenth century. American "thrifts" (known that time as "building and loans," "B&Ls" or "building societies") shared the same basic goal of their foreign counterparts – "to help working-class men and women save for the future and purchase homes."

Traditionally, a person with accumulated savings did not become a *customer* of a thrift, per se, but was accommodated as *member* who *subscribed* to a specified number of *shares* in the thrift enterprise. Such shares were paid for over time in regular monthly installments. (This business model prevailed in the savings and loan industry into the mid-20th century.)

When a reasonable number of these payments had been made, a member was allowed to borrow funds to buy a home. The amount each member was allowed to borrow could equal as much as the face value of the *subscribed* shares, so his (very few borrowers were female) loan was actually an advance on the unpaid shares. The member repaid the loan by continuing to make the regular monthly share payments as well as loan interest.

Such earned interest plus any other fees – minus operating expenses – contributed to the accumulated "surplus" of the participating savings institution. It was from this pool of funds that a "dividend" (a/k/a interest) was paid to each member.

These savings and borrowing practices prevailed throughout the 19th century, while *banking*, per se, was available only to those who had appreciable assets or wealth that needed safekeeping. Banking services were provided by institutions which were very much akin to today's commercial banks.

In the United Kingdom, the first savings bank was founded in 1810 by the Reverend Henry Duncan, Doctor of Divinity, the minister of Ruthwell Church in the Dumfriesshire, Scotland.

The first such institution in the United States, the Philadelphia Saving Fund Society, was established in 1816. It was the beginning of a "movement" that would become widespread by the 1830s. Initially, its growth would occur primarily in mid-western and eastern states.

In the second half of the 19th century, urban growth – and a concomitant demand for housing occasioned by the Second Industrial Revolution – caused the number of thrifts to explode. According to Mason, by 1890, cities like Philadelphia, Chicago, and New York each had over three hundred thrifts; B&Ls could be found in every state of the union, as well as the territory of Hawaii.

These B&L organizations – which also became known as savings associations, cooperative banks (in New England), and homestead associations (in Louisiana) – provided a safe refuge for accumulated funds and access to loans with which homes could be purchased. With respect to home financing, they gave primary attention to single-family residences. Over time, these hybrid institutions became increasingly proficient at those tasks and developed a loyal following.

Prior to the arrival of such financial entities, mortgages were not offered by traditional banks but, rather, were provided by insurance companies. The kind of mortgages they facilitated differed greatly from the home loans that are familiar today. Most early mortgages were short-term with some kind of a balloon payment at the end of the term. Typically, they were interest-only loans which did not facilitate any reduction in the principal of the loan as each payment was made. As such, a typical borrower was perpetually in debt and became enmeshed in a continuous cycle of re-financings. It was commonplace for a person to lose his home through foreclosure when he was unable to make the balloon payment at the end of the term of his loan.

By the mid-1800s, *savings banks* were beginning to proliferate in the United States. In form and function, they combined the features of both eleemosynary and business organizations. They were created by community leaders to primarily serve the needs of small savers whose unique financial needs were not perceived as an important market by commercial banks. But they also had to generate revenue (like businesses did) to support their operations.

The nation's poor immigrants, laborers, and farmers had paltry incomes but, because of their ethnic, cultural, and religious backgrounds, they were, nevertheless, inclined to habitually put aside a small portion of their weekly wages as savings. Prior to the advent of savings banks, such funds were typically squirreled away unsafely in mattresses and the proverbial "coffee cans" where they could be easily accessed during family financial crises or "lapses in frugality."

To give these hard-working savers a safe place to hoard their nest eggs, civic leaders founded "savings banks" as specialized repositories for their funds. The savings bank's founders believed they could help keep accumulated wealth within the community in which it originated rather than having it sent back to foreign homelands. In a back-handed way, these banks also served to aid the interests of commercial bankers who didn't want the expense of catering to low-balance savers.

Large, fort-like structures with imposing vestibules, massive vaults, and thick stone walls with turrets were constructed by savings banks to give the impression of security. After all, the safety of the funds they warehoused was extremely important to savers of very modest means, especially immigrants. These institutions adopted names that reinforced savers' roles in society. *Emigrant Savings Bank* was a good example. Popular names included comforting appellations like *Bowery*, *Farmers & Mechanics*, and *Seamen's*. Names like *Five Cent Savings Bank* and *Dollar Savings Bank* assured small savers that their meager set-asides were welcome.

The full-time managers of savings banks were watched over by Trustees who functioned as overseers and carried out their duties at no cost to the institutions.

These institutions grew rapidly and soon proved proficient at aggregating funds from many savers in order to make sizeable loans to individual customers for the purpose of acquiring homes. This process of procuring funds from one segment of the populace and, subsequently, aggregating them into bundles of funds that were provided under different terms and conditions to other segments was referred to as "intermediation."

Without the intermediation services provided by specialized thrift institutions, the subsistence wage level of the average worker made it impossible for him or her to muster funds in an amount sufficient to purchase a home.

Privately-owned residences were a stabilizing force in the early American economy, and home ownership was encouraged by communities' social and political leaders. Home ownership financing was especially beneficial during families' formative years when their members were young and unable to accumulate the kind of savings necessary to make a cash purchase. Here is where the up-and-coming savings banks were able to provide a uniquely valuable service. By redeploying the aggregated, small denomination savings of many workers into larger accumulations, these banks could make adequate funds available to interested – young – home buyers in the form of mortgage loans. Such lending helped build new neighborhoods and communities. It also helped generate a modest return that could, in turn, be paid on savers' deposits. Savings institutions quickly became crucial links in the important process of wealth accumulation and home ownership.

Savings banks and savings and loan associations attracted many customers because they were seen as non-profit, "cooperative," or "mutual" institutions. Furthermore, they were scrupulously overseen by reliable member-representatives. These entities were generally small (most holding less than $100,000 in deposits which were provided by fewer than five-hundred members). As such, they were greatly appreciated as *local* institutions that focused on catering to the especial needs of lower-income, aspiring homeowners.

The new banks also offered accommodating mortgage formats that appealed to prospective homeowners of the day. Prior to the turn-of-the-century, the typical mortgages offered by banks and life insurance companies were short-term, i.e. three to five years. The payments on these loans consisted of *interest only,* meaning the *entire* principal was due at maturity. On the other hand, the new types of mortgages now available at thrift institutions were longer term (eight to twelve years) and allowed the borrower to repay *both* the principal and interest over time. This type of loan, known as an "amortizing mortgage," became commonplace by the late nineteenth century.

Emerging savings institutions and established commercial banks also differed with respect to the nature of their balance sheet liabilities. The liabilities of commercial banks were primarily short-term deposits (from checking accounts) that could be withdrawn on demand by account-holders. In contrast, thrift deposits (commonly called "share accounts") were longer term. Moreover, because thrift members were considered owners of their association, savings institutions typically had the legal right to take up to thirty days to honor any withdrawal request and even charge penalties for early withdrawals. This practice augmented the stability of thrift institutions and enabled them to make longer-term, more affordable mortgage loans.

Further, the bulk of any "profits" or surpluses that were generated in the process were distributed as direct credits to depositors' savings balances, thus, affording them the benefit of compounded interest.

By and large, both savers and borrowers were pleased with these arrangements because thrifts provided home purchase loans while simultaneously safeguarding savers' funds.

By mid-century, home ownership was within the reach of average Americans. Mutual savings banks had introduced savings accounts that entailed neither membership nor a waiting period for withdrawals. Account-holders were no longer "members" but were routinely referred to as "depositors."

In his book, Dr. Mason observes that, "According to thrift leaders, they not only helped people become better citizens by making it easier to own a home, they also taught the habits of systematic savings and mutual cooperation which strengthened personal morals. This attitude of social uplift was so pervasive that the official motto of the national thrift trade association was *'The American Home. Safeguard of American Liberties'* and its leaders consistently referred to their businesses as being part of a 'movement' as late as the 1930s."

Notwithstanding this eleemosynary function, savings institution managers viewed their organizations primarily as business-type enterprises since they knew that positive earnings had to be generated in order to sustain operations.

**New bank on the block**

By 1854, the relatively new City of Buffalo was flourishing. It was aggressively building upon the spurt of growth it enjoyed following the opening of the Erie Canal in 1832, the year in which Buffalo was incorporated as a city within the Erie County.

(The community was originally founded by the French in 1758. Shortly after the beginning of the 19th century, it was organized as a formal settlement called New Amsterdam.)

Steamboat activity on the Great Lakes was intensifying. Ships of all shapes and sizes unloaded rich cargoes in the port of Buffalo and facilitated an unprecedented growth in trade, which further contributed to the expansion of the city.

Natural gas was being used for heating and for illumination on the streets, inside homes, and in commercial buildings.

New Year's Day 1854 marked the beginning of a new era as a more comprehensive and progressive Buffalo city charter took hold. City wards were increased in number from five to thirteen and the number of city aldermen grew to twenty-six from the previous ten. Buffalo, a tough city that had survived the British invasion in 1759 and an all-out war with Britain in 1812, was on the move.

Black Rock, which was Buffalo's one-time rival as a municipality and a competitor for the designation as western terminus of the Erie Canal, was annexed to the city and added 23,000 acres to Buffalo's territory. Well over $3 million in value was added to the aggregate worth of Buffalo's real estate in just one year.

It wasn't a time of wild speculation such as that which led up to the crash of the financial empire of Buffalonian Benjamin Rathburn in 1836 and resulted in the national Depression of 1837. The hard-learned lessons of those inflationary years were kept in mind and widely adhered to. The economic growth experienced in 1854 and the years immediately following was sound and judicious.

Nevertheless, a study of the economic conditions in Buffalo during the 1850s produced two significant conclusions, viz. there was a pronounced lack of capital; and, there was a rapidly-increasing need for financial assistance to small investors, home builders, and businesses attempting to keep pace with the expansion of the city.

A handful of highly-motivated, public-spirited men recognized this need for capital aggregation, and they embarked on a project that eventually led to the founding of a new savings bank that would serve the residents of Erie County in western New York.

As a result of their efforts, on January 23, 1854, New York State Senator James Earl Putnam introduced a bill for the creation of the Erie County Savings Bank. On April 29th of the same year, the bill was passed by the New York State Legislature and signed by Governor John Seymour. The bill proclaimed that the bank's general business was to "receive and deposit such sums as may be from time to time offered therefore by mariners, clerks, mechanics, laborers, miners, servants, and others."

The law office of E. Carlton Sprague at 190 Main Street was the setting for a meeting of thirteen organizers on the evening of June 17, 1854. Their intention was to build a financial institution that would serve the needs of savers and fund the needs of borrowers – principally home buyers – in Buffalo and Erie County. At the gathering, Noah P. Sprague was elected Chairman and B.A. Manchester was elected Secretary. The Honorable William A. Bird was the unanimous choice for President of the bank. Overall governance of this institution was to be provided by a Board of Trustees.

One of the first acts of these Trustees was the election of Cyrus P. Lee as Secretary and Treasurer of the Board at a salary not to exceed $1,500 per year for five years "if the bank should earn sufficient monies and be able to pay it."

At the time of his election, Cyrus Lee was Buffalo's Assistant Postmaster and was well-known throughout the city. Service to the Erie County Savings Bank was to be Mr. Lee's life's work. He and President Bird held positions of deep influence in the community through their service to the bank (which became identified by the townsfolk of that decade as "Bird's Bank" or "Lee's Bank").

In one of his early reports to the community, the bank's first Secretary summed up the bank's "mission statement" by proclaiming: "We believe in common with all our contemporaries, that the Erie County Savings Bank will produce much good. It will induce men of resources to save money they might otherwise dissipate and squander. It will be the means of placing many an honest family in independence and comfort. All amounts received on deposit will enable workers and others whose earnings are small, to lay up a little at a time, until the cents which might have been spent imprudently will reach a sum sufficient to be of material value to a poor family; the institution is entirely sound and trustworthy and will doubtless do a very large business."

At 9 AM on September 1, 1854, the bank opened its doors for the first time. It occupied an unpretentious 12 foot by 44 foot office at the corner of Main and North Division Streets in Buffalo, enjoying a three-year lease calling for rent of $500 per year. A safe was also rented. The Erie County Savings Bank would soon make its name well known and would quickly become the "preferred Buffalo banking institution."

Deposits were accepted in amounts from $1 to $1,000 upon which the bank was to pay a 6% dividend from the net profits derived from all sums on deposit. The minimum deposit accepted was $1, but the bank also offered the "ten-cent system" which permitted deposits of lesser amounts. For these small accounts, a record card was retained for all deposits under $1, and when a depositor's account reached $1, a regular passbook was issued.

For more than 125 years after the founding of the bank, the "passbook" was the primary device used to keep depositors informed about the balance of their accounts and the interest earned on those balances during quarterly periods. In this modern, electronic age, it is difficult to appreciate the fact that each deposit and withdrawal – no matter how small – of every customer was recorded along with its date by pen and ink. These notations were made in a 3-inch by 5-inch paper pamphlet (i.e. passbook) which was provided to the depositor for safekeeping. Identical information was simultaneously inscribed on a bank ledger. This was the job of a bank teller. In fact, the word "teller" was coined because one of this individual's responsibilities was to "tell" a depositor about his or her current financial status with the bank. For over a century, the passbook would be the primary means by which entitlements were recorded on behalf of the depositor and obligations were acknowledged by the bank.

In May of 1857, the bank moved to Main and Erie Streets where it remained for ten years.

Between 1855 and 1908, interest rates paid on deposits ranged from a high of 6% to a low of 3.5%. This "dividend rate" began trending downward as the bank began to prove itself and give evidence of prudent conduct. The going rate was generally offered up to a specific, stipulated dollar balance in an account. Interestingly, funds on deposit that exceeded a certain amount earned a *lesser* rate. No dividend was paid on "excess deposit funds," i.e. balances over $3,000.

This payment policy favored savers of small means, the type of unexceptional, frugal accumulator who was shunned at that time by commercial banks. Indeed, as Erie's charter reflected, one of the principal reasons that savings banks were established was "to provide a place for the people of *modest* means to save their money *safely*."

Despite the fact that commercial bankers did not want to serve the kind of customer that was attracted to savings banks, they did their utmost to make life difficult for new savings institutions. For example, in November 1859, a scant five years after Erie's founding, one or more commercial banks began a surreptitious publicity campaign against savings banks for what they alleged was "a payment of businessmen in the same manner as did the banks of discount and deposit." "Depositors' checks," they claimed "are paid as readily when presented without as with the passbook; inducements are held out by high rates of interest and otherwise to obtain deposits from capitalists, corporations, and others controlling unemployed monies..."

This was one of the first signs of commercial banks' eagerness to protect their turf, a sentiment that would prevail – and intensify – from then on.

To gain the attention of customers and, more importantly, regulators, the letter of complaint that voiced their concerns – which did not specify any savings bank by name – was widely circulated. It cited at great length the "misdeeds" of savings banks. The document, which was printed in full in the Commercial Advertiser, a prominent local newspaper, argued that savings banks "were not created to serve the convenience of businessmen or capitalists, much less to transact the ordinary business of banks of deposit; nor were they designed to furnish men with capital or those controlling unemployed funds an easy mode of investing their money at an interest nearly equal to the legal right, without risk or expense. So far as they offer to capitalists and businessmen such facilities, they work in absolute and serious injury to the commercial, industrial, and pecuniary interest of the city."

Needless to say, the Erie County Savings Bank responded with an equally self-serving (but arguably more rational) broadside.

The press noted that, in those early years, the dedicated Trustees and employees of the Erie County Savings Bank possessed "strong shoulders." "These stalwart bankers witnessed the closings and mergers of many other banks in Buffalo during its formative years but, because of its careful management, Erie County Savings Bank saw a steady growth in deposits.

By then, the proliferation of railroads and a steady westward movement of population and commerce prompted Buffalo's leaders to anticipate a possible drop in economic activity. So, in 1860, members of the business community banded together to form the Association for the Encouragement of Manufacturing, which proudly trumpeted the city's "52 miles of paved streets, 48 miles of a sewage system, and a total of 260 miles of roads." The Association's advertising circulars were sent to all parts of the country in an ongoing effort to urge businesses to locate in Buffalo. Such promotional efforts were undertaken frequently.

This kind of aggressive marketing, coupled with a surge in economic activity occasioned by the Civil War, offset fears of a local economic decline and actually contributed to tremendous growth for the Erie County Savings Bank. In contrast to the devastating personal tragedies occasioned by the war, there was full employment, more money in circulation, and more money to be saved. In the five years between the firing on Fort Sumter and the peace at Appomattox, the amount on deposit at Erie rose from $826,251 to $2,553,598.

Despite the ongoing string of disasters that constituted the Civil War, Erie County Savings Bank prospered. Needless to say, the requirements of the nation's massive national military undertaking tapped the residents of Erie County for youth and treasure. However, the industrious citizens of Buffalo continued to produce, prosper... *and save*. During the war, the number of bank depositors increased while the number of withdrawals they made decreased. The bank's conservative investment officer continued to deploy these deposit inflows in a manner that supplemented its already large store of United States Treasury securities.

The Erie County Savings Bank demonstrated concern not only for its neighbors and depositors but also for its employees. During the Civil War years, when a clerk was called to military duty, the bank set aside $300 for his family and, if he went to the front, the bank quietly cared for the financial needs of his loved ones. The bank, like many other firms in the area, held jobs open for drafted employees.

The bank's president was known to occasionally appropriate funds to "buy" a conscription substitute for a critical bank clerk who was called into service. While such a gesture would be judged inappropriate in this day and age, it was a pretty common practice among commercial enterprises during the Civil War.

To aid in the Union's cause, the bank Trustees provided some of the financial support that was needed to recruit, mobilize, and send to battle the 100th Regiment which consisted mostly of volunteers from the Western New York area. The bank also established a system whereby active volunteers in the service of the country were able to regularly "allot" (i.e. deduct) a portion of their military pay and set it aside for their dependents' welfare or for insurance. The bank administered this process "free of any cost or charge to the volunteers or the recipients of such pay."

By 1867, the prosperity that had been experienced during the war years enabled Erie to build a new "home." Constructed of Connecticut freestone, it was erected on the southwest corner of Main and Court Streets, where it served its customers for the next twenty-six years.

The bank's involvement in community affairs paralleled its growth as a financial institution. For example, in 1868, the bank went on record as opposing the extension of Batavia Street, which was later named Broadway, because it would have eliminated Lafayette Square and mar the beauty of the downtown area.

In 1871, there was an outpouring of sympathy by Buffalonians for victims of the Chicago fire which ravaged the heart of that city for almost five days. Damage was estimated at $196 million, and city of Buffalo officials asked for Erie's help in raising funds for disaster relief. The bank agreed to buy $55,000 in Chicago city bonds. Additional monies raised were sent as a gift from the City of Good Neighbors to the people of Chicago.

During the first half of the 1870s, savers in Buffalo responded to the bank's community spirit and, by 1876, the bank's annual report showed deposits of $9.4 million. However, there was a "bump" between the end of the Civil War and this grand deposit achievement. In 1873, the 10th year of the existence of a new national banking system, there occurred a financial disaster.

The "Panic of 1873" began in September with the failure of the private banking firm of Jay Cooke & Co, which had gained great wealth and prestige from its dealings in federal government securities during and subsequent to the Civil War. In short order, the First National Bank of Washington, the National Bank of the Commonwealth in New York, and other institutions collapsed and panic spread throughout the country. Depositors rushed to withdraw their funds from banks.

The "country banks," including Erie, were forced to draw heavily upon their correspondent banks in New York City. These money center banks customarily provided the liquid funds necessary to accommodate brief spikes in deposit withdrawals. Erie reacted to the fear of great withdrawal activity by notifying its correspondent banks of a possible need for funds in the short-term future. Erie's Trustees were astonished to learn that the New York City banks would be unable to furnish any currency under the circumstances. As a consequence, Erie had to resort to selling United States bonds to the Treasury. Approximately $1 million in bonds was eventually sold.

A letter written by Cyrus Lee, published in the Buffalo Courier in 1873, assured customers of the Erie County Savings Bank that their deposits were secure. The fact that, during this turbulent period, Erie continually maintained a high percentage of its mortgage portfolio in city property also helped retain customer patronage.

The bright side to this otherwise grim episode was the fact that Erie's bonds were sold at a premium of about 10½%. All in all, Erie came through the panic a winner, so to speak.

After more than a quarter-century of banking activity at the Main and Court Street address, Erie sold, in 1893, its office property to Henry W. Burke for the German-American Bank at a price of $185,000. That bank eventually became Liberty National Bank & Trust Company (which later morphed into Norstar Bank and, subsequently, was acquired by Fleet Bank and then became part of Bank of America.)

When the First Presbyterian Church in Buffalo announced in 1889 that it would move from its historic Main and Niagara Streets site (i.e. Shelton Square), Erie's Trustees saw the location as ideal for a new and larger Erie County Savings Bank building. There was, however, a competitor for the location. The United States Government wanted the land for the construction of a post office, and the local press immediately championed the government proposal. But with perseverance, and after lengthy negotiations, the bank was able to purchase the site for

$185,000... coincidentally, the same amount as the sale price of its Main-Court property.

To generate interest in such a major undertaking and to comfort many Buffalonians who opposed razing the old church, the bank launched a well-publicized competition among six of the nation's leading architects for a design of the proposed new building. The award ultimately went to George B. Post, who had created numerous landmark buildings in New York City. The caliber of the men chosen to construct the new building was exemplified by the choice of Thomas A. Edison as the consulting engineer for electrical installation.

Ground was broken in September 1890, and the bank moved into its magnificent new, castle-like home (as portrayed on the front cover of this book) in June of 1893. The total investment in the ten-story granite and brick building was $1,186,751.

Supporting a steel frame structure, the foundation varied from seven feet to thirteen feet in width. The ornate copper-crested roof set the building apart from every other downtown structure. The interior finishing was mahogany rather than the conventional oak. In addition to the spacious new banking facilities, the building boasted some 145 offices. Two bronze lions added to the striking appearance of the main entrance archway. The bank demonstrated its personal touch within the spacious new quarters by placing the president's and treasurer's desks on the main banking floor, easily accessible to everyone. A huge, walk-in safe dominated the interior landscape.

From the year that the bank moved into the new building at Main and Niagara Streets through the close of the Pan American Exposition in 1903, deposits increased by $15 million. A 1908 report on the 138 savings banks in New York State revealed that the Erie County Savings Bank had the largest resources of any savings bank, excluding those located in New York City. By 1915, there were four savings banks (Erie was the largest by far) and 32 S&Ls operating in Erie County. (These included the recently-formed Seneca Savings and Loan Association in

Buffalo, which boasted $3,100 in assets that were carefully watched over by Joseph J. "JJ" Willax, Treasurer.)

In 1910, a history of the bank was compiled which related its achievements from 1854 to the end of 1909. In it, the following testament is found: "The real history of any institution embodies in large measure the personality of the men who have made it. This is especially true of an organization which, like a savings bank, sustains a vital relation to a large part of the community. There are thousands of people to whom the bank is a guardian of savings and often a bulwark against calamity, but only a few of these people personally know its officials; all more or less consciously rest their trust on the reputation which is secured to the bank by the men who direct its affairs."

The bank's Board of Trustees was its primary governing and policy-making body. Many prominent Buffalo figures served as Trustees. Names like Watson, Sweeney, Donaldson, Wadsworth, Howard, Ogden, Letchworth, Smith, Robinson, and Whitney can still be found on Buffalo street signs. (Indeed, a Wadsworth descendent served on the bank's Board during your author's tenure.) The bank's Trustees were recognized as prominent and trustworthy citizens of Buffalo, representing industry, professions, arts, education, and government. All were men... until the first woman was elected to the Board in 1974.

In the early years, no fees were paid to Trustees for attendance at meetings. However, a stipend of $20 was paid when a Trustee, in company with the president or an officer of the bank, spent an afternoon inspecting and appraising properties for which applications for mortgages had been submitted. (This time-consuming practice continued until the 1970s.) Also, fees were paid to the members of a committee of Trustees which was appointed semi-annually to examine the securities and resources of the bank.

Meanwhile, in 1910, far from Erie County, the crowned heads of Europe met in friendship for the last time. It was the end of an era wherein people in the civilized world had confidence that a peaceful society could be maintained. Four years later, a World

War erupted, marking the beginning of a period of anxiety in an unsettled world.

At the beginning of the War, there were four savings banks and 32 S&Ls operating in Erie County. (These included the recently formed Seneca Savings and Loan Association in Buffalo which boasted $3,100 in assets which were duly cared for by Joseph J. "JJ" Willax, Treasurer.)

The following communication from Eugene Lamb Richards, Superintendent of Banks of the State of New York, was read at Erie's Board of Trustees' meeting on August 5, 1914.

"To all savings banks and private bankers in the State of New York: In view of the European situation and for the purpose of conserving currency for our domestic needs, I request that, forthwith, a resolution be adopted by your Board of Trustees requiring a notice of sixty days before repaying deposits and otherwise complying with Subdivision 1, Section 248 of the Banking Law." The Board approved this letter but no such restrictions were ever put into effect.

During the World War, dividends paid by the Erie were at the rate of 4% per annum, payable quarterly, and the legal limit on individual deposits was $3,000. During the decade 1910 to 1920, Erie's increased from $43.5 million to $61.8 million, an average of almost $2 million per year.

## A roar and a crash

The frenetic business activity and wild speculation that marked the decade of the Twenties is an oft-told tale. Once the deflationary "Depression of 1920-1921" was successfully resolved, paper millionaires were being made every day.

Accordingly, even the most prudent Americans came to regard investment in a savings account as the height of timidity and conservatism. As a result, despite the facts that the deposit limit had been raised to $5,000 and that the bank was still paying a 4% dividend (compounded quarterly), the increase in deposits for this entire ten-year period was just a little over $3 million

23

compared to an $18 million gain in the previous decade. But, even though the bank was being buffeted by competition, it worked ceaselessly to extend mortgage loans to finance the surge in commercial and residential construction in the Buffalo area.

The close watch that the State Banking Department kept on New York banks is illustrated by a letter from the Superintendent of Banks that was received by Erie in April 1924. It recommended that the salary of $5,000 per year which was paid to the bank's attorney be eliminated because the fees his firm received in handling the mortgages of the bank provided "sufficient remuneration."

During this period, the bank continued to upgrade its internal operations. Its method of keeping records and its basic system of bookkeeping had changed very little since the early days. But, in 1921, the huge, leather-bound, depositors' ledger books finally gave way to individual Remington Rand ledger cards. A short time later, Erie placed its first order for adding machines. This mechanization was grudgingly accepted by the bank's accounting personnel, who expressed serious doubts about its reliability. But, as a wise sage once observed, "all good things must come to an end."

And so they did for the '20s in the form of a stock market "crash" in October 1929, just a month after the Erie County Savings Bank had celebrated its 75th anniversary. The magnitude of this market collapse and its effect on business was reflected in the bank's mortgage activity. After almost ten years of unprecedented expansion in mortgage credit, the loans closed in the entire month of November 1929 totaled a mere $11,400.

A Great Depression had begun.

The U.S. economy started to implode after stock prices began a nosedive on September 4, 1929. This downslide culminated in a stock market "crash" on October 29, 1929, which forever after would be known as "Black Tuesday." As the global effects of this collapse ran their course through the 1930s, personal income, tax revenue, profits, and prices dropped while international trade plunged by more than 50%. Unemployment in the U.S. rose to

25% and in some nations rose to as high as 33%. All in all, records show that in the United States the value of all of its markets' stocks dropped 89% before panic subsided.

Cities all around the world were hit hard, especially those dependent on heavy industry. Private construction was virtually halted. Rural areas suffered as crop prices fell by approximately 60%. With plummeting demand and few sources of jobs, regions that were dependent on primary sector industries such as cash cropping, mining, and logging suffered the most.

Idle men and lengthening bread lines offered evidence of the serious material effects of this depression. The psychological effects upon both the public and business were equally devastating. In 1931, commercial banks, which had supplied much of the credit that helped the stock market reach its peak, were forced to lower the dividend rate they paid on savings accounts and people quickly withdrew their savings from those institutions. In contrast, the Erie County Savings Bank increased its deposits by over $9 million in just one 10-day period. In 1931, the amount on deposit at Erie increased by $17 million.

Each day, scores of homeowners who could neither pay their taxes nor meet the interest payments on their mortgages came to the bank seeking relief. Such expedients as "suspended interest" were used to help people save their homes but, in all too many cases, these practices simply delayed inevitable foreclosure.

The bank was in the unenviable position of either foreclosing or having the county or city seize properties for unpaid taxes. Therefore, in order to avoid a complete loss on those properties, the bank foreclosed on 1,200 of them. By 1939, the real estate held by the bank was valued at more than $8 million.

As people came to realize the severity of the crash, depositors began withdrawing funds from all types of financial institutions, fearing a collapse of the nation's banking system. The outflow of deposits surged to the point that, on March 6, 1933, President Franklin D. Roosevelt declared a "bank holiday." All banks were forced to close for a week so that monetary authorities could forge some order from the financial chaos that prevailed. Many worried depositors came to the bank or telephoned to express their concern. They were assured that their funds were safe and that the bank would reopen immediately after receiving permission from the government. Erie soon re-opened, but it restricted withdrawals for several more days.

To alleviate the fears of bank customers, two new institutions were organized in 1933 under the emergency powers of the New York State Banking Board. These were the Savings Banks Trust Company and the Institutional Securities Corporation. The Trust Company became the savings banks' central bank. The Institutional Securities Corporation was established to provide liquidity through the sales of real estate mortgages to the Corporation by member banks in need of ready cash.

In 1934, savings banks organized the Mutual Savings Banks Fund to provide insurance for deposits. (This Fund served as the banks' primary "security blanket" until 1943 when banks chose to become members of the Federal Deposit Insurance Corporation [FDIC], a relatively new federal entity which insured individual deposits up to $5,000.)

During this period, the Federal Home Owners' Loan Corporation Act was passed to assist savings banks with their rapidly-pyramiding mortgage problems.

At this time, because of the dreadful condition of the economy and the vast unemployment it occasioned, the bank's officers thought it prudent to limit the amount of deposits that it would accept. Therefore, Erie began to decline large deposits while the other savings banks continued to accept them.

The results of this decidedly conservative course became quickly apparent. On January 1, 1931, the Erie County Savings Bank held more deposits than any of the other savings banks in Buffalo (as it had for a number of years). Deposits at Erie totaled $65,898,291, while the deposits of its major competitor, Buffalo Savings Bank, amounted to $61,479,046. However, because of the Erie's refusal to accept large deposits, the Buffalo Savings Bank took the lead in deposit growth and by January 1, 1932, the deposit tally was: Erie County Savings Bank - $83,131,000; Buffalo Savings Bank - $85,922,000.

In 1932, in order to improve credit oversight, Erie's Trustees created an Investment Committee which was charged with making decisions concerning the granting of mortgages and the investment of funds. The offices of Secretary and Treasurer were also separated.

That same year, extensive structural renovations, costing over $135,000, were made within the bank building. These changes involved the elimination of the massive grilles and plate glass which had facilitated the protection of tellers from bank robbers. National Cash Register machines were also installed on the teller line. These devices mechanized passbook entries and reduced reliance on handwritten updating. Mortgage and other real estate accounting records were also mechanized.

Among the "modernizations" of 1932 was a new customer service practice which segregated male and female depositors at separate teller windows. (The "logic" of this routine was never officially explained.)

After a large increase in deposits in 1931, a protracted decline was experienced during the next ten years due to the enforcement of restrictions on the size of individual deposits. To abet this "no-growth" policy, the bank reduced dividend rates in 1932 from 4% to 3 ½% per annum. In January 1934, the rate was reduced to 3%; then to 2 ½% in April of 1935; and to 2% in January 1936. Efforts to reduce deposit inflows weren't relaxed until September 1936.

## Home ownership

The Great Depression was to have a significant negative impact on home ownership and, in turn, on the positive influence that housing formation had historically had on both economic growth and social stability.

Home ownership had been "the American dream" since the nation's founding. Private ownership of land was one of the fundamental enthusiasms leading to the formation of the United States. Our founding fathers fervently believed that widespread ownership of land and housing by individuals and families was crucial to the promotion of security, social stability, economic growth, and prosperity.

In America's early years, land was owned primarily for the purpose of farming. With the advent of the Industrial Revolution, however, interest in urban land ownership for the purpose of housing development grew rapidly.

The financial wherewithal provided by savings institutions was key to the creation of family housing and to the generation of economic benefits that such investment facilitated. However, despite the efforts of an expanding network of savings intermediaries, less than half of U.S. families owned their homes by 1890. In New York State, only one-third of families owned their residences. (Surprisingly, it took until the mid-1980s for that number to top 50 %.)

Home ownership spiked temporarily from 37% in 1890 to 46.5% in 1900 as a direct result of a commitment by President William McKinley to increase home ownership. This surge quickly dissipated, however, as more and more people moved to the cities where home ownership was less sacrosanct – to secure jobs that were being created as a result of the Industrial Revolution. Folks who lived in cities tended not to own their homes. In 1800, 6% of Americans lived in cities; 94% of them lived in rural areas where it was rare for someone to rent rather than own a home. By 1850, 15% of the population lived in cities.

Circumstances began to change rapidly as home purchase financing became even more readily available. By 1900, 40% of Americans were living in urban communities and, thanks to the proliferation of lending institutions and the growth of city type dwellings, 46.5% of these families owned their own homes.

Notwithstanding these demographic trends, the overall homeownership rate declined again, slowly but steadily, from 1900 to 1920. Then, a robust economy in the 1920s temporarily increased the homeownership rate once again.

Thrift institutions were playing an important role. While the average thrift institution held less than $1 million in assets, more than one hundred savings institutions each boasted over $10 million in assets. This growth in the thrift industry occurred because, as the 1920s unfolded, many upper and middle-class folks sought them out as a means to invest money safely at good returns. This growth in deposits, of course, redounded to the benefit of home buyers who were seeking financing.

Beginning in 1929, the Great Depression changed the economic landscape dramatically. The rate of homeownership plunged again, this time to its lowest level of the century. During the Depression, most banks suffered huge losses and many failed. The more conservative thrifts, by and large, fared better. According to the book From Building and Loans to Bailouts, between 1931 and 1932 almost 20% of all banks went out of business while just 2% of all thrifts met a similar fate.

But, despite thrifts' impressive survival rate, the deposit and loan flows of many of them were in a steep decline. All Americans had been impacted by the Great Depression. The number of unemployed grew and those so afflicted did not have the wherewithal to save. Almost everyone feared indebtedness and, hence, they were not of a mind to borrow money to buy housing. By 1933, almost half of all mortgages were in default and home prices had dropped roughly 50%.

In 1932, President Herbert Hoover became alarmed by the downturn in residential construction. He urged Congress to do something to encourage home building, reduce foreclosures, and increase home ownership.

The result was the Federal Home Loan Bank Act which the President signed into effect on July 22, 1932. The primary purpose of this legislation was to increase the amount of funds available to local financial institutions that supplied home mortgages.

The Act established the Federal Home Loan Bank – and its associated, regional Federal Home Loan Banks – to assist private banks in providing long-term, amortizable loans for home purchases. The idea was to accelerate banks' lending and provide realistic borrowing terms which would facilitate a growth in home ownership and the societal stability it engendered.

As he signed the Act on July 22, 1932, President Hoover said, in part: "The purpose of this legislation is to establish a system of discount banks for home mortgages, performing a function for homeowners somewhat similar to that performed in the commercial banking field by the Federal Reserve banks through their discount facilities."

"In the long view we need at all times to encourage homeownership and for such encouragement it must be possible for homeowners to obtain long-term loans payable in installments. These institutions should provide the method for bringing into continuous and steady action the great home loaning associations which is so greatly restricted due to present pressures."

As a consequence of the implementation of this Act, savings and loan associations sprang up all across the United States and ample, low-cost, mortgage-based funding for housing became readily available.

Oddly, despite all of this effort, the new credit program facilitated by this Act was a failure. While 41,000 potential homeowners applied for FHLB loans in the first two years after the passage of the Federal Home Loan Bank Act, the government agency administering the program approved just three applications. Hoover's 1928 election promise of "a car in every garage" (apparently presuming a house adjacent to every garage) was extinguished by the realities of a 25% unemployment rate.

Upon assuming the Presidency in 1933, Franklin D. Roosevelt acted quickly to ameliorate the effects of the Depression. High on his agenda was the reform of the banking industry and, by extension, the thrift industry. One of his principal objectives was to spark mortgage lending so that society's dreams of home ownership would not remain merely reveries.

His proposals for dramatic action were well received since they were seen as good for the economy – and its citizenry – in a material, financial sense. But, as most people understood, these bold actions were also part of a grand political agenda formulated by a very ambitious President. But, notwithstanding his underlying political motivations, the fact that a politician could do well for himself while doing good for many was acceptable to Americans who had for so long looked for leadership in resolving their economic hardship.

Importantly, he and other promoters of these reforms were not seeking only personal political advantage. America's leaders at the highest levels had become gravely concerned about the nation's social stability. It did not go unnoticed that economic suffering in other nations had sparked social unrest, rioting, and government usurpation. In Germany, the deprivation and inflation that surged during the final months of World War I and its aftermath forced the Kaiser to flee to Holland and raised the specter of a communist takeover. The German citizenry was bereft of resources and lacked any leadership that could realistically promise a better tomorrow.

During this period, Czar Nicholas of Russia was deposed and a socialist regime began to emerge.

Further, by the early Thirties, a demagogue named Adolf Hitler had begun an era of oppression that he excused with promises to create jobs, eliminate inflation, and restore citizens' self-respect.

At this point in history, it appeared that even rational citizens were willing to do or accept *anything* to end the personal pains induced by national economic collapse. The *anything* was what concerned political leaders in the United States. As a consequence, they began to think increasingly about expanded homeownership as a means to preserve greater social stability in a nation where ominous signs of unrest were proliferating. Millions of people were without jobs, food, housing, or hope. They constituted potent social kindling that could conceivably fuel revolution.

31

A resentment of "foreign" workers increased along with the unemployment rolls, and it sparked unruly demonstrations.

Three thousand unemployed workers in Detroit marched on the Ford Motor Company's River Rouge plant.

In Washington D. C., twenty thousand World War I veterans, who were determined to collect their now much-needed "bonus" pay for service, gathered and began setting up encampments near the White House and the Capitol. When some of these "bonus Army" members resisted being forcibly moved from their squatters' camps, violence erupted, leading to deaths of veterans. President Hoover felt compelled to order federal troops, under the command of Major General Douglas MacArthur, to assist D.C. police in clearing the city of demonstrating veterans.

"Food riots" broke out in Minneapolis and other parts of the United States. Citizen protests raged against the Federal Agricultural Program because of its orders to slaughter more than six million pigs in the name of price stabilization. Hungry citizens were riled.

A three-day dust storm blew an estimated 350 million tons of soil off the terrain of America's western and southwestern regions, smothering farms and homes and forcing the members of thousands of families to become rootless emigrants.

In January 1937, members of the United Automobile Workers struck the General Motors Plant in Flint, Michigan. The strike turned violent when strikers clashed with company-hired police.

At Republic Steel's South Chicago plant, workers and their families tried unsuccessfully to combine a picnic with a rally and demonstration. As a consequence, ten people were killed and a dozen more wounded in the "Memorial Day Massacre."

It appeared that unrest was everywhere and growing in ferocity.

Unfortunately, by this point in time, most of Roosevelt's social welfare and job-creating programs still had yet to provide meaningful assistance to the restive masses. It was feared by many that his efforts would be insufficient to dampen emotions, and that this tinderbox would remain a threat to social stability for decades to come.

Influential policy-makers at the national level eventually came to the conclusion that an important key to domestic tranquility was ubiquitous homeownership. They reasoned that if citizens had a real economic stake in the nation through their ownership of housing, they would be inclined to self-pacification in order to maintain the kind of civil order that was essential to their families' security, safety, and self-sufficiency. Since the founding of the nation, "protecting home and hearth" had always been a strong motivation. According to the policy-makers' reasoning, home ownership would go a long way toward ensuring the solidity of the nation. They believed that an ability to secure homeownership would both temper turmoil… and preserve social order.

As a consequence, much of the legislation that was forged during this period and in succeeding decades was aimed at creating paths to individual homeownership.

This same strategy for re-enforcing social stability was emphasized during the period of communist overtures after World War II and during the riots and insurgencies that erupted during the 1960s.

(Legislation that would ensure housing for needy Americans would become an even more urgent national priority during the 1960s. In the last quarter of the century, Presidents Jimmy Carter and Bill Clinton aggressively pushed financial institutions to rapidly expand the availability of mortgage loans, even to borrowers who would clearly not be able to repay them.)

Unfortunately, many of the policies, programs, regulations, consumer "protections," and competitive restraints constructed in the name of expanding home ownership would actually work to compound the nation's economic vulnerabilities and, ultimately, would help give rise to the savings and loan crisis of the 1980s.

Federal and State governments' on-going efforts to influence and eventually control free-market dynamics in the pursuit of expanded homeownership created much larger problems than they were initially designed to preempt. Nevertheless, America's leaders firmly believed that long-term programs which facilitated home ownership were essential and were worth the kinds of costs and controls necessary to implement them.

Our nation's "grand planners" were savvy enough, however, to realize that *long-term* programs would not be sufficient to ameliorate *short-term* economic and social threats. As a result, additional initiatives with a more contemporary impact also had to be undertaken as soon as possible.

It was hoped that these moves would contribute to immediate relief as well as to a placid and prosperous post-Depression future.

Roosevelt's initiatives were given form with the passage of The National Housing Act of 1934. This legislation created the Federal Housing Administration (FHA) and the Federal Savings and Loan Insurance Corporation (FSLIC). The main goals of the legislation were to:

- Make housing and home mortgages more affordable.
- Provide customers of savings and loan associations with deposit protection similar to that which the FDIC made available to depositors in commercial banks.

This legislation was also intended to create a situation whereby:

- Home loans would be made by the private sector rather than the federal government.
- Income from mortgage insurance premiums would cover the cost of the program, thus precluding the need for financial support from the government.

In addition, in order to rapidly increase the flow of money into the economy, Title I of this law allowed FHA to insure losses up to $2,000 on "loans and advances of credits... for the purpose of financing alterations, repairs, and improvements upon real property."

In 1940, the Erie began to offer FHA mortgage loans, thus enhancing its prospects and those of the communities it served.

The complementary <u>Banking Act of 1933</u> (a/k/a the <u>Glass-Steagall Act</u>) had already established the Federal Deposit Insurance Corporation (FDIC) as a federal agency. The FDIC's primary goal was to insure bank deposits and, thereby, eliminate runs on commercial banks in the United States be they member banks or nonmember banks, national-charted banks, or state-charted banks.

In 1938, the Federal National Mortgage Association (later known as "Fannie Mae") was created to provide a secondary mortgage market supported by the federal government.

Notwithstanding these aggressive efforts, deplorable economic conditions continued to prevail in almost every region of the United States until 1939, when the impacts of the Great Depression began to abate. At that point, a measure of stability was achieved, and the country's leading economic indicators suggested the dawn of more positive circumstances.

## World War II

On December 7, 1941, the attack of Japanese air forces on the American naval fleet at Pearl Harbor kicked the U.S. economy into high gear, bringing abundant economic relief from the Great Depression. The Erie County Savings Bank began to prosper once again, albeit with a severe depletion in its experienced workforce as many employees were called to serve their country.

As American industry was converted to the manufacture of implements of war, the supply of new automobiles and many other popular consumer items was abruptly stifled. But there were steady jobs for almost everyone and, with a shortage of things to purchase, money began to flow into banks. During the decade of the Great Depression, Erie had experienced more deposit outflows than inflows. During World War II, however, deposit inflows were the order of the day. At the onset of the war, no one had the audacity to suggest that the bank was experiencing the beginnings of what would be a period of eighteen consecutive years in which there would be an annual net increase in deposits.

As the impacts of the Depression began to fade, Erie commenced to dispose of the more than 1,200 pieces of property that it had taken by foreclosure. Some had to be sold at prices much below their value because the State Banking Department limited the period of time that certain of these properties could be held by the bank. One interesting example was a building on Church Street which the bank wanted to retain. But the State Banking Department sent a special agent to Buffalo to ensure that it was sold. The amount realized in this sale was $10,000. Just a few years later, the property was needed to enlarge Erie's customer parking lot... and it was repurchased by the bank for $65,000.

Because a relatively low 2½% rate of interest was paid on savings accounts throughout the War, the bank experienced a large earnings surplus each year. Most of it was used to write down – by $12.6 million – the book value of real estate taken by foreclosure during the Depression. Notwithstanding this write-off of owned property, the bank's financial condition would continue to strengthen during the War. (By 1945, Erie boasted a balance sheet surplus that was equal to 13% of deposits.)

Soon after the outbreak of World War II, the bank launched a massive effort to promote the sale of War Bonds. It also volunteered to do the bookkeeping, inscribing, and safekeeping of these bonds. At one time, there were thirty employees engaged in doing this work manually – all at the bank's expense. It is estimated that, during the War and the period immediately following, more than one million individual war bonds were issued by the bank. For this feat, bank employees received a citation from the United States Treasury Department.

Despite the gloom of the war years, Erie's management sensed that tremendous opportunities would emerge in the not-too-distant future. In anticipation of favorable post-war economic conditions, the bank began, in the early '40s, an aggressive push for a more dominant presence in both its savings and lending marketplaces.

In 1944, a department was added for the sale of Savings Bank Life Insurance. Policies were offered strictly on bank premises and at a lower cost than most other life insurance plans because the SBLI marketing methodology eliminated the costs associated with door-to-door solicitors and premium collectors.

At the conclusion of the War, in 1945 Erie promptly began to offer GI loans to help returning veterans achieve at least a portion of their long-deferred dreams.

Not much later, something "really cool" happened. In August of 1944, a form of air-conditioning was introduced to the bank's second floor (executive) offices, which, presumably, decreased discomfort and enhanced decision-making.

By the end of 1945, the bank boasted a very conservative balance sheet with cash and government bonds equaling a whopping 73.8% of deposits. By the following year, the foreclosed real estate on the bank's books had dwindled to only eight pieces valued at $1 each.

In 1946, Erie's anticipations of growth were reinforced by a new state banking law which allowed every savings bank to open two branches within the limits of the city in which its main office was located. Erie County Savings Bank opened its first branch on June 6, 1946 in one of the busiest and most heavily populated sections of the city, the Broadway-Fillmore shopping district on the east side of Buffalo. This was the first branch opened by any savings bank in Buffalo and was heralded by the press as a "bold and brave move." The branch, at 940 Broadway, became an immediate success. (Not many years later, the bank would open its second branch in the thriving Grant-Ferry shopping district.)

After the War, the Erie County Savings Bank began to research the feasibility of acquiring a new "punched card" system to further automate its existing accounting procedures. In 1947, it acquired the "machines" that were necessary for such a system from the International Business Machines Corporation. The mortgage accounting department was chosen as the site for the first phase of conversion since, at that time, the bank held approximately 10,000 mortgages. This big step would usher in a much more ambitious pace of technology adoption during the next four decades.

Importantly, the conclusion of the War marked the end of the protracted downward trend in savings account dividend rates. The return of America's industry to domestic pursuits coupled with the homecoming of eager GI consumers quickly ignited inflationary pressures that pushed up prices and interest rates.

To be sure, the '40s were amazing years. On January 1, 1940, the deposits of the Erie County Savings Bank amounted to $87.2 million; the total on January 1, 1950 was $175 million. This represented an astounding ten-year increase in deposits of more than $88 million, the largest gain in bank history to that date.

In the wake of the spate of federal economic intervention and assistance in the 1930s – and with the momentum from the nation's mobilization to win World War II – a surge in post-World War II homeownership occurred. A booming economy, favorable tax laws, a rejuvenated home building industry, and easier financing saw homeownership explode from less than a 50% level nationally to almost 65% percent in just two decades.

For Erie, it was on to the "Fabulous Fifties" and the beginning of the bank's second century!

*Chapter two*

# A SECOND CENTURY BEGINS

## A surge

Erie's outstanding record of performance as it approached the beginning of its second century of service paralleled that of the nation's economy as a whole. In the decade of the Fifties, the bank would experience a doubling of its deposits, to over $350 million. This gain was larger than the total of all the deposits the bank acquired during its first ninety-six years of operation.

This new surge in growth was triggered in 1951 when the New York State Legislature voted to increase to $10,000 the amount which savings banks could accept from individual depositors. Such limits were imposed to ensure that savings banks adhered to their original mission of serving people of modest means. Needless to say, these limits also helped to protect the turf of commercial banks. (Later, in 1962, this amount was increased to $15,000; and to $25,000 in 1965. During the 1970s, the limits were completely removed.)

Erie's investment yields were also climbing during the early '50s, enabling the bank to frequently increase the interest (i.e. dividends) it paid on savings accounts. Over a period of fourteen years, beginning in 1952, dividend rates increased and the methods of their calculation changed more than a dozen times. Rate increases were usually implemented in increments of ¼% per annum, compounded quarterly or semiannually. At various times, "extra" dividends of ¼% and ½% were declared.

There were also "special dividends" declared on funds left on deposit, undisturbed, for one or two years. The accounts benefiting from this practice were referred to as Time Deposit Accounts.

It was necessary for a savings bank to notify the State Banking Department during the first month of each quarterly calendar period when it was the intent of the bank's Board of Trustees to declare an increase in the dividend rate at the end of that period. Most banks wanted to make an announcement of "*anticipated* dividends" early in the quarter so that new deposits would be forthcoming and existing deposits would remain on account. However, in order to publicly announce an "anticipated" rate increase, the bank was required by the Banking Department to include in all of its advertising the contingency phrase "*providing favorable earnings.*" This constituted a warning to depositors in case total earnings at the end of the quarterly period turned out to be insufficient to cover the cost of the proposed increased dividend payments.

By this time, convenience was beginning to rival rates of return among customers' preferences. Since the post-war years were becoming the era of the automobile, the matter of a parking lot for the bank's customers gained importance. So, in 1950, the Underhill Building on the northwest corner of Pearl and Church Streets was acquired and torn down to accommodate approximately 28 cars... the bank's first acknowledgement of the new "mobile" generation.

The period was not totally free of "negatives," however. For example, federal income taxes were imposed on mutual savings banks in 1952. But, since savings institutions were simultaneously granted a "bad-debt deduction" as an offsetting exemption, most savings banks were, in effect, relieved of federal tax liability... for a while, anyway.

During 1951, the bank started one of its most successful community projects... the Erie County Savings Bank Exhibit Room. A remodeled area of over 2,000 square feet located on the Pearl Street level of the bank's main office on Shelton Square was made available, free of charge, to area clubs, civic groups, fraternal and social organizations, hobby groups, educational institutions, industrial firms, and art groups to showcase their work. The displays it hosted attracted large numbers of people (and potential customers) who might not otherwise have come into the bank. The Big E model train exhibit, a feature of the

Christmas season, became the number one, perennial attraction, visited by as many as 3,200 persons a day.

In September 1954, the bank formally entered its second century amidst high hopes for the future. Indeed, some wild-eyed optimists harbored "outlandish" expectations that the bank would grow to a billion dollars in assets before another hundred years had passed. This was considered by many a "wild dream," given that the bank had grown to only $300 million in the ten previous decades.

To mark its anniversary, the bank set aside $10,000 for scholarships for high school graduates, the first of a long series of generous gifts to the community. One of the highlights of the year was the opening of the bank's second branch office at the junction of Grant and Breckenridge Streets on Buffalo's West Side. The area was a flourishing retail and commercial center, populated mostly by Italian-Americans who, like the Polish-Americans that frequented the Broadway-Fillmore branch, were notoriously good savers.

The bank had succumbed to the lure of "location, location, location." After 100 years, it was truly beginning to "branch out."

During the forties and early fifties, the bank innovatively exploited the very limited powers granted to it from New York State to launch a portfolio of new financial services that further assisted its customers, distinguished it from competitors, and built customer loyalty. In retrospect, the resulting bundle of services seems like a rather paltry gaggle of benefits but, at that point in time, these initiatives helped Erie retain a substantial customer base, lay the groundwork for future growth, and generate income that would help to further the bank's development.

By 1954, Erie's exceptionally creative staff had supplemented traditional passbook accounts with a variety of new, innovative services, including: Vacation Accounts; Christmas Club Accounts; Payday Savings Accounts; School Savings Accounts; The Family Security Package (which entailed monthly "payments" that facilitated both a deposit to a savings account

41

and the payment of a life insurance policy premium); GI loans; FHA home modernization loans; and bank-by-mail services. To keep pace with the times, Erie also initiated some very specialized services for affinity groups like new mothers, bowling teams, sports organizations, etc.

To accommodate its burgeoning customer base, the bank expanded the lobby of its main office by 50% and included a new private customer elevator. A sleek counter replaced teller windows, albeit, each customer still had to queue up according to the first initial of his or her last name in order to speed up the processing of passbook and ledger entries. Mercifully, separate windows for males and females had been eliminated some years earlier.

The bank's slogan of *"Friendly service since 1854"* was delivering on its promise.

Folks in the Buffalo area at mid-decade saw plenty of reasons for optimism about the future. The region was riding on the cusp of a national industrial expansion that was initially sparked by World War II. Buffalo continued to enjoy a vibrant economy that was, to a large extent, based on its access to inexpensive and dependable electric power. (This unique asset was initially displayed at the Pan American Exposition in 1901 and it showcased Buffalo as the "Silicon Valley" of the first half of the 20th century.) The city's geographic location at the juncture of the Great Lakes and the Erie Canal was an additional economic plus. Then, too, Buffalo benefited greatly from an industrious workforce that had been created by waves of immigration.

The city's vitality was mirrored by a rapid growth in family formations and a "baby boom" that was triggered at the War's end.

During the ten years following the conclusion of World War II, the nation's personal spending had increased at a rate of over 8% a year... and unemployment had averaged only 3.6%. Buffalonians (580,000 of them according to the 1950 census) were riding high and had the foresight to save a goodly portion of their ample earnings. The Erie County Savings Bank received much of it, growing by over $100 million in just five years. (During the twenty years following World War II, the entire thrift industry grew at an average annual rate of 14%. Mortgage lending was soaring, too, with thirty million new homes built nationally during the period.)

All these developments augured well for the Erie County Savings Bank's second century.

Not seen, however, by celebrants of the bank's centennial anniversary were gathering clouds of economic upheaval that would soon conspire to ultimately create a "perfect storm" for the bank and the entire industry of which it was a part.

### The "Big E" is born

A noteworthy accomplishment of the '50s was the bank's assumption of a new, identifying "moniker" that was designed to give it increased visibility in a marketplace that was being invaded by a growing number of competitors. Its advertising agency, Gottschalff and Weil, had suggested that the bank adopt a flashier, more memorable identity. According to the agency's analyses, there was nothing wrong with the handle "Erie County Savings Bank," but it didn't quite "roll off the tongue," and it failed to really distinguish the bank from all of the other financial institutions in the area. And, it didn't connote an image of a bank that was modern and progressive. A lot had changed in the marketplace over the past 100 years, and it had become apparent that a new sobriquet was needed to demonstrate that Erie was keeping pace with such change.

The creative folks at the agency, along with the bank's young advertising director, decided to capitalize on a capital letter which, for the remainder of the bank's history, would put the bank in a class of its own. The "E" from Erie was plucked into service as a logo, and the bank became known forever after as … the *Big E*.

Legend has it that one of the principals of Erie's advertising agency was a proud Navy veteran who revered the aircraft carrier

USS Enterprise, which was fondly referred to by its crewmembers as "The Big E."

It's doubtful that anyone anticipated the awesome currency this new logo would achieve. It became the inspiring, unforgettable emblem on the "flag" under which the bank would strive and achieve for the rest of its days.

To reinforce the impact of the new logo in savers' minds, officials of the bank and its advertising agency arranged to buy the rights to the musical tune "Big D," which actually referred to Dallas, Texas. The song was a hit written by Frank Loesser in 1956 for the Broadway musical "The Most Happy Fella." An "E" was substituted for the "D" in the song and was embellished with some additional clever lyrics. The rest, as they say, was history.

The resulting jingle, for all of its innocuousness, stuck in people's minds, much in the fashion of a later Disney favorite "It's a Small World."

The bank's song went something like this:

*I bank at Big E*
*Little R, little I, little E*
*Big E*
*Ear-ie Coun-tee Saa-vings Bank.*

Love it or hate it, you couldn't forget it, and it helped the bank boost its assets to over $350 million by decade's end.

Such deposit growth was quite an accomplishment since the economy began to soften in the second half of the decade. While the 1958 US Census of Business showed that the number of manufacturing and commercial enterprises in the Buffalo Metropolitan Area – and their aggregate employment – had reached their highest levels in history, it was a pinnacle that would not be enjoyed for long.

Population began to decline from its record high of 580,000 souls in 1950. For various cost, distribution, and tax reasons, a number of major corporations operating in Buffalo closed or relocated. It was the beginning of a trend that would continue for the next several decades. The opening of the St. Lawrence Seaway and major changes in the steel and automobile industries constituted life-changing body blows for the Buffalo area. Darker days were dawning for the Erie County economy and the financial institutions that served it.

As economic conditions deteriorated in the late '50s, the local mortgage market slumped also. But, notwithstanding the reluctance among borrowers, most folks were still increasing their savings. As a consequence of record deposit inflows, the bank's Trustees were able, for the first time in history, to authorize a single investment of $7.5 million. It consisted of a package of government-guaranteed Veterans Loans that were originated *outside* of New York State. It was a practice that would expand in the future as the development of the local economic infrastructure – and its concomitant demand for mortgage loans – continued to slow.

## "The bandits are coming!"

The ebullience fueled by the bank's 100th anniversary was soon temporized by a significant event at the national level.

While commercial banks had become more aggressive competitors for savers' dollars during the first half of the century, thrifts had succeeded in defending their market positions and rapidly-accumulated market share during the Depression and the fifteen years following it.

But, by the mid-Fifties, a number of circumstances were conspiring to seriously impede Erie's capacity to compete in an increasingly-demanding marketplace.

In New York State, for example, thrifts' branching powers remained severely restricted. In contrast, commercial banks' expanding branch networks (which were not as constrained), coupled with the broad array of consumer-oriented services they had the authority to offer, began to severely cut into thrifts' market territory. For example, Erie County Savings Bank had only three branches at the time I joined it in early 1967, and this represented all of its legislatively-allowed total allotment. Moreover, thrifts' menus of banking services were still very limited, consisting principally of simple savings accounts and residential mortgages.

In addition, open-end mutual funds with redeemable shares (which had been first introduced in 1924) were becoming a more popular alternative to savings accounts as confidence in the stock market began an upswing in the 1950s. Sophisticated savers who had discretionary dollars – a segment of the population that was growing rapidly – were looking for a bigger bang for their bucks. Mutual funds accommodated this need and, as a consequence, savers' dollars were increasingly deployed in these easily-acquired "bundles" of corporate stocks that offered diversification of opportunity and little *perceived* risk. Savings institutions simply could not compete with the alluring returns that mutual funds provided.

Of course, direct investment in individual common stocks also continued to entice traditional savers as stocks' market prices and dividends rose.

As a result, less new money was coming in through the portals of savings banks and savings and loan associations while stock-market-bound *outflows* of deposits continued to grow.

Another major threat emerged within the savings industry itself. The war years and their aftermath triggered rapid population growth in the western and southwestern regions of the nation – over 120% in California where the defense industry had flourished – and the savings institutions resident in those areas expanded right along with them. Those thrifts were experiencing enormous demand for mortgage loans since the phalanx of new residents in those regions required financing for their home buying binge.

But the growth of deposits in western thrifts simply couldn't keep pace with the demand for home loans. It was evident to the managers of those savings and loan associations (there were no savings banks in the western United States) that something dramatic had to be done to acquire savings dollars sufficient to keep pace with indigenous loan demand. A new source of savings deposits was desperately needed to finance boundless housing growth in "sun country." Accordingly, the thrifts there began to look acquisitively at the surfeit of savings in America's "snow country" just a few thousand miles away.

Savings banks and savings and loan associations in the east were hosts to prodigious savers for almost a century-and-a-half, and the appetite in the east for housing loans was nowhere near that of the west and southwest. As a consequence, the aggressive western thrifts began to vigorously advertise for deposit funds in the east, commonly offering interest rates far in excess of what could be afforded by eastern thrifts.

It wasn't long before eastern thrift executives began to feel the impact of these aggressive forays into their territory. They saw a high probability that savings growth in their shops would stall as deposits were siphoned off by savings institutions in the western "badlands."

Some of the more foresighted eastern bank executives took the train of this logic to the next frightening station. The western thrifts might not only divert the *new* savings flows to their coffers, but the enticing rates they could offer just might cause interest-sensitive savers to withdraw massive amounts of *existing* deposits from the eastern shops and send them west. This could cause a frightening liquidity crisis, since all but a small cache of these savings deposits had already been deployed into long-term home mortgages... and these mortgages could not be "called" for repayment. Furthermore, the rates being charged on underlying loans could not be ratcheted upward to generate the kind of earnings required to pay savings rates that were competitive with those offered by the "bandits" from the west.

To make matters even worse, almost all of the mortgages already on savings banks' books were assumable, meaning that when a buyer obtained ownership of a mortgaged house, he or she could assume the outstanding debt of the mortgage and continue to pay it off under the *previous* terms and conditions of the loan. As a consequence, an increase in deposit costs could not be readily offset by the interest earned on mortgages.

47

Adding insult to injury, the prevailing mortgage rates were higher in the west because of the surge of demand for new housing in that region. The higher level of income generated by such loans enabled the lending thrifts there to offer higher rates for deposits than could rate-locked eastern institutions. This created a dire situation in New York State where a usury law held rates on new mortgage loans to 5% or less. The mortgage rate levels permitted by state government in Erie's markets paled in comparison to those prevailing in other parts of the country, especially the west. The state's usury ceiling was one of the major contributors to the fragile financial condition of New York State thrifts during the 1970s and 1980s.)

Frighteningly, the outlook for eastern thrifts would probably become even bleaker if inflation persisted and continued to push up interest rates overall.

To further complicate matters, New York State institutions, as contrasted to those in more progressive states, were not allowed to offer the kind of variable rate (a/k/a "adjustable rate") mortgage formats that enabled a lending bank to – at least – keep pace with rising deposit costs.

A gorilla had entered the room ... and he was from Los Angeles... and he was paying high rates on savings.

Traditional savings bankers could not envision a workable defense. They fretted: "How could banks in the east pay high competitive rates for savings if they were locked into low rate mortgage portfolios for years to come?" For example, the average yield on the Big E's aggregate mortgage portfolio was less than 5% at the dawn of the '60s. In this new competitive world, there was no way to tell how high the rates on deposits could eventually go.

This predicament was exacerbated by the fact that, given the constrictive usury ceiling, there were very few current opportunities for the Big E to originate higher-rate loans to compensate for its standing portfolio of low-yielding, fixed-rate mortgages that had been accumulated through many years of dedicated local lending. Moreover, there was only tepid economic growth in the Western New York region and little turnover in real estate.

Not a nice reward for a century of loyal service.

The increasing competition for savings forced Erie to raise its annual interest rate on savings from 3% in 1957 to 3.5% in 1958. That constituted a whopping 16% increase in the bank's cost of funds which had to be absorbed by a mortgage portfolio whose yields would, at best, rise only glacially. As the decade came to a close, the Big E, in order to remain competitive, was paying 3.75% on funds that remained on deposit for at least two years.

To make matters even worse, prevailing state laws precluded thrifts from offering demand deposit accounts. Therefore, Savings banks could not attract low-cost funds like those that were flowing to commercial banks' interest-free checking accounts.

The only alternatives open to New York State savings institutions, given prevailing regulations and market conditions, were low-cost products with minimal demand, like <u>Christmas Club Accounts</u> and <u>Stork Club Accounts</u>.

Meanwhile, West Coast thrifts were enjoying high rates of return on an ever-growing stream of new home loans. Every manager in the east coast wing of the industry fervently hoped that the siren call of "California Dreamin'" would soon lure these accursed, incursive western savings and loan association "bandits" back home to LaLa Land.

But, as presidential candidate Hillary Clinton said decades later, "Hope is not a strategy."

To be sure, many savings institution leaders – in all parts of the country – were not prepared for the new world that was dawning. Indeed, given the simplicity of their traditional business model which had – for many decades – produced profits on autopilot, they never really had to think much about either the long-term or a strategy. All of that was about to change.

# The Big E

*Chapter three*

# THE SURPRISING SIXTIES

## New economic realties

The go-go decade of the 1960s would introduce changes in mufti, music, and mores. It would also usher in some dramatic changes for the banking industry. Before it was over, a new, highly-inflationary course of events – including the Vietnam War and the establishment of President Lynden Johnson's "Great Society" – would present some significant earnings challenges for the Big E.

As the world began to morph, the asset side of the bank's balance sheet consisted primarily of old, low-yielding (i.e. 4%-5%) residential mortgages as well as a modicum of recently-originated loans whose earning capacity was still capped by the restrictive New York State usury ceiling. When contra-positioned against deposits whose costs were escalating, these rate assets squeezed Erie's net earnings immensely. (The difference between a bank's "net interest earnings" from mortgages and the "net interest cost" associated with deposits was referred to as the "net interest margin" or "NIM." This statistical measure of "gross profit" was one of the primary indicators of a savings institution's financial health.)

With a shrinking NIM, very little in the way of a surplus could be accumulated in anticipation of "rainy days."

Compounding the problem was the fact that the typical Buffalo home buyer usually held his or her property until long after the accompanying fixed-rate, long-term mortgage was paid off. As a result, Erie had little opportunity to increase the earnings provided by already-booked assets even when inflation accelerated and drove up the interest payout demanded by depositors.

Stagnant population growth in the Buffalo area also hurt because there was no substantial influx of new home buyers/borrowers who would take loans even at the very low prevailing rate of 6%.

But, there was some "good" news for thrift managers who didn't take the trouble to carefully contemplate its likely implications. The barbarians from the west were being stopped at the gates... at least temporarily. In both 1964 and 1965, the Federal Home Loan Bank Board, the principal thrift regulator, refused to make advances (i.e. loans) to thrift institutions that paid above a specified, Board-set rate on deposits. While this stemmed the assault of the invading funds-gobblers for a while, it also, for the very first time, gave the government a measure of control over interest rates paid by thrift institutions.

This "gotcha" was overlooked by many thrift leaders amidst their jubilation over their newfound insulation against the marauders from the west. They readily accepted this type of rate ceiling since it was set not far above the rates they rates currently offered. They, unfortunately, took little heed of the fact that, in an inflating economy, a ceiling could become a crushing barrier very quickly.

The Chairman of the Federal Home Loan Bank Board had been concerned that the struggle by less competitive eastern thrifts to generate earnings sufficient to cover escalating deposit costs would force them into riskier lending practices. Hence, he advocated the ceiling. But the creation of this kind of ceiling proved to be a landmark event in a pattern of ever-increasing regulatory control.

Few anticipated that this constraint would significantly affect the competitive balance between thrifts and commercial banks and eventually have a suppressing effect on deposit inflows at thrift institutions across the country. In 1963 and 1964, the growth rates of time and savings deposits at thrift institutions were 12.0% and 11.1%, respectively, while the growth rates at banks were a comparable 11.8% and 10.0%. In 1965, however, the growth rate of deposits at savings institutions was only 8.3%, while the growth rate of deposits at banks was a much greater 14.7%.

In reality, the FHLBB "remedy" constituted not much more than a "finger in the dike" which carried with it rate control consequences that would negatively impact the thrift industry for years to come. At this point, more enlightened structural reform and less kneejerk regulation would have made a big difference; but the political landscape didn't favor any kind of major overhaul of the financial system.

This was only one – of many – examples of how regulatory "tinkering" in pursuit of quick fixes fell short of the real need for basic, structural reform.

While this intervention did give thrifts a brief respite from rate wars over deposits, the new ceiling had another noteworthy – unintended? – consequence. As the "invaders" began to withdraw and costly competition for deposits subsided, the earnings of east coast thrifts began to surge. This, in turn, caught the attention of the tax collector.

As might be expected, "revenuers" in Washington swung into action. They were aroused not only by thrifts' burgeoning pots of *taxable* profits but also by a recent spate of tactless, heavy-handed lobbying by the thrift industry. The lobbyists' finagling had angered President Kennedy, who clearly wanted to smite the savings industry in the manner in which he had recently thumped the "unruly" steel industry.

As a consequence, Congress pushed through an adverse tax policy with respect to thrifts. It increased their tax bills significantly. In future years, this new tax burden would drain thrift institutions' earnings and reserves, often constituting the difference between survival and failure. The impact on Erie was painful, to say the least.

The use of interest rate "ceilings" to influence thrifts' activities did not go unnoticed by commercial bankers. They began to speculate about other regulatory levers that they might ply to their advantage. It didn't take them long to focus on Regulation Q, which had, for years, maintained restrictive deposit interest rate ceilings on savings and time deposit accounts held in commercial banks. The Regulation did not impose rate ceilings on savings institutions.

Reg. Q was the composite of a gaggle of regulations enabled by the Banking Act of 1933. It was designed to constrain the ability of commercial banks to offer excessively high rates to attract savings deposits. Advocates hoped that it would rein in commercial banks' temptations to aggressively seek funds to finance speculative deals (i.e. the kind that had occasioned the Crash in 1929).

Reg. Q had another significant raison d'être. Its backers believed that by constraining commercial banks' abilities to attract savings deposits, thrifts could continue to pull in low-cost funds to fuel residential mortgage financing, which was a national social priority.

The Regulation had no real impact during the thirty years subsequent to its enactment because commercial banks had little appetite for competing with thrift institutions for savings accounts during that period. Moreover, prevailing market interest rates during those three decades were consistently below the ceilings that Reg. Q had envisioned, so the thrift-commercial bank competitive balance was not affected. In fact, the only time the ceiling received attention was in 1957, when a run-up in interest rates caused the mandated ceiling to be temporarily raised from 2½% to 3%.

Over time, thrifts had grown comfortable with their market position since they had never come under the purview of Regulation Q. Thus, they enjoyed an ability to match market rates if and when they moved higher. Most seasoned thrift managers readily dismissed the possibility that rates would move up substantially under any conceivable economic scenario.

But the '60s were ushering in a new environment which, because of the introduction of a number of expensive public initiatives, would stimulate both public and private demand for funds and, as a consequence, cause a considerable increase in interest rates.

As interest rates dramatically escalated in the early 1960s, commercial bankers began to realize the importance of an ability to increase deposit rates in such an environment. They anticipated that they would soon be required to pay higher levels of interest on deposits to assure a continued flow of funds to support their business lending activities. This was a frightening and motivating realization, especially in light of their belief that they had, for too long, been unfairly disadvantaged in the marketplace by an oppressive rate cap which allowed thrift institutions to remain relatively "ceiling free." They feared that emerging inflation would stimulate thrifts to finally move their rates substantially above those that could be offered by commercial banks.

As a consequence, commercial bankers began to formulate plans to push for a Reg. Q overhaul which would grant them the authority to offset any substantial protracted rate disadvantage vis-à-vis thrifts.

To their delight, rate-setting regulators were accommodating. The Reg. Q ceiling was raised to 4% and then to 4½% in 1964. In 1965, it was elevated to 5½%.

While these changes were initially welcomed by commercial banks, they feared that these accommodations would not be sufficient to allow them to compete aggressively with savings institutions over the long-term as inflation persisted. It irritated them that, while they had to depend on a protracted, bureaucratic process to gain permission to increase interest rates, savings institutions could pay whatever rates they desired.

As a consequence, commercial bankers accelerated their efforts to secure legislation that would "level the playing field."

An unfettered source of funds was extremely important to commercial banks. Traditionally, the loans they extended to business firms were supported by no-cost checking accounts and low-cost corporate deposit accounts. But now, in this new competitive world, they would be forced to increasingly depend on non-corporate deposit funds... the kind that had traditionally flowed to savings institutions.

Commercial banks were facing another significant challenge, too. Many of their business customers had begun to employ non-bank financing in the form of private equity raises, commercial paper, and novel forms of attractively-packaged corporate debt. Therefore, in order to continue to be competitive in the lending marketplace, commercial banks had to offer extremely competitive loan rates... and those could be financed only through low-cost deposits.

In addition, commercial banks' consumer lending activities were becoming more popular (and profitable), and this required even greater deposit-based funding... the kind that had traditionally been the purview of savings institutions.

Therefore, as thrifts were being constrained by new regulations and taxes, commercial banks saw an opportunity to gain the upper-hand. The time was ripe, they concluded, for some regulation-free, heavy-duty siphoning from the flow of savings that had long irrigated thrifts' growth. As interest rates escalated significantly in 1965 and 1966, commercial banks' lobbyists descended in full force on Washington. As we shall see in the following pages, they would achieve a critical objective in September 1966, thanks to Senator Wright Patman and the inadvertent help of some naïve thrift industry leaders.

It should be noted that, at this stage of its history, the thrift industry generally did not welcome change. It had done very well, thank you, for one-hundred and fifty years. It had been a "quasi" eleemosynary, "sort of" non-profit, "kind of" community service institution that was never required to function as a truly competitive *business*. While some shops did stoop to employ a public relations manager to keep their images burnished, very few embraced the kind of professional management and marketing expertise that would be necessary to maneuver the treacherous waters of a competitive environment like the one that was emerging.

When things had run counter to their interests in the past, thrift execs' good-old-boy connections in Washington would routinely facilitate a rescue. Unfortunately, in most cases, these "helpful" politicians responded with only short-term, stop-gap measures that would be just enough to warrant contributions to their next election campaign... and a round of golf when they were back in their home district.

So, in the face of their most recent competitive challenges, thrift industry leaders once again turned to Washington for help. They were looking for immediate accommodation; they weren't seeking long-run, fundamental – difficult – change.

They and their trade associations implored Congress and the regulatory establishment to help them build a "fort" against the horde of competitors that was now attacking.

And, unfortunately, they got it. It was in a form that encouraged a pattern of continuous regulatory re-jiggering which would ultimately benefit neither the savings industry nor the United States Treasury. Congresspersons, not being very business savvy (few had been businessmen or entrepreneurs), didn't know how to constructively craft the kinds of regulatory measures that would accommodate an orderly, progressive, and business-like transition by thrifts into the future. So, with the housing industry at its back – pushing – Congress gave savings institutions the keys to a new protective "fort," i.e. the Interest Rate Adjustment Act of 1966.

In response to the pleas for help by the desperate managers in the savings industry, this Act "gifted" them with a *small* measure of *temporary* relief from *some* of the anxieties that came with competing in the "real world."

Not a very good deal.

The Act, which was maneuvered through Congress by Rep. Wright Patman, *temporarily* levied new interest rate controls that would – *supposedly* – advantage thrift institutions and enable them to increase mortgage lending while avoiding fierce deposit rate competition.

Importantly, the Act imposed rate ceilings on both banks *and* thrift institutions to ensure that a loss of funds from the latter to the former could be prevented in periods of rising interest rates.

A very important feature of the <u>Interest Rate Adjustment Act of 1966</u> – in addition to the imposition of ceilings – was the establishment of a "differential" between the rates that banks and thrifts would be allowed to pay on deposits. The goal was to permit thrifts to pay a higher rate and, thus, attract deposits that would facilitate loans to home buyers. In fashioning this differential, it was acknowledged that banks had an inherent competitive advantage over thrifts because of the wider array of services they could offer customers (no surprise here!). In order to offset this competitive advantage, it was argued, thrifts needed to be able to pay higher deposit rates.

Under the Act, the ceiling rates on savings deposits were initially set at 4% for banks and 4.75% for thrift institutions, a differential of 75 basis points. The ceiling rate for time deposits (i.e. contracted deposits that had to be left with the bank for a specified time period) was set at 5% for banks, while the ceiling rate for thrift institutions was set at 5¼%, a differential of 25 basis points.

Many within the old guard of the thrift industry breathed a sigh of relief, but an astute minority quickly ascertained that this Act was incredibly bad news for thrifts. *The new controls provided for in this bill unambiguously subjected the thrift industry, for the first time in history, to industry-specific deposit rate ceilings.* This limitation would create enormous financial stresses for the thrift industry in the years ahead.

Nevertheless, many thrift leaders warmly accepted this inaugural imposition of interest rate ceilings because the Act also included a permission that allowed them to pay deposit rates that were slightly higher than those offered by commercial banks. They were also pleased that this legislation was described as "temporary… to deal with unusual circumstances."

Indeed, over the next few years, many of the less-enlightened "leaders" in the thrift industry would come to view the new Regulation Q policy as absolutely essential – *in perpetuity* – for them to be able to attract deposits and make mortgage loans.

In reality, Patman's legislation created a major change in Regulation Q and reflected the dissatisfaction of the federal government with the performance of the financial system as a whole. Interest rates had risen sharply in 1965 and 1966. The three-month Treasury bill rate had jumped from 3.84% in September 1965 to 5.37% in September 1966. Over that period, interest rates on residential mortgage loans across the nation had risen from 5.80% to 6.65%.

It can be argued that the Interest Rate Adjustment Act of 1966 was crafted, in large part, to publicly demonstrate policymakers' displeasure with the competition for deposits between commercial banks and thrifts. It was erroneously believed that such competition was one of the primary causes of the general rise in interest rates nationally and that deposit interest rate ceilings had to be extended to thrifts to limit this rise.

The fans of this legislation also thought (incorrectly, it was later proven) that the escalating diversion of funds from *residential* mortgages to loans for *business* firms could be reversed by limiting the interest rates that commercial banks could pay on deposits. They further believed that the imposition of Regulation Q on thrifts would reduce their deposit costs and cause them to make more mortgages at lower interest rates.

To insightful observers, however, the action of Congress reflected a dangerous conviction that natural market dynamics could – and would – be beneficially controlled by regulation and legislation. (This kind of penchant for paternal tinkering with free market dynamics would prevail within government for many more years and would become one of the primary causative factors of the thrift crisis of the 1980s.)

By virtue of the Interest Rate Adjustment Act of 1966, the thrift industry had become willingly enmeshed in a web of new regulation that would eventually, diminish – to a huge extent – the competitiveness of its constituent institutions.

Nevertheless, many short-sighted thrift executives ecstatically embraced these governmentally-imposed ceilings and rate differentials. The walls of their "fort" were up, and the invaders were going to be held at bay.

Or so they thought.

What these risk-averse executives failed to note was that forts and prisons are architecturally identical, save for one aspect, i.e. forts have their locks on the *inside* of their doors. By giving the federal government's "wardens" the "keys" to the industry's future, they converted their protective fort into a confining prison... and the locks would forever remain on the *outside* of their doors. From that point on, thrifts' capacities to compete aggressively with commercial banks, mutual funds, the U.S. Treasury, the issuers of private and municipal debt, and – eventually – money market funds would be controlled by the federal government... a government that increasingly feared rising interest rates and a protracted inflationary economic spiral. Frighteningly, it was a government that thought it possessed insight sufficient to conjure policy that would enable it to control market realities.

Short-sighted thrift leaders got what they wanted, but it wasn't going to be pretty. Unfortunately, the Big E was going to suffer right along with them in the "Alcatraz" they had created.

In the long run, the only real losers would be savings institutions. In effect, this new legislation put the industry in "lockdown" within an otherwise free-market economy.

With the passage of the Act, commercial banks also incurred relative restraints with respect to deposit rates, but they also received some important benefits, including a *smaller* interest rate differential with thrifts and a rate ceiling that moved in lockstep with rates paid by savings institutions. Further, they still had the advantage provided by their more liberal customer service powers, including no-cost checking accounts. Their ability to scarf up funds from erstwhile savings bank customers had been greatly enhanced.

As might be expected, commercial banks began to ratchet up their competitive forays into thrifts' traditional marketplaces. When it came to the task of paying-up to snatch new deposits from their principal competitors, they carried with them a major advantage, i.e. there were very few profit-debilitating, low-rate mortgages in their portfolios.

Further, in the future, their earnings capacities – and, therefore, their rate-paying abilities – could more easily adjust to the impacts of inflation and competition. Thus, their net interest margins could be preserved. Savings institutions did not have that advantage since they were hobbled by portfolios that consisted primarily of fixed-rate loans. As a consequence, commercial banks had the muscle to continually divert savings flows from thrift institutions while simultaneously incurring a smaller hit to the bottom line than was suffered by thrifts.

To add insult to injury, the federal government was also becoming an aggressive competitor for savings dollars. Long a contender in the mortgage market, it now turned an eye toward savers. After all, money would have to be borrowed to finance President Johnson's "Great Society" and the war in Vietnam. Accordingly, the U.S. Treasury became a major player in the consumer savings market, offering gilt-edged, market-rate, small-denomination securities that were extremely attractive to savers who were becoming increasingly restive with the low interest rates that could be paid by savings banks like Erie.

Thrifts' deposit outflows were also exacerbated by increased competition from non-bank entities like mutual funds and, later, money market funds. These funds-seekers were able to offer financial instruments that carried yields above the stipulated Regulation Q ceilings. They were not subjected to interest rate controls of any kind and, as a consequence, would soon be paying rates substantially above those allowed for thrifts and banks.

Savings institutions were also being buffeted by changing consumer habits. Now that their basic, post-war needs had been tended to, American consumers began to look, increasingly, for more convenience and ease in their everyday affairs, banking included. Ready access to branches, checking accounts, consumer loans, and credit cards took on added significance in the average person's patronage patterns. Commercial banks, as contrasted to the more strictly regulated thrifts, were able to offer all of these conveniences, and they marketed them aggressively in order to draw savers to their branches.

Another significant challenge to thrifts consisted of the differences in the ways in which thrifts and commercial banks were being routinely regulated. Banks were complex entities whose operations would have ground to a halt had they been saddled with the kinds of extremely detailed regulations that encumbered thrifts. There were only a relatively small number of overly-burdensome rules that conditioned banks' operations and lending practices in the marketplaces of non-business savers and mortgagors. For most of history, the primary mission of commercial bank regulators was to ensure that banks were operating in a safe and sound manner in the *business* world.

Thrifts, on the other hand, were generally perceived by their regulators as community service organizations that were originally enfranchised to serve individuals of limited means. As such, thrifts provided regulatory bureaucrats with abundant opportunities to introduce, with relative impunity, all manner of detailed proscriptions, guidelines, rules, and mandated procedures that focused intensely on the provision of consumer benefits but had little regard for the bottom-line earnings and surpluses that thrifts had to create in order to continue to serve.

For example, the New York State Banking Department, the principal regulator of state savings banks, clung rigidly to the belief that thrifts could survive and serve the housing market without any significant change in their powers to compete. Branching within the state was highly constrained and supervised, often to the point of ridiculousness. For example, because of municipal zoning issues, the drive–up facility at one of Erie's new branches was constructed 105 feet from the main building (as contrasted to the 100 foot maximum distance stipulated by state banking regulations). As a consequence, we had to construct an expensive man-tunnel between the two structures before the Department would sign off on the project as consisting of just "one" building (which would not be subjected to the mandate concerning the "distance between structures").

This petty stuff was the least of the state's savings banks' problems. A continuing unrealistic usury ceiling and strict geographic restraints on lending activities made it difficult for savings banks to book profitable assets to offset the increasingly expensive deposit liabilities they were accumulating. For example, savings banks could make mortgage loans only in New York State and its five contiguous states, i.e. Pennsylvania, Massachusetts, Vermont, Connecticut, and New Jersey.

Moreover, despite the fact that deposit costs were continuously increasing as national interest rates climbed, the New York State Legislature was not willing to consider adjustable rate mortgages or higher-rate consumer lending powers for savings banks. New fee-generating services were also denied.

Commercial banks had great influence over the state's Senators and Assemblymen. Their large political donations were highly effective. In fact, many members of the Legislature depended upon commercial banks to finance both their personal endeavors and their professional enterprises. Moreover, many Legislators were attorneys who derived a great deal of business from commercial banks and their business customers. Savings banks began to wilt amid an intensifying squeeze between national market realities and the rigid, provincial operating constraints imposed by the state government and federal agencies.

There did emerge, however, a glimmer of hope on the national level. The Chairman of the Federal Home Loan Bank Board, the principal regulator of savings and loan associations, recruited Dr. Irwin Friend of the Wharton School of Business at the University of Pennsylvania to compile a comprehensive evaluation of the thrift industry and its prospects. In 1969, his incisive report was published. It called for thrifts to be empowered to book a more diversified array of assets, including variable rate mortgages and consumer credit products. It also called for a more relevant mix of liability (i.e. deposit) offerings, including checking accounts. If implemented at that time, these major modifications in balance sheet composition would have probably precluded a lot of thrift failures during the "crisis" of the 1980s. However, since the rate wars of the early '60s had abated somewhat by 1969, there was little motivation on the part of government to act on Dr. Friend's proposals.

This was not a surprise since, as history has amply demonstrated, governments are typically stirred to action only in cases of acute crises... when almost any action is too late to make a difference.

Then, too, most of the old-guard leaders in the thrift industry pooh-poohed Dr. Friend's suggestions because his proposals included the abolition of Regulation Q, the anti-competitive device that had become near and dear to their hearts.

## More frontiers for the Big E

Fortunately, the first year of the 1960s saw the introduction of the "right man at the right time" into the top executive position at the Big E. His leadership was to have a great impact on the Erie County Savings Bank and on the industry as a whole. He appreciated the need for sweeping change in the thrift industry and he was eager to prepare the Big E to play a winning role in the new consumer banking system he envisioned.

Harlan J. Swift, a lawyer who had served as second in command at the bank since 1957, was elected President of Erie. He was the eighth president in the 106-year history of the institution, and he brought with him the intelligence, savvy, determination, and demeanor that would be needed as the challenging decade unfolded.

When he was hired, he was told that banking was really "a pretty easy business" and that it ran by the "3-4-5 Rule." In the parlance of the industry, that meant: pay three percent on deposits; charge four percent on mortgages; and get to the club by five o'clock. The 1960s proved that no less-true words were ever spoken. Harlan Swift would never abide by that rule.

During the first half of the decade, he and his small team (the bank had only 280 employees) launched a number of initiatives to make the bank competitive and profitable. In 1960, the bank took advantage of the New York State Omnibus Banking Bill which allowed it to open a new branch outside of the city limits. The office was opened in the Northtown Plaza in Amherst and was dubbed by the press as "one of the most modern, striking, and functional structures of its type in America, with many exciting new features designed especially for suburbanites."

On the consumer front, the bank began to aggressively promote student loans, which it was authorized to do in 1960. It also introduced "second mortgages" (which it called "home-based loans"); personal savings (passbook) loans; payday savings accounts for employees of Buffalo companies (which facilitated automatic deductions from an individual worker's wages); property improvement loans; and a telephone-based Time and Temperature service (844-6161) to which over 13 million calls were placed in its first year of operation. (There were more than 78,000 calls on a single day in October 1965.) These initiatives marked the introduction of the art and science of marketing into the Big E.

The bank also showed its progressive side. In 1960, a woman was elected an officer of the bank for the first time since its founding.

During this period, the Big E began to *compound* dividends (i.e. interest) on savings accounts, thereby increasing the effective rate of return earned by depositors.

At the mid-point of the decade, the bank announced its participation in the redevelopment of downtown Buffalo. A wide-ranging acquisition of land by a bank-supported development group resulted in, among other things, the construction of the Main Place Mall and its adjoining 26-story Big E office tower. It was a much-needed addition to downtown Buffalo, and it spurred substantial complementary development of the area.

The bank's first "real" computer, an IBM 360, was delivered in mid-decade with the promise that it would soon provide faster and more accurate customer service. Indeed, the Big E was to become one of the first banks (including commercial banks) in the nation to put account data "on line" to all branches.

In 1964, a full page bank advertisement boldly proclaimed that the Big E had reached the "five...oh.. oh..oh..oh..oh..oh..oh..oh" mark in assets (i.e. a half of a billion dollars). The ad further proclaimed that this achievement "means that hundreds of thousands of people in all income groups have one important thing in common – the important and wholesome habit of *THRIFT*."

This growth did not come without a high cost, however. In order to retain existing deposits and garner new ones, the bank had to continue paying the highest interest rates allowed by prevailing law. In 1962, it raised its regular dividend to 3.75% and offered 4% on balances remaining for over one year; in 1963, the regular rate rose to 4% and the one-year deposit rate jumped to 4.25%, the highest in 81 years; by 1965, the bank was paying 4.25% on all deposits. Meanwhile, the rate on the bank's earning assets – principally mortgages – had risen only slightly... and *very* slowly.

As the second-half of the decade commenced, the rapidly-growing financial needs of the federal government sowed the seeds for rampant inflation. The resulting scramble by private financial institutions, the Treasury, and other government agencies to meet mounting demands for funds – at *any* price – caused interest rates to spike and pulled savers' dollars away from thrifts. It forced a substantial cutback in the Big E's mortgage lending for the first time in the bank's recent history.

The menacing interest rate "Genie" had managed to get out of the bottle... *with a vengeance.*

The Big E responded by offering a special dividend rate of 5% on savings accounts. The 5% rate plateau had long been envisioned by bank officers as the "line in the sand" between normalcy and an economic Armageddon. No one could believe the "dreaded future" had come so fast; few expected that it would keep right on coming.

The consequent earnings squeeze did not go unnoticed by President Swift. He was mindful of the long-term threat that it posed to the bank. He was convinced that, despite its many accomplishments to date, the bank had to become even more aggressive in the marketplace and that it would have to cope with increasing competition from enterprises of all stripes, including non-banks. Accordingly, he began to search for a marketing manager who understood the evolving economy's implications for the thrift industry – and the Big E in particular – and could lead a fitting response.

## My great opportunity

For a number of years, Erie's senior vice president, William "Bill" Schreiber, had routinely attended the monthly meetings of the Buffalo Chamber of Commerce "Breakfast Club." A regular feature of those get-togethers was an economic briefing which was presented by a young staff economist at the Chamber. As Director of Research and Education at the Chamber, the "kid" who prepared and delivered those presentations was also involved in the Chamber's regional development and marketing initiatives. (At that time, the Buffalo Chamber of Commerce was the fourth largest Chamber in the nation.) In a report to Harlan Swift, Bill said that this twenty-seven year old, wet-behind-the-ears economist – *your author* – seemed to have "a lot of savvy and energy" and should be a candidate for the bank's newly-established "marketing manager" position.

After a number of discussions with Harlan Swift and a "vetting" by Dr. Austin Murphy, a bank Trustee (who also happened to be an economist and the "kid's" major professor at Canisius College), I was offered the position of Marketing Officer for the Big E, and I formally signed on in December 1966, the 150th anniversary of savings banks in the United States. It was a big day for this life-long resident of East Buffalo and the city's "Fruit Belt"... this son of a bank teller... this proud new Erie team member.

It should be noted that I'd previously learned the importance of saving and had *some* experience in banking. In 1946, while in second grade at St. Ann School in Buffalo I became the class teller for an Erie County Savings Bank in-school savings program. My job, under the stern supervision of Sister Mary Raingardis OSF, was to ledger-in deposits from my classmates. I bundled up their pennies, nickels, and dimes and shipped them to the Big E every Tuesday, like clockwork. St. Ann's, located at Broadway and Emslie Streets, was built primarily with the savings (and personal labors) of its frugal German parishioners more than a half-century before I arrived on the scene. Sensitive to my Germanic heritage, and with the fear of a stint in purgatory or a ruler on my knuckles, I knew that my deposit ledger simply *had* to balance.

I was also my mother's banker, trekking weekly to the Community Savings and Loan Association at Genesee and Johnson Streets to make weekly deposits of twenty-five cents to each of three Christmas Club accounts. I also had the onerous duty of occasionally apologizing to the austere but cordial teller/manager when the Willax family was tardy in meeting its "commitment" to the fifty-two week process of saving for Christmas.

I was my own personal banker, too. A number of jobs during my teen years – bookstore manager, neighborhood theater manager, printing salesman, mailman, etc. – enabled me to amass, by age 18, the princely sum of $1,400. That was enough to cover two years of tuition at Canisius College or the University of Buffalo. Happily, by the time I was ready to enter college, I had snagged a New York State Regents Scholarship in the amount of $1,400 and, thereby, had sufficient funds in hand to pay for *four* years of college education.

Now the choice was, "where to go?" My frugality played a role here, too. I had initially considered attending the University of Buffalo but, in 1957, the local transit authority levied a two-cent fee on transfers from one bus line to another, thus greatly increasing the daily expense of a trip on *both* the Jefferson Ave. and Main St. lines (which would have been necessary for UB attendance). In comparison, the Jefferson line, sans transfers, provided a direct, fee-free trip to the Canisius campus. Not incidentally, the daily four-cent difference equated to the price of a carton of milk in a college cafeteria. Once again, saving money was a big factor in my decision-making. So, it was "off to Canisius."

My first *real* bank job – at age sixteen – entailed using small rags and Q-Tips to scrape the preservative grease from the myriad of sharp interior crevasses on bank vault doors at newly-opened branches of the Marine Trust Company (later HSBC). Scores of finger cuts ensured that this assignment would be looked back upon as the least pleasant job of my entire banking career.

During my college years, I was able to work full-time at the Marine Trust Company as a relief teller during the summer and other vacation seasons. I was proud to work at the same bank that had employed my father since 1918. (By the time he retired in 1968, he had worked for almost 40 years as a teller at a single Marine Trust Co. branch. He finished his 50-year career as an assistant manager at that very same branch.)

Needless to say, all these personal banking experiences taught me the value of banks to savers. But they never suggested a career path. Indeed, as a life-long witness to my father's hard work in the banking business, I easily conjured up a career scenario of long, tedious hours at very low pay. (In fact, the year that I started to work at the Big E, my annual salary was almost fifty-percent greater than my dad's... and he had been employed by a bank for a half-century!)

In my youth, I saw him serving customers through a metal security "cage" in a less-than-stylish beige "office coat." At day's end, he would update all transaction records by hand (a pre-computer practice that was still in place during my years as a teller). For a time during the 1920s and 1930s, he also packed a revolver. (Dillinger was not going to take *his* cash drawer!)

Since the Jefferson-Utica neighborhood was a major shopping destination at that time, my father also had to report to work on Saturday mornings and afternoons (with a three-hour intervening break) to service neighborhood merchants.

He never complained. He loved the customers. Every night at our family dinner table, he would recount each customer transaction of the day, *at least once*. And the customers loved him. The owners of some of the biggest businesses in Buffalo would travel to Jefferson Avenue to do their banking because "Os" would take good care of them.

And he loved the bank. It provided him with security during the Depression. It gave him a pension to look forward to. The bank's Mariners' Club gave him opportunities for socialization, not the least of which was bowling. We lived in the vicinity of his branch, so convenience was also a benefit. Most importantly, it allowed him to help people with their financial affairs. Interestingly, he also trained many employees during his years at Marine Trust, and three of them went on to become bank presidents.

He never looked forward to retirement until the 1960s when muggings, fire bombings, and robberies forced us, in 1964, to move from our city neighborhood to a $16,000 "mansion" in suburban Cheektowaga – with the help of a sizeable mortgage from the Big E. Sadly, our two-family house on the East Side – my father's residence for almost forty years – sold for only $1,200.

In his final years with the bank, I could see that new-fangled things like computerization, personal loans, highly-structured marketing programs, and employee evaluations (which, in order to be "fair," he labored over at home for hours at a stretch) were beginning to take their toll. So was the deterioration of the neighborhood around his branch. His old, faithful customers had left. He, too often, was driven home from work at night by a friendly police officer from the local precinct after his car was stolen from the bank parking lot. As much as he loved the bank, he began to realize that the time to move on was approaching.

So, in the spring of 1968, Os was offered early retirement (four months early) and he took it in order to get a jump-start with his garden. Four months later, he was in a nursing home, never to return to his beloved vegetable patch.

I always knew that as much as he loved the people, the security, the bowling, the pension, and "striking the accounts" to a perfect balance, he never really *wanted* to a banker.

As a young man, he wanted to be an architect; but for that profession you had to have attended high school and college, which he hadn't because of family obligations. He also nurtured a dream of being a farmer, and he acted that out superbly, part-time, with a vegetable garden that was the envy of many full-time farmers.

Like my dad, I never really wanted to be a banker, either. I had seen too much of a banker's life and wanted to pursue something different.

During my five years of service at the Chamber of Commerce, I had been offered several employment opportunities – one with the Marine Trust Company – and by mid-decade was considering three of them seriously. These included a major television network's on-the-job training program for news correspondents; a job in New York City with the largest public relations firm in the world; and a marketing/member education position with the National Association of Manufacturers. Unfortunately, each of them required me to leave Buffalo.

As attractive as these opportunities were, I wanted to stay in Buffalo. My stint at the Chamber had shown me that there was much that could and should be done in a community that had begun a menacing – but, to a young person, exciting – metamorphosis.

But I was still not interested in banking. That's when the call came from Harlan Swift. After a telephone chat and a meeting with him, I became intrigued by the career opportunity he offered me. He wasn't talking about banking; he was describing an institution – an entire industry – in transition. He was presenting me with an opportunity to help change the very nature of a bank... to become a leader... to make a difference... and, to do it in a community that I loved.

Of great significance was Mr. Swift's admission that he really didn't want to hire a banker. He wanted somebody who was willing to take some chances in changing an "establishment." Moreover, he said he needed somebody who could sell uncomfortable change to others. He wanted somebody to help him make banking different, and to move Erie in new directions.

And *that* I could buy into.

However, the biggest inducement to join the Big E was Harlan Swift himself. He and Austin Murphy were the kinds of leaders I wanted to emulate. Harlan was recruiting a change-maker; I was recruiting a role model. He was smart, experienced, approachable, articulate, friendly, affable, and decisive. He was a thinker and an innovator. He was a true gentleman.

Of course, he was also a graduate of Princeton and Yale, a member of Buffalo's "establishment," and a well-to-do pillar of the community. But this "baggage" didn't stop me from buying into the man. I knew we "could go places together," and I quickly took him up on his offer to become a non-banker at the Big E. to this day, I have never questioned my decision.

I assumed my duties as Marketing Officer in January 1967, settling into an office on the third floor of the Big E "castle" on Shelton Square. (See rendering on the front cover of this book.)

It was to be the first year the Erie County Savings Bank suffered a financial loss since the Great Depression.

The next twenty-three years were to be busy ones for Paul Willax.

**The tasks at hand**

Soon after I came aboard, the bank opened a branch office (it's fourth) on Transit Road in Amherst, New York, across from an enormous, barren field that housed only a small Grant's department store. The landlord promised that a vast project – to be called Eastern Hills Mall – would eventually open on that site and that our tellers would be busier than we could imagine. He was right.

My first order of business at Erie – other than to assist in the opening of a new branch – was to formulate a plan for change, a plan that would make the Big E more than "just" a traditional savings bank.

It was an easy job. There were so many talented, forward-thinking, hard-working employees in the bank who were willing to participate. Harlan had developed many believers, both young and old, and they wanted to be part of the great adventure that was envisioned in the bank's first marketing plan, which I completed in the spring of 1967.

Of course, there were some naysayers among the old guard, and they often made life miserable for the "young Turk" who was responsible for this disconcerting "change in direction." To be sure, they wanted what was best for the bank; but, they weren't convinced I was offering it.

However, one by one I began to win their support. To paraphrase Winston Churchill, I had never before, nor have I ever since, witnessed so many talented people work so hard and make so many sacrifices to create a promising future. Nor have I ever seen so many people having so much fun doing it. To this day, I encounter former Big E staffers who happily claim the bank was the best place they'd ever worked. And, they inevitably add, "It was great fun, too."

There was an amazing culture at the bank, the onset of which preceded my arrival. It offered opportunity for an ambitious team to build the most exciting, innovative, progressive bank of its time. It wasn't going to be "my father's bank," but it was going to be the kind of bank he would have loved.

Much of the positive atmosphere in the bank was derived from its busy social calendar. The bank funded (dues were nominal) an "Employees Club" that facilitated a wide range of social, sports, and professional activities in which staff members could participate. Bowling, basketball, and baseball attracted not only eager and able players but hordes of spectators from every department of the bank. Win or lose, there was always a party after a game… and Big E parties were festive, to say the least. Indeed, parties were a way of life and work at the Big E. There was a weekly "fifth floor" party at the old Shelton Square headquarters. (The party, of course, migrated with the staff as we moved from building to building while our new Main Place Mall headquarters took shape.) There were parties for holidays, birthdays, and for many reasons less defined. Picnics, sporting events, and kids' days at the park got families involved as well.

Camaraderie was prevalent and pervasive; a team atmosphere energized almost every aspect of bank life. It transcended gender, age, and rank within a rather informal bank hierarchy. When I joined the institution, there were still Thursday afternoon poker games in the basement furnace room that beckoned all, from maintenance man to senior vice president. Atypically for a bank, everyone worked and played on a first name basis.

I firmly believe that the bank prospered for as long as it did in large part because of the personal bonds that connected all of its team members in both work and play. To this day, I advise my students and clients that a company must carefully attend the social dimension of its organization at the risk of becoming too formal, stultified, and ossified for its own good. I learned quickly at the Big E that the creative juices and operational energies that feed any ambitious business entity are correlated closely with its "fun" factor. Our success, I believe, demonstrated that fun should be part of any job.

The Big E team's amalgam of talent, spirit, and competitiveness allowed it to continually innovate and prosper. As the following pages will reveal, even the loftiest goals of this ambitious band of brothers and sisters became realities during the next two decades. From the "Surprising Sixties" forward, the bank consistently introduced significant innovations that eventually became widely accepted in the thrift industry.

The second half of the '60s saw the first batch of these new products, services, and business practices successfully introduced by the Big E as the bank's first ever business plan gained traction.

A broad range of new accounts was introduced to attract savers. EZ Save statement accounts (complete with an ID card featuring a color picture of the depositor) were offered as a convenient and simplified alternative to the passbook.

In cooperation with local employers, a Payday Provider service facilitated an allocation of regular deductions from their employees' paychecks to a combination of accounts designed to achieve their education, retirement, general savings, and vacation goals.

The bank brought to market Fun Accounts to encourage savings for things other than "rainy days." These special accounts had pre-printed deposit slips to encourage saving for fun times. Also introduced were retirement accounts for self-employed individuals (under the federal Keogh Act of 1962).

Other, non-account services were also introduced to attract and retain customers in an increasingly competitive marketplace. The Money Minder service offered a customer a personalized, computer-generated "target" budget based on his or her life's circumstances and on the practices of typical Western New York residents in a similar income group.

At the bank's sprawling main office, fashionably-uniformed, in-lobby hostesses were provided to personally assist customers. In addition, customers of all branches could make appointments with bank personnel, thus obviating irritating queues.

Despite a surge in bond rates in 1968 and 1969, which offered the Big E an attractive investment alternative to mortgage lending, it continued to provide a ready source of loans for housing in Erie County. In 1968, for example, Erie made more residential mortgage loans and more student loans than any other local savings bank... over $50 million, which was 22% of all the lending done by the fifteen other banks and savings institutions in the Buffalo area combined. In the decade of the '60s, the bank invested more than a quarter-of-a-billion dollars in mortgage loans, which financed over 20,000 homes.

In 1967, Big E tellers in every branch went "on line" with a central computer, making Erie the first bank in the nation to accomplish such a feat.

A little later, the Sheridan Drive – Northtowns office became the first savings bank branch in New York State to attain $100 million in deposits.

Growth was taking place in downtown Buffalo, too. In 1967, the bank's historic main office on Shelton Square (which is depicted on the front cover of this book) was demolished. There were very few dry eyes as the wrecking ball crashed into the building's stately facade. While many wished otherwise, there was no other option. Both the interior and exterior walls of this building – which was opened in 1893 – had begun to crumble, and its electric wiring could not be upgraded, thus making modern heating and air conditioning impossible. The "castle," regrettably, had to come down.

In its place, there arose a three-story shopping mall and a twenty-six story office building anchored by the headquarters of the Erie County Savings Bank (displayed on the back cover of this book). At the formal dedication (a/k/a *What a Party!*) on March 31, 1969, Harlan Swift said: "This structure was not built merely as a symbol of faith in our city's future, but in the knowledge that its future will be great..."

To reflect Erie's new stature in the marketplace, beginning in 1969, all bank advertising was embellished with a new angular Big E logo that was to endure for the life of the bank. It was conceived by local artist Peter VanScozza – with a little help from your author – on a napkin over lunch in Chef's Restaurant in Buffalo. It was based on an inspiration Peter had after noticing the "E" on United States one, ten, and twenty dollar bills.

By decade's end, the bank had truly become – as its advertising trumpeted – *"The bank that's on the move."*

*Chapter four*

# A BUSINESS MODEL MORPHS

## The good ol' days

From 1854 through most of the decade of the 1960s, the business model employed by savings institutions was pretty simple. A certain interest rate was paid to savers on their deposits; let's call it three percent. A slightly higher rate was charged to borrowers who wanted to use those funds to buy a house; we'll say four percent. The one percentage point difference between what was charged to borrowers (i.e. mortgage interest) and what was paid to savers (i.e. interest or "dividends" on deposits) was the "net interest margin" (i.e. NIM). From this NIM, all other operational expenses were paid. If any surplus remained, it was stashed away to accommodate future opportunities and challenges.

In a stable economic environment, this model worked beautifully. In fact, in Erie's heyday, senior officers could occasionally wrap up their duties early in the afternoon, taking the downtime to stop at their brokers' offices to check the stock "ticker" or, as legend had it, traipse across Main Street to catch a matinee at the Palace Burlesque Theater.

Depositors also liked the business model because they had a safe place to salt away their savings and actually earn money on the funds so hoarded. It surely beat stashing greenbacks in a mattress or coffee can.

Likewise, borrowers were pleased. They probably never would have been able to save enough to buy a house for cash during their years of family formation. But, savings institutions helped them to use OPM (other peoples' money) – along with a modest down payment – to "buy now and pay later." Since interest rates were fixed and loan maturities extended twenty to thirty years (enough to pay off the loan), their housing cost was predictable and stable.

This rewarding intermediation model was the raison d'être for the entire thrift industry, and it was successfully sustained for almost one hundred and fifty years. In this construct, savings banks "intermediated" or "came between" savers and borrowers to provide benefits to each.

A number of social and economic conditions – which are enumerated below – facilitated this powerful and profitable intermediation model.

- **Inefficiencies in the marketplace:** As any freshman economics major knows, the marketplace does not always provide for an efficient matching of buyers and sellers. Since the needs and resources of savers (i.e. funds providers) and borrowers (i.e. funds users) vary considerably from time to time and from place to place, significant arbitrage opportunities become available to an institution that is able to deftly position itself between these two marketplaces. Savings institutions flourished for decades as an arbitrageur in this milieu. They provided an otherwise unachievable interface for the supply and demand elements that were so essential to satisfying the needs of both savers and borrowers.

  The following paragraphs describe a number of long-standing, socio-economic factors that assisted thrifts in utilizing this arbitrage opportunity to serve customers and to, simultaneously, sustain their own operations.

  o **Uninformed savers:** Historically, most thrift institutions' depositors were middle-to-low-income, "blue collar" individuals with average-to-below-average formal education. Typically, they knew little about investment theory or the opportunities to apply it that were offered by brokerage firms and other sophisticated financial service organizations. These customers were risk averse and were motivated primarily by a desire to preserve their accumulated savings. Their personal or folkloric experiences with financial crises, especially the Great Depression, served to accentuate this particular bent. Furthermore, the availability of FDIC and FSLIC insurance enhanced the attractiveness of thrift institutions to them.

- o **A dearth of alternative conduits:** There were very few established institutional links between funds providers and funds users in the savings/mortgage marketplaces. Like commercial banks, stockbrokers focused on erudite investors and eschewed middle-income and lower-income customers. Commercial banks profited as intermediaries that converted *corporate* deposits into *corporate* loans. It wasn't until the mid-point of the twentieth century that commercial banks began to aggressively expand this intercalating function by using both corporate *and* individual savers' funds and to supplement their corporate finance activities and fund consumer credit services. Up until then, only savings banks and savings and loan associations concentrated primarily on maintaining a bridge between small, non-corporate savers and private borrowers who needed residential real estate financing leverage.

- o **Artificial price "controls":** For over a century, the thrift industry business model worked because its constituent institutions could easily set, in accordance with their view of prevailing market conditions, the interest rates that would be paid to savers and the loan rates that would be charged to borrowers. Their "rate schedules" were often further finessed by informal "agreements" between competing bankers or according to a "monkey see; monkey do" interest rate matching methodology. Needless to say, the "similar" rate structures that resulted from this tactic helped to preclude disruptive incursions into each other's customer clienteles via profit-debilitating "rate wars." (From the 1970s onward, prudence, the prospect of punishment as a consequence of antitrust violations, and

79

the introduction of Regulation Q killed such interest rate "coordination" practices.)

- **Relative balance in the capital markets:** Except for infrequent aberrations, supply and demand in the capital markets remained reasonably well-balanced from the time of the Industrial Revolution to the middle of the twentieth century. Corporate and personal savings were sufficient to fund the nation's capital requirements and preclude distortions that might squeeze an intermediary's profit participation (i. e. NIM).

- **Lack of incentive:** During most of the thrift industry's early history, depositors lacked any real incentive to find other avenues to deploy their savings accumulations. The rate of inflation rarely exceeded one percent; and IRS 1099s were just a glimmer in the tax man's eyes. The after-tax, *real* yield afforded by savings accounts easily satisfied the average depositor. There was no need for thrifts to narrow their established profit margins by testing the price elasticity of savers' markets. As a result, the interest rates offered by thrifts tended to hover around satisficing levels and to be relatively static. The interest rates charged in mortgage markets were also rather stable. Over time, this kind of equilibrium allowed the typical thrift institution to accumulate a respectable capital surplus (i.e. net worth) and maintain sufficient liquidity. Since savers were perfectly willing to let their accumulations "rest," and since there were few opportunities – or motivations – for thrifts to achieve investment rates that were higher than what they were already earning, thrifts had no reason to fix a business model that wasn't broken.

As a result of the above conditions, profitable stability prevailed in the thrift industry for generations. A manager who could cloud a mirror could easily achieve – between trips to the country club – a healthy 100 to 200 basis-point spread on the services his thrift provided. It could be safely said that the savings industry, during the first century-and-a-half of its operation, was in "fat city."

## "The times they are a changin'"

The jolting experiences of the late 1960s gave ample warning to bankers that, as Bob Dylan proclaimed, *"the times they are a changin'."* But it was heeded by very few. The typical thrift executive was relatively oblivious to the trends that were taking hold and to the probability that his (there were very few women in management positions at that time) "cake" job was ideally positioned to become a "pie in the face."

Nevertheless, the reasons to anticipate calamity were many.

As the decade of the '70s opened, the nation was suffering a huge balance of payments deficit, anemic growth, and inflation.

In August 1971, a meeting of White House and Treasury Department officials at Camp David resulted in a decision to break up the postwar Bretton Woods monetary system, devalue the dollar, raise tariffs, and impose the first peacetime wage and price controls in American history. Historians referred to this as the "Nixon Shock" and blamed it for a decade of one of the worst inflations in American history and the most stagnant economy since the Great Depression. According to the Wall Street Journal, the policy that was generated by President Richard Nixon and his cohorts "sowed chaos for a decade. The nation and the world reaped the whirlwind."

Consequently, the thrift industry's world began to change dramatically as deleterious events in the economy conspired to make the industry's basic business model obsolete. The most disruptive impacts are outlined in the following paragraphs.

- **Inflation**: The advent of the '70s gave force to an economic phenomenon that began in the late '60s... *stagflation.* It was a new word in America's lexicon and it described a slumping economy coupled with escalating inflationary pressures. This condition so debilitated the nation's economy that even a staunchly conservative

President like Richard Nixon embraced stringent wage and price controls. But, despite this and other policy efforts, including the abandonment of the gold standard, inflation continued unabated and the economy feebly struggled on.

(The average yield on long-term Treasury securities provided an indicator of the severity of this inflation. The rate rose from 5.4% in 1968 to 7.1% in 1973; to 9.3% in 1979; and to 13.7% in 1981. Average six-month Treasury bill rates rose from 5.4% in 1968 to a high of 13.8% in 1981.)

From 1973 to the decade's end, the year-to-year percentage change in consumer prices ranged from five to ten percent. This provoked a shocking diminishment in the real value of the dollars that savers were accumulating. The purchasing power of the dollar dropped more than 50% during the '70s. As a result, savers began to avoid the obvious penalty associated with hoarding depreciating dollars. They came to the disheartening realization that, during extended periods of inflation, dollars were their most adversely- affected assets.

As a result, many savers went off the "dollar standard" and began to reduce their savings in order to redeploy their dollars into appreciable, non-monetary assets. Increasingly, they invested in common stock, antiques, real estate, collectibles, commodities, etc., the value of which, they believed, would move in harmony with the rate of inflation. Individuals who desired safety, liquidity, *and* return on investment began looking for alternatives to savings accounts, e.g. unregulated – but safe and high-yielding – money market funds (which were introduced in 1971). For those individuals who opted to maintain dollar-denominated liquidity, the *real* rate of return (i.e. the current rate adjusted for inflation) offered on their savings became of paramount importance.

Consequently, the interest rate ceilings on deposits that had, only shortly before, been embraced by thrift industry leaders as their salvation became rigid constraints which severely limited savings institutions' abilities to pay (*if* they could afford it*)* the kinds of returns that would enable them to retain deposits and stabilize their liquidity.

Their erstwhile "forts" against change – which provided protection in the form of "walls" of interest rate regulation – quickly became "prisons" in which thrifts' flexibility to compete was *restrained* by the very same walls of regulation. Regulation Q was preventing them from paying competitive interest rates on deposits, and a threat of massive deposit outflows loomed.

(The government tried to keep pace with escalating interest rates by gradually lifting the ceilings on rates that thrifts could pay on deposit accounts. Upward adjustments were allowed in 1970, 1973, and 1978. By 1979, it was apparent that attempts to control rates paid to depositors were futile. The rate control strategy that was trumpeted by Congress in 1966 was abandoned in 1979.)

Interest rate ceilings were causing problems on the asset side of thrifts' balance sheets, also. Long-established state anti-usury laws imposed ceilings on the interest rates that could be charged for loans (including mortgage loans, which were the primary source of income for thrifts). This delimited the returns that thrifts' invested assets could generate. Usury laws, which were especially onerous in New York State, had originally been designed to protect borrowers from exorbitant loan rates. In this hyper-inflationary market, however, even "normal" market rates had become exorbitant. (By the end of the decade, mortgage loan rates would approach 16%.) As a consequence, usury ceilings began to unreasonably constrain thrifts' (especially those in New York State) abilities to charge what had become – during this period of super-hot inflation – reasonable, competitive *market rates* on mortgage loans.

Therefore, given the high rates that had to be paid for deposits, almost every new mortgage loan that was booked by a savings bank was a loser from day one. It should be noted that New York State also prohibited variable-rate mortgages and short-maturity mortgages, the kinds of loan configurations which could have enabled thrift institutions to gradually mitigate the interest spread deficiencies that escalating inflation was causing.

By their very nature, inflation and regulation constituted supreme threats to the proper functioning of an intermediary that specialized in bridging capital markets and that depended upon a relatively stable economy in which to do it.

As a consequence of spiraling interest rates, the 1970s witnessed a severe liquidity crisis as both banks and thrifts hemorrhaged savings deposits. This stress occasioned the first spate of thrift failures since the Great Depression.

The outflow of deposit dollars from thrift institutions in response to the high interest rates that were being offered by other intermediaries (like money market funds) created a phenomenon that is generally referred to by economists as "disintermediation." In plain-speak, this means that traditional financial intermediaries were being replaced by new market "bridges."

While gradual, secular change in an economy's configuration can be seen as a positive consequence of growth and development, a *rapid* dislocation of essential monetary conduits will typically cause extreme short-term difficulty and perilous long-term consequences for established financial intermediaries. Few observers, analysts, and policy-makers were taking into account the probability that emerging long-term trends would cause severe disruption, dislocation, and terminal disability within the savings industry. Too few anticipated the enormous economic and social costs that would be levied on the nation by such rapid, abnormal change.

While an alteration in savers' habits was the most obvious contributor to the turmoil, borrowers were also abetting the escalating downward spiral of the savings industry. Existing borrowers were slowing their mortgage payoffs in order to continue to enjoy the low borrowing cost guaranteed to them by their long-term, fixed-rate mortgage contracts.

Ironically, thrift institutions' loyal borrowers had unwittingly and unintentionally become (in the financial jargon of the *next* century) "subprime" borrowers. Their perfectly legal mortgage contracts allowed their loans on their lending institution's balance sheet to precipitously depreciate in value as interest rates rose. In effect, savings institutions were being penalized for their compliance with long-standing usury ceilings and for their efforts to accommodate borrower preferences – and regulatory mandates – which called for long-term, fixed-rate mortgage contracts.

In addition, *potential* borrowers became hesitant to take on debt in an environment of extraordinarily high interest rates.

During a short period in the early 1970s, the nation's inflationary surge abated somewhat and regulated savings intermediaries attempted to get back to "business as usual" – with renewed but diminished confidence in their "forts." But, as the latter half of the decade approached, inflation resumed... this time with a vengeance.

- **Taxation:** Taxation also took its toll. Social Security taxes, federal income taxes, and state and local tax burdens spiraled relentlessly. Furthermore, the impact of inflation on family income continually pushed the average taxpayer into higher tax brackets, despite the fact that the "real" income he or she was earning was not appreciating measurably, if at all. Between 1965 and 1980, taxes on individuals as a percent of their total personal income rose from less than 19% to more than 22%. The combination of taxes and inflation on the average family's financial status was devastating. As events evolved, a family that had an income of $ 10,000 in 1970 needed an income in 1981 of $22,477 simply to maintain a constant level of purchasing power. The tax burden in New York State was particularly onerous. In the Buffalo area, residents suffered the third highest aggregate tax bill among the thirty largest cities in the nation.

As a consequence, contemporary savers were becoming, perforce, more sophisticated in the task of money management. They began to carefully gauge the impact of inflation and taxes on the returns afforded by their savings accumulations. To protect the value of their personal assets, they explored a myriad of alternative savings and investment vehicles now available to them. An eclectic array of tax and inflation hedges – including condominiums, cattle, commodities, and collectibles – emerged to serve the saver as, at least, a partial surrogate for the traditional savings account. It became all too apparent to a growing number of savings institutions' customers that – after discounting for inflation and taxes – a high, 8% nominal rate of return on a time deposit account was insufficient to preserve the true value of their initial savings deposit. During the latter years of the 1970s, the proud holder of a passbook which paid 5.25% interest actually experienced a *negative* annual real rate of return of approximately 10%.

Naturally, these conditions militated against the kind of habitual patronage that savings institutions had come to rely upon.

- **Savers' increased risk tolerance:** The growth in social benefits provided by the public and private sectors during this period emasculated the traditional "rainy day" motivation which had helped to propel the savings process in past generations. Personal catastrophes like ill health, accidental injury, or unemployment were substantially offset by public and private insurance and social welfare programs implemented in the 1960s and early 1970s. The need to save for retirement was similarly diminished by the expansion of social security benefits, the growth in private pension plans, and a longer working life.

In addition, a family's traditional financial responsibilities were being offset somewhat by the trend toward smaller families. Young couples, in growing numbers, were delaying the family formation process until later in the life cycle. Furthermore, public funding and loan assistance programs were expanded, reducing a family's need to save for its members' educations.

In sum, the typical family had less reason to nurture the traditional "rainy day" savings habit and more incentive than ever before to *spend* the monies available to it... or to deploy its funds in non-bank *investment* vehicles.

- **Changes in savers' proclivities:** Rampant inflation and escalating taxation also began to change typical savers' habits, motivations, liquidity preferences, and investment strategies in the new economic world that was emerging.

   An issue of MONEY magazine that circulated during the height of this inflationary turmoil reflected the plight of a young couple who *saved* for one year to buy a three hundred dollar stereo system instead of buying the unit immediately *on credit*. In return for their frugality, they lost – in real terms – $21.50 and a year's worth of "discoing" because they were savers instead of borrowers.

   Traditional savers were being shocked out of habits that were based on a rapidly-obsolescing perception of the "benefits" offered by thriftiness and the institutions that accommodated it. An inflation-sparked psychoneurosis gripped typical middle class Americans, spurring their spending and depressing their proclivity to save.

This malady was similarly conditioning the *next* generation of potential savers. In the 1970s, the more hedonistic behavior of an emerging "cultured," permissive, and avant-garde society produced a "live for a sunny day" syndrome to supplant the "save for a rainy day" habit.

Ironically, Depression-conditioned savers had spawned a generation of inflation-conditioned spenders. The theory of "rational expectations" was at work, and it depressed any tendency to save in the face of anticipated protracted inflation. Euripides' observation of two millennia ago, "the thrifty man does every thing aright," had come into question.

These conditions were particularly troubling for Erie. Our customer research had consistently shown that Erie's savers were less educated and affluent – and maintained smaller account balances – than did the customers of other local commercial banks and savings institutions. Buffalo Savings Bank, Erie's major – and larger – competitor, was perceived as serving a "silk stocking" clientele, while Erie was seen as a servant of "meat and potatoes" folks. Indeed, for many years, Erie had successfully directed its marketing efforts to this socio-economic segment. Our market surveys showed that Erie's customers more frequently shopped at Sattler's (a local "discount" store) than they did at trendier department stores. In fact, the bank's advertising jingle (very similar in "melody" to that of Sattler's) tended to appeal to – and attract – middle-class and less-privileged Buffalonians.

But this did not mean that Erie's savers weren't savvy. The same studies showed that Erie's customers were among the most bargain-focused, price-sensitive, and able shoppers in our marketplace. They watched their money carefully and were acutely aware of the interest that their accounts were earning. They were also becoming increasingly more informed, thanks to local and national news media that had begun to focus on the returns being offered by newly-emerging financial services like money market funds. Our customers asked excellent questions about the products we offered and they were careful and deliberate in their decision-making.

Nevertheless, the high returns now being offered by mutual funds and money market funds were dramatically affecting the financial decisions of erstwhile docile patrons of savings institutions. Given inflation and high taxation, savers were more willing to move their stashes to the repositories that offered them the best bottom-line deal. As a consequence, thrift managers began to see huge swings in net deposit flows. It was going to be much more difficult to manage their shops in the years immediately ahead. The old "three-four-five rule" had become just a nostalgic memory.

- **Deregulation:** Along with the radical changes that thrifts were experiencing in the retail marketplace, there were some significant negative impacts resulting from a new spate of deregulation. Legislatures on both the state and federal levels – along with the scores of regulatory bodies they created over years of effort to "fine tune" the economy and the institutions that served it – began to second-guess their previous actions. They accurately concluded that regulatory fiat of earlier years had failed to productively "control" and condition the nation's free market economy (just as rational observers had earlier predicted).

As a result, they began to dismantle *some* of the regulatory mandates and "protections" that they had assiduously constructed over preceding decades. They had come to the conclusion that their earlier fiats – which were initially designed to ensure a flow of savings to support the mortgage market – simply weren't working in the nation's new economic milieu.

Unfortunately, in their place, Erie's newly "enlightened" regulators created even more deleterious "rule books" for the industry. The shifts in the regulatory landscape that they now introduced overlooked the fact that savings institutions had, over a period of many years, metamorphosed to structurally and operationally accommodate prior regulatory dictums. As a result, the rapid elimination of those long-standing "givens" in the chaotic economic environment of the late 1960s and 1970s simply further confused and confounded the managers of savings institutions at a critical time.

For example, the long-term maturity features of small denomination certificates of deposit were abolished in favor of much shorter six-month time deposit accounts. In the wake of this move, it quickly became apparent that even a six-month maturity was too long to satisfy the needs of contemporary savers, especially in light of the advent of money market funds which offered one day maturities. As a result, savings institutions – which were geared to function in a less rapidly-changing environment – were suddenly forced to offer terms as short as a single day on high-rate accounts. Thrift managers, who were long-conditioned by regulation, were simply not prepared to expeditiously invest or lend their cash in ways that would enable them to immediately pay the high rates associated with such short-maturity deposits. It's important to keep in mind that these escalating rates also had to be extended to *existing* depositors just to keep them from moving out the door.

At the same time, the interest rate protections that were afforded thrifts by Regulation Q were being emasculated, thereby submitting the new – and still unfamiliar – process of rate-setting by thrift treasurers to the machinations of wild, open-market bidding.

The new maturity structures that had emerged as a consequence of recent stabs at deregulation were now forcing thrift managers to make interest rate decisions on a daily basis. Neither they nor their inflexible balance sheets were prepared for this new reality. They faced a long learning curve before they could effectively hold their own with competitors that had been organized from the get-go to operate profitably in these kinds of volatile economic conditions.

Other regulatory changes emerged, too, including a statutory prohibition of a "due-on-sale" clause which was a contractual requirement of a mortgage loan that disallowed the assumption of that loan and its extant rates and maturity terms by a new buyer.

A reduction of deposit withdrawal penalties was also mandated by regulators at this time.

Deregulation was a "game-changer," and thrift managers had not yet learned the rules of the new game.

- **Increased demands for capital:** In the decades following World War II, global economic development and rapid growth in demand for high-cost technology exacerbated the private sector's need for capital. The thrift industry was one of the primary aggregators of capital and, as such, the substantial flow of funds to it became a juicy target for commercial banks and other sophisticated intermediaries.

  At the same time, governments – and their treasuries – began to demand greater and greater amounts of funds for their own purposes. This growing appetite was a strong incentive for new capital conduits to come into existence and supplant the traditional savings aggregation activities of thrifts. Commercial banks, investment banks, and other financial enterprises designed unique methodologies for capturing and redeploying the funds that historically flowed to savings institutions. Unencumbered by a blanket of pervasive regulation, these competitors enjoyed operational and cost efficiencies that gave them the capacity to pay high rates. As a consequence, savers and borrowers were encouraged to bypass traditional savings intermediaries in favor of other types of funds gatherers.

- **Increased economic cyclicity:** In the mid-1960s, the nation and its constituent financial institutions had begun to experience aberrant economic cycles of reduced duration, increased amplitude, and distorted periodicity. As a result, interest rate levels began to bounce erratically and violently.

Needless to say, such wildly-fluctuating interest rate cycles made "trading on the yield curve" (i.e. borrowing short-term funds at low rates and re-lending them for longer-terms at slightly higher rates) a highly risky undertaking. The volatile economic environment dramatically impacted thrift institutions' traditional intermediation strategies. Their long-established, conservative, and moderately profitable arbitrage techniques were rendered ineffective as savers expanded their liquidity preferences to hedge against roller-coaster rate cycles. Many thrift institutions were unable to fine-tune their cash flows properly and, as a consequence, the costs of unanticipated liquefaction of assets to accommodate withdrawals began to significantly diminish their profits and accumulated surpluses.

- **Emergence of new competition:** The upheaval in traditional capital markets served to invite new competition. As a consequence, a host of new conduits was born to give savers new, more direct, and less expensive (in terms of the conduits' profit participations) access to funds users. This kind of competition further enlightened and informed savers, thus making the capital markets even more efficient and, simultaneously, providing fewer opportunities for a traditional intermediary like a savings bank to achieve a positive net interest margin via established arbitrage techniques.

All thrift institutions began to feel the pinch created by their emboldened competitors. An example illustrates their problem. In mid-1981, in order to achieve sufficient liquidity to continue operating, a prominent New York City thrift institution was compelled to compensate for deposit outflows by bidding on a three-month deposit of a New York State pension fund that demanded an 18.82% yield. The thrift was competing with a leading commercial bank which was able to invest the pension deposit in 90-day commercial paper with a yield of 18.99%. The commercial bank's aggregate loss on the proposed deposit transaction, even after taking into consideration the cost of franchise taxes and bank operations, was infinitesimal in comparison to that of the thrift, whose only offset to the prospective pension deposit consisted of mortgage loans that yielded an average of less than 10%.

In 1971, Bruce R. Bent and Henry B. R. Brown had established what was to become the greatest threat to thrifts' abilities to garner savings deposits. Their "money market mutual fund" was the first significant alternative intermediary of its kind to be introduced in the United States. Their Reserve Fund was offered to savers and investors who were interested in safely preserving their cash *and* earning a *market rate* of return. The fund was, in effect, a new type of financial intermediary which was not subject to Regulation Q. It could pay any rate it desired and imposed no term requirements since it invested primarily in very short-term government securities. The fund was a de facto substitute for bank accounts, but it operated with very low overhead since it maintained no branch offices and employed a simple investment technique, i.e. investing in safe, readily-available, short-term securities. (In three years, the original Reserve Fund grew to $390 million in assets; over the next seven years it grew to $80 billion.)

It wasn't long before a horde of brokerage firms began to offer their own version of this new, incredibly attractive, and easily-accessed product for savers. Naturally, the kind of market "efficiencies" that these funds provided bode ill for the types of arbitrage that single-purpose savings intermediaries had provided for almost a century and a half.

The outflow of deposits that money market funds provoked at traditional thrifts was testimony to their appeal. Savers had begun to use "sharp pencils" when calculating the returns they were willing to accept. Erie was particularly vulnerable to deposit outflows since, between 1960 and 1970, its deposit growth had doubled. By 1972, deposits had reached $2 billion. To be sure, Empire was, from day one, a juicy target for money market funds. (Four decades after their inception, money market funds would boast assets of almost $4 trillion, about a third of the total invested in all mutual funds.)

## A capital crunch

As a result of the circumstances cited in the preceding pages, the net intermediation margins of most savings institutions began to narrow significantly and in a growing number of situations, they turned negative, ravaging their earnings and capital surpluses. During the '70s, the interest cost of Erie's deposits approached double digits, while the average return on its mortgage portfolio was only slightly above 5%. Under these conditions, the bank lost money on every new dollar that was deposited unless it could be redeployed quickly in a high rate mortgage. Given the prevailing usury ceiling and market conditions in the Buffalo area, this kind of opportunity was rare.

To make matters worse, the maturities of most of the mortgages in Erie's extant portfolio ranged from ten to twenty years. This meant, of course, that Erie's depressed level of earnings would persist for a considerable period of time.

Consequently, thrift institutions like Erie faced a "Hobson's Choice," i.e. either pay unaffordable interest rates to retain deposits *or* liquefy low-yielding assets in the open market at a significant loss in order to satisfy withdrawals. These alternatives would axiomatically result in either dramatic cash outflows as deposits were withdrawn *or* enormous losses as below market-rate mortgages were sold at a discount. Either option would occasion a massive deterioration of the capital base (i.e. surplus) that provided a stable foundation for a thrift's operations.

Most savings institutions opted for gradual self-immolation by continuing to pay high, market-rate interest on deposits. This was, at best, a short-run, finger-in-the-dike strategy. Such excessive interest payments would rapidly deplete a bank's accumulated surplus and force it to turn to the other, equally obnoxious, option of offering *less*-than-market rates on its savings accounts. The consequence of this latter strategy would be massive deposit outflows that would eventually cause the institution to collapse.

Eventually, it became evident to even the most hide-bound savings institution manager that either of their current options would lead to disaster unless dramatic changes were made in the traditional thrift industry business model. Obviously, one of the most pressing needs was a mechanism by which savings institutions could affordably supplement their capital bases.

Admittedly, the high-cost, "pay-up now" strategy to stabilize savings flows did buy time; and its advocates hoped that inflation would soon abate and that deposit rates would drop back down to historical "normal' levels. The Nixon and Ford Administrations and Congress worked feverishly during the '70s to achieve such normalization but had not been successful.

To put the problem of accelerating capital depletion in perspective, at the midpoint of the twentieth century a typical thrift institution's surplus account was equal to as much as 15% of the amounts owed depositors. Thrifts in rural areas enjoyed even higher capital ratios because they experienced far less costly competition for savings in the marketplaces that they served. For a long time, that kind of capital cushion afforded savings institutions a robust safety net.

But circumstances were changing rapidly. When I joined the Erie County Savings Bank in 1967, the published reserves of Erie were only 7.92%. Just twenty years earlier, they had been 13.43%.

The significance of a savings institution's capital surplus was not very well understood outside of the industry. Thrifts contributed to such ignorance since they typically did not publish detailed financial statements. The first public financial disclosures were voluntary and didn't occur until the late 1960s. Erie was one of the first banks to make such disclosure.

But, even then, thrifts weren't required to display their full array of surplus and reserve accounts. They were allowed to maintain some "dedicated" reserve accounts "off the balance sheet." Thrift managers believed that surplus accumulations provided a vital financial safeguard and they were afraid that a full disclosure of surpluses when it was not legally required would trigger new taxes and governmental confiscation. History had demonstrated that such set-aside accumulations of surplus were essential to the weathering of uniquely stressful times like those during the Great Depression and other national financial crises.

(The monumental depletion of institutional surpluses that occurred as the '70s unfolded was little noted by the press, politicians, and the public at large, but it was to become the core cause of the eventual "thrift crisis" of the '80s. Indeed, this lack of awareness and understanding was to contribute greatly to the public sector's future misguided policies for dealing with the industry's meltdown.)

Erie's capital base was becoming increasingly fragile because of its need to "subsidize" the housing costs of its borrowers who had mortgaged their properties in previous years. The use of the term "subsidize" might seem like a harsh indictment of borrowers. It is not. Subsidization was, in fact, occurring, but our borrowers had no direct, intentional hand in implementing it. They *deserved* such a "subsidy" since they had entered into mortgage contracts with provisions that were, at the time the loan was granted, justified by market conditions and embraced both by the borrower and the lender. The fact that these borrowers were ultimately "advantaged" as interest rates rose, simply reflected the upside-down posture of the savings intermediation business in a highly-inflationary economy.

The interest rates associated with these older mortgages were the true market rates *at the time of their origination.* Only the recent run-up in interest rates made those previously-booked mortgages a great deal for borrowers and an extremely poor investment for banks.

Given this unique legal and moral obligation to "subsidize" *past* borrowers, Erie's *current* earnings and accumulated surpluses had to make up the difference between the low rates on those old loans and the higher rates that subsequently had to be paid on deposits. This "phantom subsidy" that former borrowers enjoyed was roughly equal to the difference between the rates charged at the time they borrowed money and the inflation-spiked deposit rates of the 1970s.

The net impact of these kinds of financial circumstances on lending institutions like Erie amounted to an expense identical to a real, direct subsidy.

In Erie's prevailing situation, most – if not all – of the dollars required to accommodate such a deficiency in its earnings had to come from the surpluses created by borrowers and savers during the previous one hundred years of Erie's operations.

Erie, as a financial intermediary, had to honor both its previous contracts with borrowers *and* the current demands of its savers for higher interest rates. Unfortunately, the resulting depletion of its surplus put Erie in great jeopardy because, in order to continue in operation, it had to maintain minimum regulatory surplus and reserve levels. Failure to do so could trigger a bank takeover by government authorities.

Hope, theories, promises, and rants abounded within both the industry and the public sector but none constituted a substantive *plan* which Erie, and institutions like it, could employ to surmount these difficulties and move forward.

It was clear to Erie's management team that it had no alternative but to independently create a bold, aggressive, ambitious – probably unconventional – plan for increasing its income and supplementing its surplus. Greater earnings and capital would be necessary in order to convert the daunting realities the bank had inherited into an enduring opportunity. We concluded, as General Dwight Eisenhower had often observed, "you have to play the hand that's dealt you."

The Big E team committed itself to the tasks necessary for the bank to survive the current crisis and eventually rise, Phoenix-like, from whatever ultimately remained of the savings industry.

*Chapter five*

## THE SOARING SEVENTIES

### Making headway

Because of its deteriorating economic environment and diminishing capital base, Erie kept a laser focus on customer satisfaction. It was essential that the bank prevent major deposit outflows or declines in lending. Accordingly, during the '70s, many new services and products were initiated to help preserve and expand its client universe and to provide the stability and strength that Erie needed to cope in the decade ahead.

For a few years commencing in 1971, the bank's slogan was *"More than just a bank,"* reflecting our desire to expand services to customers in a way that would invite their loyalty and continued patronage. However, for most of the decade, the bank's advertising slogan was, appropriately, *"The Big E – Number One where it counts."*

Of course, first and foremost in everyone's mind were the interest rates paid on savings accounts and time deposit accounts. While rates moderated a bit in the early Seventies, by late 1974 they were escalating rapidly. Rates paid on savings increased continuously during the remainder of the decade. In 1971, Erie was paying 6% on two-year time deposit accounts. By 1978, it was offering 9.5% (yielding 10%) on its highest rate savings accounts. By late 1979, the bank was providing an effective yield of 10.78% on $10,000 deposits in its Inflation Fighter six-month term accounts.

These kinds of rates allowed for fresh inflows of savings that were critical to Erie's solvency. Such inflows were also essential to the kinds of expanded lending that would increase our NIM. To achieve such necessarily ambitious deposit and lending goals, the bank had to increase its market reach. Accordingly, the Big E launched an aggressive branching program (which was allowed under recently-liberalized New York State banking statutes).

In quick succession, it opened additional Erie County branches in: Cheektowaga on Union Road (1972); Hamburg (1973); Cheektowaga on French Road; Tonawanda on Colvin Boulevard and Sheridan Drive (1974); Williamsville at Main Street and North Forest (1976); and Orchard Park (1978). It also opened a Savings Bank Life Insurance Office in Como Mall in 1977. In addition, during the early '70s the bank merged with Frontier Savings and Loan Association in Cheektowaga.

Our merger with a savings institution in Olean, New York in 1975 and the opening of a brand new branch (in a converted funeral home) in Jamestown, New York, that same year reflected our territorial ambitions beyond the borders of Erie County and ultimately prompted a name change – to Erie Savings Bank – which occurred on September 19, 1977.

## Success in "Aisle 2"

Our management team understood that the bank would not be able to satisfy depositors' growing demands for convenience solely by opening additional branches. First of all, full-service branching was an expensive proposition. Furthermore, there still were state regulatory constraints on branching

Even as we implemented our branching program, we knew that new ways had to be found to "touch" savers who were favorably disposed to Erie but who lived and worked outside of its established branch service areas.

A savings and loan association in Nebraska had recently attacked this problem by opening small, limited service outlets – that were governmentally sanctioned – in local Hinky Dinky Supermarkets. Unfortunately, no such branching option was explicitly allowed by New York State banking statutes. But that wouldn't stop the creative team at Erie.

Sometimes, the simplest approach is the most effective, as it was in this case. It occurred to me that we were defining the term "branch" in a very traditional way... the way that the New York State Banking Department was accustomed to dealing with it, i.e. a building dedicated to the execution of customer financial transactions. The only distinctive features of a "branch" were: tellers employed by the bank to assist customers; a vault in which modest amounts of cash were stashed temporarily; dedicated telephone lines connecting the in-branch transaction terminals to a main frame computer at the "home" office; and, sometimes, a drive-up window that added convenience. Surely, similar facilities could be utilized by non-bank companies (e.g. supermarkets) to perform the same functions if they had a monetary or marketing incentive to do so... *and* if they had the "blanket" of a legitimate bank charter to work under. Importantly, there were precedents for such an arrangement.

For many years, Erie's school savings program installed student "tellers" in classrooms to foster the savings habit by collecting weekly deposits and forwarding them to the bank. This was an obvious antecedent to providing banking services through a vehicle other than the traditional branch.

Also, the U.S. Postal Service had been facilitating bank transactions for decades as part of a "bank-by-mail" service. The involvement of the post office demonstrated the fact that, as long as the *final* "booking" and validation of a transaction was conducted on fully-sanctioned *bank* premises by *bank* employees, the conduit that initiated the transaction could utilize non-bank personnel at non-bank locations to facilitate it.

After considerable investigation, speculation, and hypothesization during 1974, we became convinced that we already possessed sufficient precedent and quasi-branching latitude to move ahead with an in-store banking initiative. We felt that we could redeploy these "entitlements" in a way that would allow us to open facilities in retail establishments – especially supermarkets – which enjoyed a high volume of regular traffic.

We decided to make a case to the New York State Banking Department for establishing "supermarket branches" and to go to court if necessary to use precedent as a path to this kind of alternative "branching." All we needed was a willing "co-conspirator" in the local retail industry.

An acquaintance, Burt Flickinger, was an owner and top executive of S.M. Flickinger Co., the largest wholesale food distributor in the state and principal supplier to the extensive Super Duper chain in New York, Ohio, and Pennsylvania. At the time, Super Duper was the second largest retail grocery chain in Western New York. I knew Burt enjoyed a curious, creative mind, and that he harbored an adventurous bent. Further, he was always looking for ways to enhance his company's market position in the area. At the time, Super Duper markets were slugging it out with Tops Markets and Bells Markets for market share in Erie County.

I approached Burt with the idea of collaborating with Erie in our "attack" on the Banking Department. He quickly became an enthusiastic supporter, enlisting the cooperation of the independent owner of the chain's largest and busiest store. We carefully worked out details like: operational interfacing; marketing; remote transactional support; non-employee responsibilities; and "rent." Soon, we were good to go.

Back at the bank, we decided to forego a formal "application," which was the traditional path for securing Banking Department branching approval, and formulate, instead, a document that simply *informed* the Department that, in the name of customer convenience, we would, as of a certain date, be using already-sanctioned procedures for processing simple customer transactions... *in a different venue*. We cited the precedents of in-school banking and bank-by-mail. We emphasized that supermarket employees would simply be "facilitators," and that all transactions would be finalized on bank premises by bank employees. We also, not-so-subtly, suggested that, if Erie wasn't allowed to cooperate in this endeavor with Super Duper, the supermarket company might very well decide to cooperate with an out-of-state financial institution.

Since the Banking Department was always apprehensive about being perceived as "advantaging" one financial institution over another (particularly if it meant giving a savings institution an edge over a commercial bank), we indicated that our bank would be willing to share these in-store locations with other banks, savings and loan associations, and credit unions. Essentially, we stood ready to offer (at a modest price) the computer-based network necessary to facilitate transactions for other institutions. This not only diffused the static we anticipated from other, competing banks, but it also substantiated the assertion that these were not Erie branches.

Last but not least, we suggested that our venture would ensure that the New York State banking system would not run second to some "hinky-dinky" outfit in Nebraska.

We submitted our declaration of intentions to the Banking Department in mid-1975 and braced for the kind of firestorm of bureaucratic resistance that we had encountered on other, previous occasions.

We were surprised and delighted by the response. The Department asked us for a short postponement in our timetable to enable them to shape the regulatory language necessary to govern such "non-branches" in the event the concept was pursued by other banking institutions in the State.

In September 1975, the Banking Department promulgated its regulations; and we were soon in business with the first shared, "point-of-sale" banking network in the nation. This experience was a lesson in the benefits associated with employing simple, consumer-friendly innovation. It was a lesson that I never forgot... and that I had the opportunity to apply on numerous occasions in the future.

In less than twenty-four months, we opened fifteen supermarket locations in Super Duper and Bells supermarkets and "shared" these sites with four other savings institutions. These were the first "remote" branches in New York State; they constituted the first multi-bank shared network in the nation; and they comprised the most successful point-of-sale banking system in the country in terms of transactions and dollar deposits.

While the per-transaction fees charged to other banks using these facilities were small, the aggregate amount of income generated by them constituted a major revenue stream for Erie over the next fifteen years. We discovered, to our delight, that, while "pennies-a-click" seemed to be a puny return for a transaction, they could produce a torrent of cash as transactions multiplied. Here, I learned the important lesson of combining "small" with "scalability."

Another lesson we learned pertained to the importance of organizationally accommodating different operating cultures. Up until this time, the internal customs of a bank had been quite different than those of non-financial businesses such as retail stores. Given the historically simple premise and function of savings banks, getting to a "bottom line" each year had not been a complex endeavor for over 100 years. If deposits flowed in and mortgage funds flowed out at the "right" prices, a profit rather predictably appeared. Up until the 1960s, there was competition from other savings institutions but it was generally civil, tepid, and "collegial."

The supermarket business and – as we were to learn – almost all other non-bank businesses were a different story indeed. In those sectors, costs, margins, customer satisfaction, product diversification and availability, ease of access, price, accommodating technology, and efficient delivery mechanisms were routine drivers. The lessons we began to learn from working in a supermarket environment were eventually to be of great assistance to us as we toiled to change the nature, culture, and operations of an institution steeped in tradition and custom.

Having operated several businesses of my own, I knew that the modus operandi of the traditional thrift – even though it was changing – would not allow for this new "supermarket banking" initiative of Erie's to flourish if it were departmentalized within the bank and delimited by the prevailing bank culture. In my opinion, it had to function like a stand-alone *business* enterprise if it were to succeed. Most of the bank's senior managers agreed, signaling, in addition to a willingness to get this venture off to a sound start, an acceptance of a new, more innovative, business-like approach to banking.

Accordingly, a standalone corporation, initially dubbed Consum-R-Serve Systems Corporation, was formed to run the evolving remote banking network. The rather unwieldy name was soon changed to Metroteller Systems Inc.

This new subsidiary afforded us the opportunity to install non-bank management, create a board of directors that was singularly focused on the commercial success of the undertaking, and create a financial structure that allowed for close monitoring of operations. It also enabled us to establish compensation and incentive packages that were necessary in this kind of operating environment (but were not necessarily compatible with prevailing bank personnel policies).

This "subsidiarization" approach also allowed us to install entrepreneurial top management personnel who were opportunistic, aggressive, bottom-line-focused, and creative risk-takers. By the end of the decade, this business grew to encompass 160 individual, in-store Metroteller locations with 32 different banks sharing its facilities and paying per-transaction fees to Metroteller (whose income was consolidated annually with that of Erie). This subsidiary business flourished for over fifteen years and, on the occasion of the bank's dissolution in 1990, was sold to a larger bank for a handsome profit.

Importantly, Erie used this organizational model for all of its new ventures from then on. (Ultimately, Erie's non-bank operations grew to include over fifty corporations and partnerships.)

Our experience with this non-bank subsidiary validated our assumption that there were opportunities outside the realm of *traditional* banking that would enable us to generate supplementary income for Erie. Economic conditions during the 1970s demonstrated the difficulty of creating respectable profit margins from conventional intermediation activities, even with a multi-billion-dollar-plus asset base. The Metroteller initiative, and the profit contributions it brought to "mother" bank, convinced us that our long-term strategy would have to include revenue-generating business activities beyond our historical savings bank functions.

Another important lesson we learned related to the critical importance of putting the right person in the right job. It sounds like a simple philosophy, and it is. It's just very hard to execute. In following years, we had numerous stumbles in this regard when it came to selecting the CEO's of our many subsidiaries, even when we were assisted by experienced consultants and accomplished head-hunting firms. We quickly learned the importance of seeking people who understood our unique mission and who were focused, industrious, profit-oriented, and capable of building a winning team. In most cases, "experience" was not as important as these entrepreneurial traits.

Few people had experience doing what we were trying to do, so we had to find and motivate our own "intrapreneurs." We gradually found the "right" person for every initiative, and assembled an outstanding team of venturers.

### Checking accounts?

By mid-decade, a new attack strategy in our competitive battle with commercial banks was evolving. Time and again, our customer surveys revealed that our clients wanted more convenience when it came to accessing or transferring their deposited funds.

As a response, in 1973, Erie introduced passbook-free EZ Banking statement accounts that could be easily accessed in every branch with only a plastic card (which could be carried much more safely and conveniently than the traditional paper passbook.)

We also began to offer the EZ Billpayer service that functioned very much like today's popular Quicken bill-paying service (which was introduced ten years later). Our version, however, depended on the U. S. Postal Service rather than the Internet and PC, neither of which was available to us at that time.

Each month, an EZ Billpayer customer was sent a computer generated list of payees that he or she had previously selected to receive payments. The list included specific payment dates for each, and the amounts that should be paid. Customers could easily add or delete parties from the payment list and also change the dates and amounts designated for payment. Once the proposed payments were reviewed and, where necessary, modified, the completed list was returned to the bank in a postage-paid envelope. Upon receipt of the form, Erie executed payment directly to each vendor on behalf of the customer. Routine payments were made automatically until the payer indicated otherwise.

Depositors could also arrange payments by telephone twenty-four hours a day by dialing a special number or by visiting any one of Erie's branches. At that time, EZ Billpayer was the only service of its kind offered by a bank.

These kinds of services had great appeal to many of our customers, but they weren't the "big guns" we needed in order to "out bank" commercial banks.

The most popular banking tool for accessing and transferring funds was the checking account. This type of an account – officially titled a "demand deposit account" – had been denied to thrift institutions since their inception. However, in the new consumer-centric marketplace of the '70s, it was obvious that our lack of statutory authority to offer this service was contributing to our deposit outflow woes. People simply wanted to be able to employ their funds quickly and without hassle.

In 1972, a small savings bank in Massachusetts had introduced a savings account on which "negotiable orders of withdrawal" could be written. It operated like a demand checking account but, thanks to the blessing of Massachusetts legislators and regulators, it was considered a savings account *that could pay interest*. Up until the introduction of this account, checking-type accounts did not pay interest. These new Now Accounts (Negotiable Order of Withdrawal Accounts) gave savers a double bang for their bucks, i.e. easy transferability of funds and interest earnings on their idle balances.

In 1974, a bill was introduced in the New York State Legislature which would have allowed thrifts in the State to offer Now Accounts. Unfortunately, this governing body, which was still greatly influenced by the huge commercial bank lobby, ran true to form and adjourned before taking action.

Since, based on previous experience, we didn't anticipate any great help from the State, the members of the "brain trust" at Erie had donned their thinking caps months earlier to devise a plan to offer a service that was *similar* to a Now Account but that did not violate existing State banking laws. It was to be a hybrid account that combined features similar to – but not identical to – those of checking accounts and Now Accounts.

We were encouraged by the fact that neither checking nor similar money transfer powers were specifically denied to savings banks under existing statutes. The regulatory "door" appeared to be open a tiny crack... and that is all that the inventive minds at the Big E needed.

Helping our cause was the fact that Erie had, for many years, been selling "money orders" in its branches – over 65,000 of them per month by 1974. This product was remotely similar to a checking account in that money order "instruments" allowed for funds to be transferred from one party to another. These instruments – which cleared through the financial system in a manner similar to that which processed checks – were originated, for a fee, by a bank employee using payee information that was provided by a customer. The dollar amount of each money order was simultaneously withdrawn from the payer's savings account. The bank's customer was responsible for sending the instrument to the designated payee who would ultimately "cash it" like a check.

Demand for money orders at our branches emanated from the fact that 60% of our customers had not yet opened checking accounts at commercial banks. The popularity of money orders among our customers was a strong indication that our customers would benefit greatly from a bank-based, dedicated funds transfer service that was akin to a checking account.

The big stumbling block to offering such a checking-like service was structural. The Federal Reserve System was the only facilitator of the process for clearing checks through the banking system, and only commercial banks could be members of the Fed. We were neither a commercial bank nor could we become one.

But, we were not deterred. We speculated that, perhaps, we could implore a commercial bank to handle the essential interface with the Fed for us... as an intermediary and as our representative. No existing statute or regulation seemed to preclude this. We already used the "correspondent services" of commercial banks for other functions, and commercial banks enjoyed considerable fees from the savings industry for providing those services.

We reasoned that the revenues accruing to commercial banks by virtue of the services that we routinely purchased from them could be used as leverage to solicit the cooperation of at least one major commercial bank in implementing our envisioned "Rube Goldberg" process for providing checking-like services to our customers.

We passed the idea by our existing correspondent banks but none responded favorably. Based on their objections, we created a more attractive proposal, and approached the Marine Midland Bank - Western, a large commercial bank that was headquartered in Buffalo (and which eventually became HSBC Bank). The folks at Marine quickly appreciated the potential for new income and worked with us in preparing the systems, procedures, and documentation necessary to accommodate Fed requirements.

As a consequence, immediately after the close of the State's legislative session in June 1974, Erie became the first non-commercial bank in New York State to offer an account that provided the convenience of a checking account.

Previously, we had enlisted the Bowery Savings Bank in New York City – the largest savings bank in the nation – in our "scheme." The Bowery had the resources, clout with the Legislature in Albany, and a reputation that would be helpful in attracting other savings banks in the state to our cause. Encouragingly, the Bowery had also been considering a similar foray in the world of consumer checking.

Within days our Erie's introduction, the Bowery Savings Bank followed suit. We were soon joined by the Roslyn Savings Bank on Long Island. Not long after, Buffalo Savings Bank came aboard. Soon, more savings banks were rushing to follow suit. By year's end, 35 of the state's 199 mutual savings banks had opened over twenty-two thousand jerry-rigged "non-checking checking accounts" that, by then, boasted over $9 million in deposits.

Technically, we were not offering a classic demand deposit account. We had deliberately built a tiny speed bump into the "on-demand" feature of the traditional check processing protocol. It involved a provision that *enabled* Erie to require, *at its option*, a sixty-day notice from a depositor before he or she could withdraw funds from this kind of account. This, in effect, made it a *non-demand* deposit account. Clearly, this was a provision that both the bank and its customers realized would never be implemented. While this added step in the established check clearing process would be transparent to the saver, it enabled us to legally position this new service as a statutorily-authorized *deposit* account rather than as a presumably-prohibited *demand* account.

Dubbed the EZ Pay Account, this hybrid account initially eschewed the payment of interest. This exception was (temporarily) implemented because we wanted to do everything possible to mitigate the resistance that was sure to erupt in the commercial banking industry and in the New York State legislature. We also wanted to make our product initiative as defensible as possible when we were dragged into court (as we were sure we would be; and as we soon were).

Before long, we were invited to help more savings banks in the state offer this revolutionary (to savings banks, at least) service.

In contrast to most fee-based checking accounts offered by commercial banks, we offered the account as a *free* service to our existing customers, hoping to garner a large number of satisfied customers *and* supportive New York State voters (who would be of great assistance should we ultimately have to "pressure" the State Legislature for sanctioning).

In a matter of days, we opened over 500 accounts, most of them for existing customers. This was an incredible achievement, given the totally new and controversial nature of the product.

To our astonishment, only a few more weeks passed before the State Banking Department issued enabling regulations governing the offering of such "non-checking" accounts. They were only modestly restrictive and did not encumber our marketing efforts.

Needless to say, commercial bankers were infuriated. They said we were "sneaking" checking accounts into the market in "ducks' clothing." They reasoned that if the EZ Pay Account looked like a duck, walked like a duck, and quacked like a duck, it must be a duck (i.e. checking account). It was clear that, *in their opinion*, savings banks were not entitled to offer checking-type accounts... or *ducks*. The war was on!

As we expected, the New York State Bankers Association and three small affiliates – the Bank of Akron, Alden State Bank, and Evans National Bank – quickly brought suit in State Supreme Court to cause us to cease, desist, and quit "quacking." They charged that the accounts were "illegal" and constituted a competitive threat to small commercial banks.

We were bemused, however, by the fact that Chemical Bank (a huge commercial bank in New York City), almost simultaneously, announced that it was going to compete with Marine Midland Bank – Western in the business of offering check clearing services to savings institutions. This service constituted a significant opportunity for commercial banks since, at that time, the savings banks' industry in New York State was $60 billion in size. (Commercial banks' assets totaled $149 billion.) In December, the appellate panel of the New York Supreme Court ruled 4-0 against the savings banks, declaring that "there was no clear legislative intent for these accounts."

We had lost the first round... and it was *on to an appeal.*

By this time, Erie had opened thousands of accounts. This was ample evidence of consumer interest and provided grounds for appeal. The case was on appeal until December 30, 1975, when the New York State Court of Appeals unanimously upheld the ruling of the lower court and ordered that such accounts be liquidated by May 31st of the following year.

By then, there were six-hundred thousand savers in New York State enjoying a convenient, free service. Not incidentally, they were also voters who, if the prohibition of these accounts was upheld, would soon lose an important convenience *and* would have to begin paying commercial banks, once again, for checking services.

Of course, we had been lobbying state legislators all during 1975 and making them acutely aware of the devastating effect that the Courts' actions would have on their constituents. Given this kind of unrelenting, pro-consumer pressure, it wasn't too long before the legislators passed a law that enabled savings banks to keep "quacking" and to provide their customers with an important free service. In 1976, Erie formally introduced checking with overdraft privileges, and in 1978 it began to pay interest on checking account balances.

We had added an important competitive weapon to our arsenal. Moreover, our successful efforts represented a milestone on the path to empowerment for savings institutions throughout the nation. It offered hope at a critical time.

**Still more service**

Beyond "checking" services, other banking products like Individual Retirement Accounts and Social Security Direct Deposit Accounts were introduced by Erie in the 1970s.

To enhance our relationship with the customers who meant the most to us, we launched, in 1970, the Money Managers' Club (MMC), a preferred "membership" club for depositors who maintained a savings balance of $10,000 or more. The purpose of the Club was to demonstrate the bank's appreciation for its savers' patronage and to reinforce, in a substantive way, the bond that such involvement entailed. The Club offered numerous benefits, including: a photo ID/membership card; discounts on a wide array of merchandise and travel excursions that were offered by local businesses; a newsletter; seminars; customized, computer-generated budgets; discounted, guided vacations; and televised infomercials and their accompanying scripts. (Erie was the first bank in the industry to produce "infomercials" which consisted of short, videotaped money management "lessons" that were broadcast to assist Erie's customers with their personal financial management tasks.)

Members were also entitled to participate in the bank's Installment Savings Plan through which a customer was sent a "bill" each month to prompt – but not mandate – a deposit of an agreed-upon amount.

An arrangement with a professional tax preparer in the Buffalo area enabled the bank to also offer tax preparation services to MMC members. In addition, to ensure speedy service, members could make appointments to conduct business at their favorite branch.

By the end of 1971, MMC membership had grown to 19,000 customers and would expand to twice that number in just two more years. In 1971, Ralph Nader, arguably the most prominent consumer advocate nationally at that time, spoke at a Club membership gathering at the prestigious Kleinhans Music Hall in Buffalo.

By 1977, membership in the Money Managers' Club hit 70,000, making it the largest consumer organization of its type in the nation. The benefits of Money Managers' Club membership were extended to *all* customers by the end of the decade. (It would ultimately embrace more than 80,000 members.)

In the late 1970s, no other bank or thrift in the nation offered a more comprehensive a package of financial products and consumer services to its customers.

Erie's efforts were not applauded in all quarters, however. After a speech I gave to the New York Stock Exchange Annual Conference in 1972, a reporter for Institutional Investor magazine wrote that he overheard one brokerage firm executive say: "I thought all we had to worry about was IDS, Prudential, and Sears (some of the companies who, at that time, were expanding into the traditional turf of brokerage firms), but if every two-bit mutual savings bank in the boondocks and God knows who else has one of those smart-asses plugging it, we're going to get murdered." His observation stung a bit, but I was pleased that I had managed to make our intentions so clear. The war was gaining momentum.

Erie had always been a socially progressive bank with great concern for its customers and employees. In 1970, in order to keep customers fully informed about the health of the bank that they entrusted with their funds, Erie became the first local savings institution to publish a *complete* income statement showing the profit/loss from operations, gains on sales of investments, and transfers to and from surplus and reserves.

In 1974, the bank elected its first woman trustee. Our existing Trustees (all male) sported a few Cheshire grins as she arrived late for her first meeting. It was an understandable incident since she had not been provided with instructions concerning our rather convoluted parking arrangements. It broke the ice as nothing else could. Her aplomb in handling the situation demonstrated to all that she would be an important addition to the Board... and she was.

Throughout the decade, the bank found new and different ways of serving its host communities. It launched a six-story high Big E hot air balloon (with free rides for residents of our marketplaces); sponsored free days at the zoo; and put a Crime Stopper van on the road. It sponsored SummerFest Super Stars competition; a Big E Relay Carnival; and Labor Day in the Park. The Buffalo Philharmonic Orchestra, Studio Arena Theater, and the March of Dimes were also beneficiaries, as were many other community organizations in New York State.

During the gasoline shortage in the mid-Seventies, Erie created the Computer Car Corps to match riders with drivers in a car pooling effort. The bank also financed a Neighborhood Improvement Program (NIP) to serve the distressed communities in the area with specialized rehabilitation funding and related housing services. (At the time, the NIP initiative for urban renewal and development was cited by the federal government as one of the best in the United States.)

Erie even served well during the great Buffalo Blizzard of '77 which began on Jan. 28, 1977 and, over a three day period, produced zero visibility, seventy-plus mile an hour winds, countless feet of snow, and a wind chill factor that plunged to sixty degrees below zero. As the storm took hold, Erie broke out a thousand blankets which had been purchased for use as new account premium giveaways and made them available to chilled workers who were stranded, many for days, in downtown Buffalo. Needless to say, this storm prompted a prolonged party for trapped Big E employees at which, because of scarcity and prudence, the goodies were carefully rationed.

## California, here we come

Small, rural communities and tertiary suburban areas seemed to be enjoying the greatest immunity from the "rate wars" that were breaking out in larger, metropolitan markets. For example, in the Western New York Area, the Lockport Savings Bank (later, First Niagara Bank) was not feeling the kind of customer pressure for higher rates that Erie was. In fact, Lockport Savings Bank was actually *growing* its surplus. Across the country, small communities served by only one major savings institution seemed to be enjoying more stable interest rate environments.

The opportunities provided by such markets were appealing. Accordingly, I compiled a profile of an "ideal," non-New York market for Erie. I envisioned a community that was small and prosperous, and that hosted only one significant thrift institution. My ultimate goal was to find a profitable, shareholder-owned thrift that could be purchased outright using the little known statutory provision that had previously enabled us to establish and fund Metroteller as a stand-alone subsidiary.

New York State banking law had long-contained a "leeway provision" that permitted a chartered thrift to invest up to 1% of its assets or 10% of its net worth in non-traditional investments, as long as the investment was not a commercial bank or life insurance company. As the decade drew to a close, Erie's asset base exceeded $2 billion, meaning that we had over $20 million available for deployment in non-traditional assets. Since the leeway provision did not specifically preclude investment in business enterprises like Metroteller, I optimistically concluded that a stock savings and loan association might be a permissible acquisition target for Erie under these guidelines.

Provided with a clear vision of a preferred marketplace, the Big E team began to search for a small, profitable, acquirable savings and loan association (no savings bank in the nation was a shareholder-owned company at that time) in a growing, moderately competitive marketplace that met our criteria. We culled the archives of libraries, trade associations, regulatory agencies, and data brokers. As might be expected, in those pre-Internet days, it took a bit of time to find candidates that fit our criteria but, eventually, we had a short list of prospects.

The most appealing one of the bunch was a little thrift in a (then) small agricultural community thirty-five miles east of Los Angeles, California. The Ontario Savings & Loan Association reported $60 million in assets and operated five branches in the

San Bernardino Valley. Ontario had the best profit performance of any savings and loan association of its size in the United States, earning a whopping 3.68% on its assets. It had a net worth of $7 million or 11.7% of assets. (Erie's net worth ratio at the time was only 5.93 %.)

We felt that expansion into a prosperous geographic area like Southern California would give Erie the opportunity to build a branch network that could tap into the kind of growth it needed. Importantly, such an acquisition would also allow Erie to convert to a stock institution. (A merger of Erie and Ontario would enable us to move Erie's legal headquarters to California where thrift institutions were permitted to engage in offerings of stock to private investors and the public.) This would afford us the type of corporate status and statutory power that was necessary to attract much-needed capital.

Also favorable was the ownership structure of Ontario. Only seven shareholders controlled 98.5% of its stock, and its president wanted to retire for health reasons. It didn't take much more analysis to prompt me to fly west and meet the president of Ontario face-to-face.

He already had a dozen other offers on the table, but we immediately hit it off. He liked the idea that I had started my career as a bank teller and that I was personally familiar with the Southern California area. I also had a special interest in railroading, which was the second largest source of income for the Ontario area.

Over a period of a few weeks, Erie completed due diligence and I presented him with a purchase offer which he and the other major shareholders promptly accepted. The president of Ontario was in a good mood since he had recently completed a very lucrative deal to sell hundreds of acres of land he personally owned to the highly trafficked Ontario International Airport (later to be designated the LA/Ontario International Airport) for the extension of its runway.

The deal we forged for the purchase of Ontario was a great one for all involved parties. The acquisition contract was signed

117

in December 1978 and it represented an $11 million investment by Erie. Importantly, the sale price constituted only slightly more than one-half of one percent of Erie's assets but, when the transaction was completed, the earnings from Ontario, which would be consolidated with Erie's, would represent over 13% of Erie's after-tax profits.

Needless to say, at this juncture another battle with regulators began. There was no precedent for a transaction like this and, as a consequence, we were required to obtain formal approval from the Federal Home Loan Bank Board, the California Department of Savings and Loans Associations, the Federal Deposit Insurance Corporation, and the New York State Banking Department before we could formally close the deal.

Despite the simplicity and practicality of the proposed transaction, our efforts to consummate it would constitute a Sisyphean regulatory struggle that would last for two years. We soldiered on, however, because, in our opinion, an acquisition like this was well worth any amount of effort. Success would see a strengthening of Erie's balance sheet and income statement; give us access to a lucrative market; allow us to book a rapidly-appreciating asset; and enable us to raise capital as a public company. It gave us hope that Erie would enter the 1980s on a profitable and promising new footing.

Unfortunately, the wisdom of our Ontario initiative became increasingly obscured as it was dragged through the regulatory jungle. As we approached the third year, the Federal Home Loan Bank Board (the principal regulatory agency that had the *final* say with respect to such transactions) still had not seen fit to take formal action on our proposed purchase.

Our anticipation, it turned out, was analogous to leaving the runway lights on for Amelia Earhart. We were obliged, therefore, to release the owners of Ontario from their sale contract. It was a sad day for everyone.

**Personal happenings**

The '70s were great years for me, personally. I had always been fortunate when it came to career advancement. I never had to *ask* for a challenging assignment, promotion, or salary increase from the time of my first full-time job with the Buffalo Chamber of Commerce to my retirement many years later. Money was never a big motivator for me. I gained my greatest satisfaction from tackling difficult projects and completing them beyond expectations. I always enjoyed a challenge and took great Germanic pride in working hard and innovatively. I figured that a smart boss who wanted me to keep doin' it would take care of the rest. Indeed, my achievements in business were derived principally through the auspices of bosses who let me do my thing... bosses who would generously collaborate to ensure that *we* did it effectively.

Boy, was I fortunate.

I was elected Senior Vice President of Erie in 1972 and Executive Vice President in 1973. Two years later, I was elected Chief Operating Officer and a member of the bank's Board of Trustees. In December 1978, I was elected President of the bank and, at age 39, became the youngest officer in the bank's history to have achieved that position.

Given my age and penchant for being aggressive and somewhat unconventional, these promotions were gutsy steps for Erie's Trustees to take.

Each of these moves along my career path was an honor that I cherished then and thereafter. Never did that kid on Grey Street dream of earning $75,000 a year.

Only in America.

**Early "social media"**

One of the non-traditional bank responsibilities I especially enjoyed was serving as the bank's spokesperson in the media. I had gained familiarity with the requirements of this role during the early 1960s when I served as a radio and television newscaster and commentator in the Buffalo area. So, not long after I joined Erie, Peter King, a principal in our advertising agency, encouraged me to become the radio and television "mouthpiece" for the bank, appearing in commercials and in bank-sponsored audio and visual educational programs (which were later commonly referred to in the television industry as "infomercials.") The bank had decided to replace Bob Wells, its long-time, on-air spokesman and a very popular radio personality during the 1950s. (Bob had pioneered the "dance party" format that would later take Dick Clark to the pinnacle of national popularity.) Our advertising agency wanted a spokesman who could *personalize* Erie's marketing messages and deliver them as an official representative of the bank.

A short time before, a Chevrolet dealer in town by the name of Dan Creed began to personally promote his product on the air. His enthusiasm and sincerity captured the attention – and dollars – of local car buyers and pushed his previously little-known dealership to the head of the pack. On a national level, Frank Purdue and Orville Redenbacher enjoyed similar success promoting their chickens and popcorn on television. Our advertising gurus concluded that, if Dan, Frank, and Orville could pull it off, so could Paul. And so, I became the bank's "media mascot" and proudly related the bank's values to its customers and the public for the next twenty years.

Judging from our market studies, this gambit paid off. The bank's recognition as "believable," "sincere," "progressive," "genuine," "helpful" and "a friendly place to do business" soared. Apparently, talent wasn't essential; sincerity was.

In addition to delivering traditional commercials, I was also tasked with the presentation of five-minute segments concerning personal money management that appeared on the local morning television program, Dialing for Dollars. The bank was recognized as one of the first commercial entities in the nation to successfully employ this non-commercial "infomercial" format in its institutional marketing.

120

By the mid-1970s, I assumed that Buffalonians had suffered enough of my mug and for a few years the bank engaged a series of much more professional and widely-recognized spokespersons for its over-the-air commercials, including Arthur Godfrey, ("Talent Scouts"); Jackie Vernon ("Frosty the Snowman"); Rod Serling ("The Twilight Zone"); and the popular fictional characters "Ernest" P. Worrell and his unseen friend "Vern" played by Jim Varney ("Ernest Saves Christmas," et. al.)

I continued to do infomercials during this period and was eventually called back into service to do regular commercials when the bank expanded into the national marketplace.

In 1977, the bank's infomercials were syndicated nationally to interested broadcast and cable stations. In 1982, four-minute versions began to appear weekly on the nationally-syndicated television series PM Magazine where they aired for several years.

(Years later, when I left the bank's employ as it was coming increasingly under the control of the federal government, our regulators requested that I continue my media presence – even in retirement – to help dissuade, in their words, "a run on the bank" which they believed was entirely possible if a government takeover occurred.)

During my hiatus from the airwaves, I had a personal experience that convinced me of the power of television as a marketing medium. I was completing a purchase at a downtown clothing store when the clerk who was filling out the purchase order asked my name. "Paul Willax," I replied.

"Isn't that Paul 'A' Willax?," he asked.

I acknowledged the middle initial and inquired as to how he knew what it was. He informed me that he saw it on my television commercials. I was astonished, since my name appeared in very small letters at the bottom of the screen for only one or two seconds during each commercial. Nevertheless, thanks to the might of the medium, he remembered the "A."

(Of course, there is such a thing as too much customer awareness. In 1971, a popular local disk jockey who was featured in many of the Big E's radio commercials – and who apparently was in considerable debt – availed himself of a ski mask and toy gun and held up one of our suburban branches to the tune of $503. A customer recognized his distinctive voice, and he was arrested at his home as he returned from his caper.)

In my mind, the most important part of the bank's advertising stratagem involved making an official bank representative both visible and accessible to its constituencies. It was hoped that, as a consequence of my direct messages, Erie's customers would feel that they had a *personal* connection to the bank.

Big E depositors and borrowers quickly showed that they appreciated this link by using it liberally. Through correspondence, telephone calls, and in-person contacts I was inundated with questions, problems, and concerns... almost all of which were legitimate and most of which would probably not otherwise have been voiced if the bank had not used the media to encourage their communication. I tried to emulate my dad's practice of "customer focus" by personally involving myself in the process of answering every customer inquiry and comment.

Eventually, the swelling flow of communication mandated that I be joined by a dedicated – and internally well-connected – staff assistant who would quickly research the issues brought to our attention and prepare useful responses for inquiring customers *and* provide corresponding feedback to any bank personnel involved in the issue at hand. I continued, however, to review and sign every letter of response and personally follow-up on every telephone call directed to me. I frequently jotted a personal handwritten note to the inquiring customer or to the bank employee(s) who could help us build positively upon the feedback we had received. This practice continued until I retired, and it produced a wealth of helpful comments and suggestions for improved performance on the part of the bank.

**"Help" arrives**

As the decade of the '70s drew to a close, federal and state governments – and their regulatory apparatuses – still had not productively engaged the critical issues facing savings institutions. Policymakers in the public sector were struggling to cope with "stagflation," accelerating inflation, historically high interest rates, escalating energy costs, poor economic growth, and gasoline shortages which were creating long lines at filling stations (along with pleas for rationing).

Throughout the decade, a smidgen of optimism had persisted in the thrift industry. Its constituent managers clung to the hope that federal and state governments would eventually provide, at the very least, a measure of accommodating legislation and regulation.

But such constructive assistance proved to be hard to come by.

Thanks to politics-as-usual, the Federal Home Loan Bank Board (FHLBB), the principal national regulatory body for thrifts, would "enjoy" five different chairpersons in quick succession, each with a different take on the metastasizing problems confronting it. Meanwhile, the capital and surpluses of thrifts continued to erode.

Ironically, in a moment of supreme counter-intuitiveness, the FHLBB did manage to mandate the imposition of a higher capital requirement – 5% – on savings institutions. This, of course, only compounded thrifts' problems of disappearing earnings and eroding capital.

It wasn't surprising that, by the end of the decade, there were 17% fewer thrift institutions than there were at its beginning. Almost all of this decrease was occasioned by inadequate capital. Profit margins in the industry had been slashed by more than 60% during the period, making it almost impossible to maintain a respectable capital base.

As the folks at Erie had anticipated, a growing number of out-of-state thrifts addressed their capital insufficiencies by selling themselves to stockholders via public offerings. In 1961, a federal ban had been placed on such mutual-to-stock conversions in order to "minimize the risk posed by rapidly expanding thrifts," but this prohibition was repealed in 1975. Unfortunately for Erie, in New York State there still was a *constitutional* prohibition against stock thrifts (which was to continue well into the 1980s).

A number of other restrictive statutes and regulations that were peculiar to New York State made it extremely difficult for banks like Erie to accommodate the rapidly-changing economic landscape. My personal experiences with the state's governmental leadership gave me little hope for quick relief. I recall one especially disheartening encounter on the occasion of a luncheon hosted by the bank's senior managers for New York State legislators. The purpose of this gathering – like that of other confabs we arranged for federal legislators and the press – was to explain Erie's take on the emerging crisis and to outline some of the things that we thought the government could do to alleviate it.

At the conclusion of this particular luncheon, a prominent State Assemblyman took me aside to ask a personal favor. He wanted to inspect the inside of the vault at our Main Place headquarters, admitting that "I always wanted to see what a billion dollars looks like." Further discussion with him, along with our visit to the bank's "cash catacomb," convinced me that he was serious. He actually believed that all the money the bank gathered in deposits was kept inside our vault. His belief was alarming. If an elected representative didn't understand the very basic operations of the financial intermediaries he oversaw, what hope was there for meaningful reform in the State?

(Among the most memorable of these luncheons was one attended by Senator Patrick Moynihan. Aside from Jack Kemp and Ronald Reagan, he was probably the most erudite and affable politico I had ever met. I recall having to suspend the bank's long-standing rule that prohibited alcohol at luncheons to allow for an ample supply of Irish whiskey on this particular occasion. Indeed, the libation seemed to fuel his prowess and wit.)

Several governmentally-sponsored studies were conducted around that time to figure out what had to be done to stem the growing crisis in the savings industry. In 1969, a three-year study by the Friend Commission had proposed some helpful new powers for thrifts, including variable rate mortgages, checking accounts, consumer loans, and more flexible investment and deposit powers, but Congress took no action.

Businessman Reed Hunt headed up the President's Commission on Financial Structure and Regulation in 1972 and proposed other enhancements for the industry, including credit cards, mutual funds, and subordinated debt. A phased elimination of interest rate controls was also advocated by the panel.

However, before any action could be taken, Senator Wright Patman, chairman of the House Banking Committee, made a play to steal the spotlight and issued a "white paper" advocating even more radical changes. As a consequence, the Financial Institutions Act emerged in Congress in 1973 and again in 1975. Given the prevailing confusion and consternation in Washington, neither was enacted.

Shortly thereafter, a Congressionally-inspired study – entitled Financial Institutions and the National Economy – was undertaken and the Financial Reform Act of 1976 was introduced. Predictably, the Act died before reaching a vote.

Alas, the only legislation that was enacted during the '70s was the Financial Institutions Interest Rate Control Act of 1976 which had little impact on the industry's spreading predicament.

Conflicting political and economic agendas had produced gridlock with respect to reform on the federal level. The significant changes in the makeup of Congress which followed the Nixon-Ford era contributed also. Moreover, in many areas *outside* New York State, thrifts already had powers that enabled them to grow and achieve profitability in the mortgage market. Needless to say, those thrifts were reluctant to campaign for more change.

In the final analysis, there was no obvious "mandate" for change coming from within the government or the savings institutions it regulated. In fact, it can be argued that one of the greatest stumbling blocks to initiatives for progressive change in the thrift industry was the industry itself.

Change was not a comfortable prospect for the majority of thrifts, most of which were small and lacked adequate financial and management resources. Their managers tended to be older, more conservative, and traditional. They were not familiar with the lending and marketing practices that would be required in a more progressive – and competitive – industry of the future which (irrespective of their hesitancy) was rapidly and relentlessly emerging. They fervently "hoped" that things would soon return to "normal" and that they would be able to thrive once again simply by employing the "plain vanilla" operational methodology they had come to know and love.

The big threat, as they saw it, was the possible neutering of Regulation Q. Its elimination was already being called for in progressive legislative and regulatory reform proposals. However, the "old guard" in the savings industry had become dependent on the regulation-based competitive "advantage" that they perceived was associated with the continuance of Reg. Q. But, in reality, Reg. Q had become merely yesterday's "security blanket." Nevertheless, their pleas for its continuation persisted despite the fact that in recent years the margin of interest rate benefit that Reg. Q provided had been significantly diminished.

The operators of small thrifts doggedly opposed any new, substantive reforms. Their vociferous opposition was heard loud and clear in Washington and in state capitols. The extremely powerful U.S. League of Savings Institutions, the savings industry's trade association, had, over the years, become a formidable force with tremendous, well-greased leverage in the political and regulatory arenas. As a consequence, small thrifts, which constituted the majority of its membership, were able to enlist its efforts to forestall meaningful reform with the hope that better days were surely on the way. Their reluctance to adapt was one of the principal reasons for the eventual decimation of the industry. As Charles Darwin once noted, "The primary reason for the survival of the human species was not superior strength or unmatched intellect. It was mankind's ability to adapt."

Many years later, in 1993, a retrospective report to the President and Congress by the <u>National Commission on Financial Institution Reform, Recovery, and Enforcement</u> (NCFIRRE) concluded that:

"The years 1966 to 1979 were critical in determining the ultimate fate of the (savings) industry. Had fundamental reforms been implemented during this period, particularly the early part of it, the S&L debacle could have been avoided.

"From 1969 to 1979, the industry became increasingly vulnerable as a technological revolution integrated financial markets and as fluctuations in inflation and market interest rates intensified. By the mid-1960s, it was well appreciated by academic economists and many other observers that forced specialization should end. The S&Ls needed the flexibility to diversify both their assets and liabilities. Yet, despite the changes that were occurring and the warnings being voiced, specialization of the industry in long-term, fixed-rate mortgage loans continued. Congress's insistence that S&Ls continue to function almost totally as vehicles for achieving national housing goals prevented needed adjustments from occurring.

"Attempts to achieve required reforms failed because of fears that any actions to disturb the status quo would hurt housing. Representatives of home builders and realtors actively opposed fundamental reforms. With nothing obvious to replace the mortgage activities of S&Ls and with strictures to 'leave home finance to the market' too abstract and uncertain, opponents to reform easily prevailed. The home builders, realtors, and consumer groups, fearing a negative impact on housing, convinced Congress to block federally-chartered S&Ls from granting adjustable rate mortgages (ARMs) despite appeals by the U.S. League, the Bank Board, and academic experts that S&Ls needed ARMs to protect them from mounting interest-rate risk.

"The S&L lobby generally resisted reform because the industry did not want to stray too far from housing finance for fear that it would lose its political influence."

## A bleak ending

The 1970s were not to end on a happy note. Despite all of the financial, structural, and service innovations implemented by Erie, the decade closed without producing a public policy that practically addressed the bank's most troubling economic and financial issues... issues that were similarly hammering other savings institutions throughout the nation.

Interest rates were still inordinately high and threatening to move higher. Inflation was having a serious negative impact on savers and prompting them to look beyond banks for surcease. A saver, who put $1,000 in a time deposit account at a 7.75% interest rate in 1974, saw his actual purchasing power *drop* to $890 in just five years. In one month in 1978, the savings banks in New York State experienced a net deposit outflow of over $350 million.

In June 1978, federal bank regulators took note of these circumstances and granted thrifts the power to introduce six-month, $10,000 certificates of deposit with interest ceilings linked to the rates of six-month Treasury bills. The allowable rate at that point was 7.14%. This would help Erie to stem deposit outflows but would wreak havoc with its bottom line. Over 75% of our deposits reposed in 5% passbook accounts. If a significant portion of these funds were to flow into these new short-term, high-cost (to the bank) CDs, the bank would suffer un-survivable financial duress.

In addition, the regulators also permitted an eight-year, $1,000 certificate of deposit that could be offered at 7.75% by commercial banks and at 8% by savings institutions. While these accounts helped offset deposit outflows (and reduce the threat of *illiquidity*), they substantially increased savings banks' interest costs (thus escalating the threat of *insolvency*). These high rates represented a major threat to the bottom line of every New York State thrift since the recently "liberalized" state usury law still kept the earnings rate on new mortgages at 8.5% or less.

The state legislature finally voted to further increase the usury ceiling at a pre-dawn special session in December 1978. It allowed for a new ceiling of 9.5% but only until December 1980, when it would revert to the old level. In the meantime, the rate could increase a maximum of ¼% per quarter until it reached a level two points above the Constant Maturity Yield Index of Federal Treasury Securities. Lamentably, the legislation still did not make provisions for variable rate and short-term mortgage formats. Again, it was too little, too late.

As a consequence, newly-originated mortgages would still entail long maturities and fixed rates, and, thus, would not be able to keep pace with market rates of interest and the interest rate demands of depositors.

The usury rate concession was too little and too late. The cost of new deposits at Erie (including those rolled over from less expensive passbooks) was already exceeding the new usury ceiling. In the rest of the country, the permitted mortgage rates ranged from 11% to 12%; and even those high rates merely matched the cost of deposits, leaving no margin to cover all of the other costs of operation. The handwriting was on the wall, and it was written in red ink.

The assets and liabilities on Erie's balance sheet were being referred to as "rocks" and "hard places."

As the decade came to a close, deposit funds (i.e. the "rocks") continued to flow out of savings banks and savings and loan associations at an unprecedented pace, threatening thrifts' liquidity *and* solvency.

Institutions in competitive, mature markets in the Northeast were being hit particularly hard. In fact, Buffalo was recognized as one of the most competitive in the nation; it was home to savers who harbored a keen appreciation for a "deal." The demographic, ethnic, and financial composition of our community dictated that Erie pay top dollar for savings deposits.

Other kinds of woes were ravaging the asset side of Erie's balance sheet (i.e. the "hard place"). Most of Erie's mortgage portfolio still consisted of loans featuring interest rates of 4.5% to 6%. Even under the "liberalized" usury law, every new mortgage would be a long-term loser as far as our bank's bottom line was concerned. Each of these mortgages would have to be "subsidized" by the surpluses created by savers during the past 120 years. This subsidization constituted a massive shift of wealth from savers to homeowners during the 1970s.

Incredulously, as the stressful decade closed, the "ostriches" in leadership positions in the thrift industry elected to defer thinking about the future until it happened.

Not a good sign for institutions that had insufficient wherewithal to carry them through the next decade.

*Chapter six*

## THE EIGHTIES ARRIVE

### An escalating threat

As the 1980s opened, it was becoming apparent that despite innovations like checking accounts and in-store banking, traditional savings institutions still lacked sufficient competitive clout in the evolving marketplace. The technology, credit expertise, service packages, and branch networks of commercial banks and other contemporary financial services providers – coupled with the growing sophistication of thrifts' customers – were contributing to an escalating, probably inexorable, erosion of deposits, profits, and surpluses in the savings industry. The long-standing, government-facilitated interest rate advantage enjoyed by thrifts had been neutralized; it no longer contributed to the competitive wherewithal that was necessary for survival and success.

Thrifts were being hit on all sides.

- Money was streaming out of them and into money-market mutual funds. By the end of 1982, these funds held over $240 billion in assets.
- Corporations, investors, and individual borrowers were turning to non-bank mortgage companies rather than to banks and thrift institutions for their real estate funding needs. These non-bank lenders were taking advantage of new methods for the "securitization" of loans (i.e. the packaging of individual loans into securities that can be marketed to investors).
- Traditional, conservative savers were being attracted by large mutual funds which offered diversified bundles of stocks featuring attractive dividend yields and substantial potential for appreciation. Those who

sought both a reasonable return and safety were turning increasingly to thrifts' new competitors.

Inconceivably, at the same time, the regulatory establishment continued to use every ancient cudgel of repression at its disposal. In New York State, as in many other states, those artificial, regressive obstacles included: unreasonable usury ceilings; unrestricted assumability of mortgages; mandated fixed-rate, long-term loan formats; and geographic limitations on bank operations which constituted a *cordon sanitaire* against serving customers in out-of-state markets where deposit sources and contemporarily-priced mortgages were more plentiful.

Despite the titanic changes that were occurring and the dire warnings that were being voiced, the public sector persisted in its demands that the savings industry continue to function, almost exclusively, as a conduit for affordable housing finance. In New York State, this meant that the primary role assigned to the thrift industry required its constituent savings institutions to provide long-term, assumable, fixed-rate mortgage loans… at rates well below the national average. Congress, the New York State Legislature, and the regulatory establishments they deployed were essentially insisting that savings institutions continue to function like they did during the previous 100 years, i.e. as vehicles dedicated almost exclusively to ensuring the availability and affordability of housing finance.

I found it difficult to accept the convoluted logic that had, for too long, been employed by public policymakers in this regard. For more than a century-and-a-half, thrifts had provided the vast majority of funds for private housing in the nation. Understandably, affordable housing was a continuing national priority. But, by forcing one segment of lending institutions (i.e. thrifts) to continue to function in the 1960s and 1970s in ways that imperiled them financially, politicians merely served to jeopardize an essential flow of funds to homebuyers. In order to successfully continue their activities as the nation's primary housing lender, thrifts had to be freed from the antiquated legislative and regulatory constraints and mandates that were now preventing them from competing – and surviving – in an otherwise free marketplace. Thrifts desperately needed new products, powers, and lending formats that would enable them to generate the revenues required to sustain traditional mortgage lending operations in the "new world." It was clear to most informed observers that savings institutions were being denied these essential tools in response to political pressures mounted by commercial banks, the real estate industry, and well-meaning but misguided consumer activists. As a consequence, by the beginning of the '80s, self-interest in both public and private arenas was strangling the "golden goose."

Some promising attempts to achieve prudent reforms in the 1970s had failed because of fears in "high places" that any action to disturb the status quo would "hurt housing." The staunch opponents of fundamental reforms argued that "there were no obvious alternatives" to the mortgage services provided by S&Ls.

On the other hand, the proponents of reform – like Erie – argued that government should "leave home finance to the natural dynamics of an *open* and *free* market."

Ultimately, the opponents to reform – *including a preponderance of small savings institutions* – prevailed. Home builders, realtors, and consumer groups who feared a negative impact on housing ultimately convinced Congress to block federally-chartered S&Ls from granting adjustable rate mortgages (ARMs). Many state legislatures followed suit.

(In the 1990s, similar government efforts to force banks to provide "affordable" housing finance – even to borrowers who could not afford it – would precipitate what is now referred to as the Global Financial Crisis of 2008-2009. Congress's blind pandering to vocal constituencies with respect to housing finance contributed to both the S&L Crisis and the Great Recession, two of the most damaging economic debacles in American history.)

During 1981 and 1982, the industry sank to a collective *negative* net worth in excess of $150 billion, based on market values of its assets. In other words, it would have cost *at least* that amount to shut down insolvent S&Ls and pay off their depositors. On the basis of book values, tangible net worth for the industry as a whole was only six-tenths of one percent of deposits.

Erie Savings Bank shared the plight of the industry. Its capital base had diminished by $17 million in 1981. At one point, the bank's Controller produced projections that showed that it could lose another $54 million in 1982, thereby taking its net worth down to 1.68% – well below the level that could trigger intervention (perhaps a takeover) by its regulators. Such capital erosion had been responsible for the recent failure of one of our principal competitors in Buffalo, the venerable Western New York Savings Bank.

In addition, we could reasonably expect even greater deposit outflows which would further exacerbate the strain on our liquidity. Competitors were aggressively chasing our valued depositors. For example, the Oppenheimer Money Market Fund was offering a 17.82% yield with free checking. The Vanguard Money Market Fund of government-backed securities was offering 17.16%.

Tough competition, indeed.

As the National Commission on Financial Institution Reform, Recovery, and Enforcement later concluded in a 1993 report:

"Interest rate increases of unprecedented magnitude
during 1979-82 revealed the extent of interest-rate
risk to which the industry was exposed. The S&Ls'
deposit costs rose far above the return from their
portfolios of fixed-rate mortgage loans. There were
huge operating losses and many institutions were
bankrupted."

Discouragingly, it was becoming evident that this situation was going to be a long-term, chronic problem. One of our Controller's more pessimistic scenarios intimated continuing losses that could total $335 million over the nine-year period ending in 1991. It was estimated that the bank's negative net worth could reach as much as $250 million by 1988.

Obviously, in this kind of scenario, the Erie Savings Bank – without an aggressive turnaround plan and fresh capital – faced discouraging prospects.

## The government's response

Sharp increases in interest rates in late 1979 and early 1980 had triggered large outflows of deposits from both banks and thrifts. In a relatively short period of time, money market mutual funds had become extremely powerful predators.

Faced with these kinds of threatening circumstances, the federal government finally began to realize the enormity of the problems facing the savings industry, and it decided to introduce a dose of "corrective" action.

As the decade began to unfold, the government took a number of specific actions to alleviate the burgeoning crisis. Apparently, "better late than never" was its reasoning. Unfortunately, "too late" was the reality.

Realizing that Regulation Q was not yielding the desired results (i.e. restraining competition for deposits and increasing the supply of mortgage credit), Congress passed the Depository Institutions Deregulation and Monetary Control Act of 1980 (DIDMCA) which provided for a phase-out of all deposit rate regulation.

Importantly, the Act called for great deal more than the abolition of rate ceilings on deposit accounts. It put into law an initiative by President Jimmy Carter that was aimed at eliminating many of the distinctions among different types of depository institutions. Unfortunately, most of these late-to-the-party provisions pertained only to *federally*-chartered savings institutions and would not help Erie and thousands of other state-chartered institutions like it.

The major elements of the DIDMCA provided that:

- All *federal* depository institutions could issue interest-bearing checking accounts and would have to hold reserves at the Federal Reserve.

- *Federal* S&Ls could have up to 20 percent of assets in a combination of consumer loans, commercial paper, and corporate debt instruments.
- *Federal* S&Ls could offer credit card services and engage in trust activities.
- A statutory capital requirement of 5% of deposits was replaced with a range of 3% to 6%, to be set by the Federal Home Loan Bank Board.
- Deposit interest rate ceilings were to be phased out over a six-year period and the interest rate differential for S&Ls would also be terminated. Interest rate deregulation was to be administered by the Depository Institutions Deregulation Committee (DIDC) with the Secretary of Treasury as Chair and the heads of the Federal Reserve, the Federal Deposit Insurance Corp., the Federal Home Loan Bank Board, and the National Credit Union Administration as voting members.
- The deposit insurance limit would be raised to $100,000.
- A Federal preemption of state usury laws would be introduced for mortgages and certain other loans.
- Statewide branching for *federal* S&Ls would be permitted.
- There would be an elimination of geographic limits for lending and subsidiary company operations.
- Expanded authority would be granted for *federal* S&Ls to make acquisition, development, and construction (ADC) loans.

Surprisingly, no power to offer adjustable rate mortgages was provided for in this Act.

But, in 1980, the Bank Board did reduce the net worth requirement for insured S&Ls from 5% to 4% of total deposits; and in 1981, it was reduced again to 3%.

In light of the many benefits afforded to federally-chartered thrift institutions by this legislation, Erie's Board of Trustees decided in 1981 to surrender the bank's long-treasured New York

State savings bank charter and convert the Big E to a federal savings association. Our Board had reasonably concluded that the commercial bank lobby and other activists would continue to pressure New Your State Legislators to "protect" non-business borrowers and savers by forcing state-chartered savings institutions to function as they always had.

As a result of its conversion to federal status, the Big E was able to pursue implementation of the new powers granted by the DIDMCA.

Notwithstanding this conversion, however, the New York State Constitution still prohibited a savings institution headquartered in the State from issuing stock to New York residents. This onerous restriction continued to make it necessary for Erie to move its federal charter and legal headquarters to another state if it wished to get the authority to implement a capital-generating stock offering.

In early 1981, Richard Pratt, a protégé of Senator Jake Garn (Chairman of the Senate Banking, Housing, and Urban Affairs Committee) was appointed by President Ronald Reagan as Chairman of the Federal Home Loan Bank Board, the chief regulatory body for thrifts in the United States. Pratt had great familiarity with the industry since he had served as senior economist for the U. S. League of Savings Institutions in the late 1960s. He understood the enormous problems that the industry was facing, and he quickly began to formulate a program of practical deregulation to deal with them. This approach was in total alignment with President Ronald Reagan's philosophy which discouraged "bailouts."

He teamed up with Roger W. Mehle Jr., who had just been named Assistant Secretary of the Treasury – Domestic Finance. They quickly formulated an agenda for both legislative and regulatory change. Their basic strategy called for actions which would preclude a run on savings institutions while, simultaneously, granting S&Ls the powers to *gradually* increase their earnings potential.

Their regulatory initiative was designed to:

- Quickly merge failing thrifts into healthy thrifts or banks.
- Provide thrifts with many of the powers that previously were exclusively reserved for commercial banks.
- Allow temporary forbearances from the type of capital and operating requirements that were contributing, at that point, to the rapid demise of savings institutions.
- Permit the issuance of notes – or "Net Worth Certificates" – by the FSLIC which could be used to bolster thrifts' capital bases.

At that time, the FHLBB maintained a list of thrift institutions that could be categorized as follows:

- "Dogs" that were on the verge of imminent collapse;
- The "terminally impaired" which would not recover over time.
- The "possibles" that *might* survive.
- The "probables" – like Erie – that would likely survive *if given sufficient time.* (In subsequent years, the Board conducted a series of "viability" tests which confirmed that Erie/Empire had been appropriately included in this category.)

Pratt's strategy accommodated the needs of thrifts like Erie since it "bought time" for work-outs, re-financings, and the occurrence of a downturn in interest rates. He believed that acute interest rate cyclicity was the fundamental cause of thrifts' (hopefully transient) problems.

Dr. Pratt's policy also encouraged the conversion of mutual savings institutions to stock companies which had the legal authority to publicly solicit supplemental capital from investors.

Pratt's was a pragmatic approach since the estimated cost of a bailout of the industry at that time was $60 billion... and Congress had not yet allocated *any* funds for such a purpose. (Soon after, the estimated cost of a bailout was raised to $178 billion, or about $350 billion in 1990 dollars.)

The Pratt/Mehle initiative quickly morphed into a regulatory platform upon which the Big E could implement a "Phoenix Plan" (as outlined in the next Chapter) to guide its recovery and resurgence.

While Pratt's aggressive regulatory approach promised to give well-run institutions like Erie a new lease on life, his legislative proposals to "level the playing field" for thrifts, commercial banks, and securities firms ran into stiff opposition from Fernand St. Germain, Chairman of the House Banking, Finance and Urban Affairs Committee, and an array of lobbying groups representing the securities, insurance, real estate, and commercial banking industries.

As a result, the only worthwhile piece of legislation that emerged during the Reagan administration was the 1982 <u>Garn-St. Germain Depository Institutions Act.</u>

This Act granted *federally* chartered S&Ls additional powers to diversify their activities.

Its major provisions:

- Effectively eliminated deposit interest-rate ceilings.
- Expanded substantially the asset powers of *federal* S&Ls by permitting them to allocate:
  - Up to 40 percent of their assets to commercial mortgage loans.
  - Up to 30 percent of their assets to consumer loans.
  - Up to 10 percent of their assets to commercial loans.
  - Up to 10 percent of their assets to commercial leases.
- Eliminated the previous statutory limit on the loan-to-value ratio, i.e. the dollar amount of a loan made by an S&L expressed as a percentage of the appraised value of the project for which funds were provided.
- Expanded the powers of the FSLIC to deal with troubled institutions, i.e. authorized the FDIC and the

FSLIC to issue "net worth certificates" to supplement the capital foundations of troubled thrifts.

- Restricted the ability of bank holding companies to acquire failed S&Ls. This limitation was designed to discourage commercial banks from increasing their market presence by taking unfair advantage of distressed thrifts. (As we shall see in a later Chapter, this provision did not preclude the ultimate, piecemeal acquisition of Erie/Empire by a number of commercial banks.)

Interestingly, the bill's full title was <u>An Act to Revitalize the Housing Industry by Strengthening the Financial Stability of Home Mortgage Lending Institutions and Ensuring the Availability of Home Mortgage Loans</u>. The title, once again, illustrated Congress's overriding concern with the availability and affordability of housing despite the negative impacts that such an exclusive focus would have on the thrift industry's financial stability and its capacity to provide residential loans in the future.

The <u>DIDMCA</u> and the <u>Garn Act</u> did, however, offer an important measure of hope to federally-chartered savings institutions like Erie. These Acts – along with other regulatory changes implemented in the early '80s – finally provided us with some of the desperately-needed asset and liability powers that had been proposed so often during the 1960s and 1970s. They also sent a signal, for the first time, that Congress and its regulatory machine were beginning to realize the impracticality of using the thrift industry as a "public service tool" to facilitate homeownership. They were, at last, acknowledging that prevailing economic realities had circumscribed their long-standing perceived prerogative to mandate that a single industry of *private* enterprises assume near-total responsibility for the accomplishment of a huge, financially-demanding, social task like national housing finance.

In further pursuit of its thrift rehabilitation goals, the Bank Board also eliminated restrictions on the minimum number of stockholders required for a publicly-traded S&L. Previously, it mandated that a publicly-owned thrift had to have at least 400 shareholders, of which at least 125 had to be from the local community served by the S&L. These prior regulations had stipulated that no individual could own more than 10% of an S&L's stock and that no "controlling group" more than 25%. With the new regulation, there could be a single owner.

This proved to be a double-edged sword. On one hand, it encouraged wealthy, well-meaning investors to bring new capital to the industry. On the other hand, it prompted many overly-ambitious developers, aggressive non-bank companies, speculators, quick-buck investors, and a few out-and-out crooks to take over S&Ls. Takeovers were made even easier by allowing acquirers to put up land and other real estate as non-cash "currency" to buy stock in thrifts. Often, such purchases were enabled by exaggerated appraisals of the real property that was invested.

Small institutions could, therefore, be acquired at low cost and quickly expanded into large enterprises, thanks to investors' ability to attract savers with recently enacted, higher levels of federal insurance on deposits. Too many of the S&Ls acquired in this manner became "rogues" in the marketplace. They constituted a competitive force that clobbered other prudent thrift operators like Erie.

The ceiling imposed by Regulation Q was being relaxed with the *hope* that, if thrifts were able to pay competitive rates, they could stem the outflow of deposits to money market funds. Regulators fantasized that higher permissible deposit rate ceilings would enable thrifts to retain deposits, thus averting a liquidity crisis. What they failed to realize was that most thrifts, because of their low-rate loan "baggage" from the past, could not afford to pay current market rates of interest without annihilating their capital bases.

To address this problem, the Federal Home Loan Bank Board introduced, in 1982, the concept of regulatory "forbearance" under which the savings institutions that faced insolvency as a result of (judiciously) paying unprecedented high interest rates would be allowed to continue to operate. It was hoped that, by providing selected troubled thrifts with limited forbearances from mandated capital requirements and operating constraints, they would be able to endure extreme – temporary – duress until interest rates returned to historical – moderate – levels.

Commercial bankers voiced strong opposition to such temporary forbearances since they had long been counting on participating in the "feeding frenzy" for market share – or the outright redistribution of thrift ownership – that would likely accompany the collapse of the savings industry. Fortunately, their very vocal resistance served to highlight the fact that forbearances were extremely important to the majority of thrifts that had all but exhausted their supply of ready cash.

It was perilous for thrifts to sell mortgage loans in their portfolios to raise liquid funds because most previously-booked loans typically carried interest rates that were below prevailing market levels. Thus, any sales of loans had to be made at a discount to their portfolio value. As a consequence such transactions would simply create new losses – and additional capital diminishment – for the sellers. Forbearances were important, therefore, because they could provide a significant offset to the impairment of capital that was occasioned by the sale of assets at a loss.

The importance of forbearances would most certainly grow over time as the twin specters of illiquidity and insolvency continued to menace the thrift industry. Indeed, the number of failures in the thrift industry that were triggered by capital insufficiency continued to escalate. Institutions in Western New York had become especially fragile, and Erie Savings Bank did not escape the trauma. At the dawn of the 1980s, its surplus and reserves had been decimated, and prospects for new, offsetting earnings contributions were practically non-existent.

A number of smaller local thrifts had already bowed to the inevitable, and the Erie Savings Bank had acquired several of them. In 1981, Western Savings Bank, the third largest thrift in the Buffalo area, failed and the gravity of the situation really hit home. (In the next few years, over a dozen of the remaining sixteen savings institutions in the region would disappear. By 1991, only one locally-based thrift would still be in operation.) In this kind of an environment, forbearances could play an extremely positive role.

To complement the forbearance component of its effort to "re-regulate for success," the Federal Home Loan Bank Board decided to allow thrifts to adapt their accounting practices to "generally accepted accounting principles" (i.e. GAAP), the universally accepted accounting standards for all types of business enterprises. Importantly, GAAP allowed for the use of "goodwill" on a savings institution's balance sheet. This type of accounting treatment had been in use for decades by corporations of all stripes. It promised to have a particularly salutary effect in the deteriorating thrift industry where mergers between soon-to-fail thrifts and healthier institutions could be "arranged" in order to "buy time" to structure long-term workouts in anticipation of an eventual decline in interest rates. With the application of the principle of goodwill as provided for by GAPP, the tangible negative net worth of an acquired institution could be written off against the earnings of the acquiring institution over a period of forty years.

This fillip made mergers economically practical and affordable and, thus, reduced the number of institutions that regulators would have to bail out with cold, hard cash. The government gave its "blessing" to this technique since it would help forestall the need to immediately liquidate failing institutions. This goodwill "solution" made it possible for "good banks" to carry "bad banks" until economic conditions returned to "normal."

In a typical savings institution acquisition transaction of this type, the "purchase price" to the acquirer was the assumption of the acquiree's deposit liabilities. (In some cases, an additional contribution of cash by the buyer was required.) The difference between the dollar amount of the extant deposit liabilities acquired and the current *market* value of the tangible assets which were simultaneously acquired typically constituted a significant negative gap. This gap existed because the assets of the acquired institution were principally troubled loans or loans carrying relatively low rates. Therefore, as a consequence of recent dramatic increases in prevailing national interest rate levels, the true market value of these loans was significantly less than their book value.

As a result, from day one, a surviving merger partner was liable to its newly-acquired depositors for an aggregate dollar amount that was considerably in excess of the value of the assets it had obtained via the merger. (The procedure used in revaluing assets to reflect their current market worth was referred to as "marking-to-market.")

In such acquisition transactions, a universally accepted accounting technique called "purchase accounting" was used. (This practice is described in detail in the following Chapter.) The application of this method, in effect, offset the negative value gap that the mark-to-mark process produced by ascribing a professionally estimated market value to the *intangible* assets that were also conveyed in the transaction. These assets were considered "goodwill." Technically, goodwill was an impalpable asset that had monetary worth ascribed to it in an accounting context in order to reflect the value of incorporeal items acquired in the merger, e.g. advantageous branch locations; unique customer affiliations and loyalties; unmatched geographic reach; skilled staff talents; special niches in the marketplace, etc. These were things of true value that, absent a merger, would not be reflected on a balance sheet as individually identifiable assets.

The inclusion of this intangible bundle of assets enabled most resulting post-merger balance sheets to "balance." The goal always was to offset the negative gap between tangible assets and deposit liabilities with intangible assets of sufficient value.

Especially important was the fact that thrift regulators allowed S&L acquirers to include the value of goodwill in their calculations of resulting regulatory capital. Using this new approach, an acquirer was able to preserve – even expand – its capital base as a consequence of merging with a struggling institution.

With this new goodwill "tool" at its disposal, the Federal Home Loan Bank Board began to encourage "non-seizures" of struggling or failing thrifts through "goodwill mergers." This pragmatic practice enabled the Board to attract a number of qualified acquirers, including Erie.

But there was an important "hitch." The FHLBB required acquirers to gradually amortize (i.e. write off against earnings) such acquired goodwill, typically over a period of forty years. This was acceptable to acquirers, however, since they reasonably anticipated that the reconstituted merged entities would generate future operating income supplementations that would be far in excess of the mandatory write-offs.

Further, GAAP allowed the difference between the market value of acquired assets and their book value to be gradually accreted as income by the acquirer over the remaining expected life of the assets. The income product of this approach, commonly referred to as the "discount," provided an immediate stream of reportable earnings for the surviving institution.

Supervisory mergers, therefore, provided benefits for all parties involved, i.e. the acquirer, the acquiree, and the federal government.

While many purists – and commercial bankers – attacked this process as an accounting "fabrication," it was arguably the best legal way for a government with no cash bailout funds at the ready to stem the surge of failed thrifts. If the then-current rate of failures were to continue, it would soon levy a crushing financial burden on the federal government. Moreover, it would have created a devastating loss of confidence in the entire United States banking system and, possibly, spark a cataclysmic depositor "run" on all banks.

This merger process provided potential acquirers – like Erie – with much needed time to reconstitute their balance sheets;

achieve supplementary earnings; and expand their branch networks into fertile, rapidly-growing regions of the nation.

The FSLIC and FHLBB quickly identified a small number of savings banks, including Erie, as prime potential acquirers, given their performance records over the previous decades.

In conjunction with this approach, the Federal Home Loan Bank Board occasionally allowed for a "good bank; bad bank" strategy by which an acquirer of a failing thrift was allowed to segregate the resulting accumulation of assets and deposits of both the acquirer and acquiree into separately-chartered banking entities. One of these institutions would embody most of the "bad assets" while the other would carry the "good" assets which would, over time, generate sufficient earnings to carry both institutions. (This kind of good/bad coupling would be employed in a number of banking crises during the next three decades.)

The thrift industry – and, along with it, the real estate industry – were also aided for a short time by the Economic Recovery Tax Act of 1981, an ambitious tax-reduction initiative of the Reagan Administration. It reduced the depreciable life of real property to fifteen years, replacing the previous complex schedules that had mandated depreciable lives of up to sixty years. This Act increased the up-front tax shelter that real estate investments provided and, consequently, enhanced the attractiveness of real property as an investment.

Importantly, the Act also made such depreciation available to passive investors (i.e. people who were not professional real estate investors), so a huge, new source of demand for real state was quickly created.

The shortening of depreciation schedules for real property greatly increased the profitability of real estate investments. By leveraging a real estate investment, it was possible for an investor to enjoy a cumulative tax deduction that was greater than the amount of cash he or she originally invested. After-tax returns on real estate investment became so attractive that initial investments could be earned back in only a few years.

The Act, which was sponsored by Representative Jack Kemp of Western New York and Senator William V. Roth, Jr., of Delaware, produced a boom in real estate development, and it provided unusual profit opportunities for lenders like S&Ls, banks, and insurance companies.

Sadly, many of the real estate investors and lenders who availed themselves of this tax benefit soon experienced considerable losses when a key provision of the Act was reversed by Congress in 1986 as part of a "re-thinking" of the tax code.

*****

Erie took advantage of most of the applicable, pertinent, and workable aspects of the new statutes and regulations that emerged during this period. Many of these provisions would be embodied in Erie's "Phoenix Plan" (described in the next Chapter of this book) which was formulated to aggressively, innovatively, and responsibly meet the challenge of the "new world" that was "a dawnin'."

## Choose your poison

In reality, the legislative and regulatory changes contrived during the early Eighties provided savings institutions with only a few strategic options. They constituted a fuzzy blueprint for what "might" work... but had never been proven. None of the proposed regulatory changes constituted a "silver bullet." (Not incidentally, they *did* provide a means for government kahunas to avoid being tagged with a "do-nothing" label.)

Complicating matters, was the fact that the operators of traditional savings institutions had little opportunity over the prior fifty years to become familiar with the new-fangled financial products, technologies, and investment strategies that were suggested by the current flood of re-regulation. Many thrift infrastructures, distribution networks, and – most importantly – key staff members were inadequate to the challenges involved in taking profitable advantage of these newly-proffered regulatory initiatives.

For many savings institutions that had evolved in a much different era, the spate of re-regulation in the early '80s was too late, too complex, and too daunting to be properly utilized. Ostensibly, the "good news" was that the managers of long-bridled thrifts were now going to get to play in the big leagues. The overwhelming "bad news" was that, in too many cases, their previous experience had been limited to sandlot stickball.

For over fifty years, state and local governments had fashioned and promulgated mandatory rules, policies, regulations, constraints, and prohibitions that were designed to keep thrift institutions focused on providing housing to the masses. The public sector had tinkered incessantly with various ways to implement progressive housing policies; but they demonstrated little regard for the costs or perils they might generate within the thrift industry and the economy as a whole. It was a quintessential example of government trying to strong arm a free marketplace to do a bureaucracy's unrealistic bidding.

With respect to the federal initiatives of the early '80s, the private sector institutions generally had to take most of the risks and incur most of the costs.

Essentially, the government's latest putative reform tactics only provided the thrift industry with an opportunity to pull itself up by its own noose so that it could – possibly – live a little longer. Savings institutions were being abruptly tasked with the kinds of reformation efforts that should have been methodically nurtured by the government over the previous half century.

Consequently, thrift leaders now had only four dubious options:

- **Change nothing and attempt to continue business as usual.**

  Unfortunately, in the prevailing environment, efforts to carry-on the operating practices of the past were simply a recipe for continued decline, at the very best. It should be noted, however, that this approach was a reasonable option for a few savings institutions that had built up enormous capital surpluses over many decades. These were generally institutions in small, rural, or remote communities that were insulated from the blistering interest rate and service competition that had prevailed in major markets since the end of World War II. But the vast majority of savings institutions couldn't continue to operate "the old way" for very long, given their eroding capital bases. Unfortunately, those that opted to stay the course were, in reality, simply "playing out the string" until their larder was bare and the government arrived to arrange a marriage of convenience with another, better capitalized (if only barely so), financial institution.

- **Rapidly exploit newly-granted powers**

  This approach required thrifts to maximize institutional growth in the short term. Such a strategy had to assume, perforce, that hasty growth, in and of itself, would *immediately* generate earnings that were sufficient to create a positive spread between the interest paid on new deposits and the interest earned on the new loan acquisitions that those deposit dollars made possible.

  Unfortunately, loans that were generated quickly in a distressed environment usually increased the risk of loss. While many panicked managers had come to believe that their only option was "growth at any cost," the consequence of such a "hustle-up" approach was typically the booking of less-than-prime real estate loans. These, in turn, further exacerbated their institution's original earnings problem. Furthermore, even solid, newly-booked loans could not make adequate contributions in the limited time available.

- **Beseech their regulators to "arrange" a sale of their institutions.**

  This strategy required interested investors who saw thrift ownership as an avenue to previously unavailable opportunity. Unfortunately, many of the investors who emerged turned out to be "high-rollers" who had previously only dreamt of getting the keys to other people's "piggy banks." Now, they accurately perceived that, since deposits were insured by the government, relatively low cost funds (compared to the costs of borrowing in the open market) would be available to them. These monies would allow them to finance aggressive – often high-risk – investments in large-scale real estate projects and property developments.

  The financial leverage afforded by equity ownership of a thrift institution had great appeal to ambitious investors, especially those with a covetous eye on the real estate market. Further, Uncle Sam's guarantee to protect depositors from loss ensured that these investors would have a virtually bottomless pot of funds to put at risk. (In reality, the kinds of "dream gains" these nouveau thrift investors sought proved to be difficult to achieve. In too many situations, only the owners of thrifts reaped gains while the long-established institutions they acquired continued to flounder.)

- **Cherry-pick the new powers and permissions.**

  To make this strategy pay off, thrift operators had to create an expanding mix of customer services, loans, and investments that offered immediate revenue supplementation, a promise of solid, long-term growth, and acceptable short-term risk. Innovation and carefully planned growth in a variety of financial service arenas were critical keys to success with this option.

## Erie's choice

The Big E team chose the latter option because it offered the highest probability of effecting the kind of pragmatic turnaround strategy that would facilitate a Phoenix-like rise for a stressed but not-yet-failing institution like Erie. This option would provide a framework within which Erie could:

- Grow its portfolios of assets and liabilities in markets which were more fertile – in comparison to those in Western New York – thereby generating significant, supplemental positive earnings. Such earnings would offset the continuing losses created by the existing, miss-matched portfolios that had been created over many years as the bank worked to accommodate the need for housing finance in its market areas. This type of growth would necessarily entail the generation of new, higher-rate asset products like consumer loans, credit cards, and automobile loans.

- Secure additional capital to support the expanded asset base that would be occasioned by growth.

- Field an extremely qualified and disciplined cadre of specialists and experienced managers who could guide growth both wisely and, to the extent possible, conservatively.

- Implement new techniques for increasing earnings without necessitating a concomitant expansion in the bank's capital base. For example, assets could be originated for sale to other investors (at a profit). Such assets would not be added to the bank's balance sheet where they would require an additional capital offset. These assets – including mortgages, consumer loans, and automobile loans – would continue to be "serviced" by Erie and, thus, produce additional income. Such off-balance-sheet loan aggregations would allow Erie to garner supplementary income without diminishing its all-important capital ratios.

- Create non-portfolio-dependent income through fee-based services that could be provided to existing and new bank customers. New regulatory powers coupled with ingenuity could facilitate profit-generating investments in non-bank enterprises such as real estate sales agencies, insurance agencies, transaction servicing companies, brokerage firms, employee relocation companies, and the like. Such investments could produce substantial, non-traditional, income for Erie.

In 1981, Erie's Board of Trustees gave me the responsibility for preparing a rehabilitation strategy based on the "cherry-pick" option. I immediately began to formulate a plan designed to enable the Erie Savings Bank to succeed in a foreboding, adverse environment

Naturally, I dubbed it the "Phoenix Plan."

## Preserving pre-plan progress

Of course, the new plan had to build upon the bank's achievements of the past. It could neither interfere with nor dilute Erie's already initiated turnaround efforts which were experiencing great success.

For example, to ensure that the bank would not perpetuate the fixed rate mortgage "box" that had long squeezed its income, Erie had recently become – thanks to its new federal charter – the first bank in New York State to introduce variable-rate mortgages. The contractual configuration of these loans allowed their associated rates to be renegotiated every three years, based on an FHLBB index.

The bank had also formalized and expanded its activities in the secondary mortgage market by "packaging" locally-originated mortgages for sale in the national market. This process provided Erie with an immediate financial return (in some cases, also including servicing revenue) on loans that were sold subsequent to their origination. This packaging technique provided an opportunity to continually "recycle" available mortgage money to new borrowers, a process similar to "turning over" inventory in a retail enterprise. (We bundled only *whole* loans, thus precluding the kinds of trouble created during the banking crises of 2008-2009 by the "sliced-and-diced" mortgage securities that were created in the 1990s.) Unfortunately, our success in this endeavor was somewhat muted by the fact that new housing construction in our primary lending markets dropped 79% during 1979-80. (Such securitization would help in later years, however, as the mortgage market became re-energized.)

In addition, thanks to recently-introduced federal permissions with respect to the origination of consumer loans, Erie had begun to offer credit cards, auto loans, personal loans, and the Uncharge Card, which was a VISA debit card. The latter was an extremely popular product. Uncharge Card transactions increased 400% in a very short time, making it the most successful VISA savings product in the United States.

To further supplement our income while we were planning for the long term, we had incorporated Shelton Square Agency, an insurance agency subsidiary which was the first entity of its type ever owned and operated by a mutual savings bank. We also accelerated the expansion of our established Metroteller subsidiary.

Our Phoenix Plan would have to nurture these extant initiatives as well as create new ones.

While dividend and interest costs continued to surge, Erie managed to realize a net *operating* profit of $1.9 million in 1980. We were one of a few thrifts in New York State to achieve positive earnings performance. As a consequence, we were able to undertake some portfolio restructuring in order to enhance our future earnings potential.

But, economic pressures continued. In early 1980, the prime rate approached 20%. The cost of Erie's deposits was averaging 10.22% while less than 25% of our mortgage portfolio was earning that much.

It was clear to us that, given the intransigent drag of the low-rate mortgages we had generated over the past several decades, it would be virtually impossible for us to grow out of our financial bind conventionally if our operations continued to be limited to traditional bank activities in the low-growth Western New York region. Erie would need higher volumes of deposit and loan growth – with profitably-matched rates – in order to approach the kinds of revenue streams that would support it and its accumulated impedimenta. Of course, the bank would require additional capital to support such growth. Supplemental revenues from other, non-traditional financial services would be needed, too.

Accordingly, we rushed to have the "Phoenix Plan" – which would incorporate all these objectives – ready for implementation by early 1982. Our talented and aggressive team members worked diligently to prepare for the dramatic changes and adjustments in bank operations that would be necessary to launch a formidable – and successful – response to the mounting threats in our environment.

*Chapter seven*

# THE PHOENIX PLAN

## A sense of urgency

While the Phoenix Plan was being completed, the rate of thrift failures continued to escalate, and the regulatory agencies that oversaw them became responsible for a rapidly-growing roster of "ghost" institutions.

No federal money had been appropriated by Congress to support resolution efforts. In fact, regulators had neither a mandate – nor an operational structure – to deal with the swelling tide of failures.

Moreover, regulatory bodies were seriously understaffed. Too many examiners had insufficient experience with the highly-sophisticated techniques that were being employed by thrifts like Erie. Regulators would often visit with our management team to be briefed on the complex practices that were becoming essential to the modern thrift.

As we noted in an earlier Chapter, the government's belated response to the crisis was to deregulate interest rates and give federally-chartered thrifts permission to offer a limited array of heretofore prohibited services. All this was done in the *hope* that the managers of deteriorating institutions would be able to: immediately offer – at a profit – complex new services in a world of experienced competitors; deal with one of the most adverse economic environments that had ever emerged; and, somehow, put the portfolios of the past behind them.

Needless to say, this hope was unrealistic.

Many honest managers were in over their heads. The prevailing circumstances pretty much relegated them to the arena of high-rate deposit-sourcing and, high-risk lending. The good guys in the industry – who had managed their shops conservatively for years and who would have preferred to continue to do so – were pressured into doing some counterproductive things in the cause of survival. Indeed, many state and federal regulations that were promulgated at the time actually encouraged such action.

It was hoped by Congress, regulators, and the public at large that thrifts could – with a modicum of regulatory relief – *somehow* work their way out of their dilemma without tangible assistance. It was becoming painfully apparent, however, that further relaxation of long-standing repressive regulations – an attractive option in theory, and probably workable if it had been introduced earlier and implemented gradually with forethought – could not now adequately serve as an immediate, stopgap solution.

### Rising from the ashes

With these circumstances as a backdrop, the Phoenix Plan was adopted by the bank's Board of Trustees in the spring of 1982. The survival strategy and tactics it embodied were designed to provide Erie with the time and capacities necessary to:

- Complete the kind of organizational and operational restructuring that would allow Erie – which became a federal savings institution in 1981 – to fully exploit the powers that the <u>Garn Act</u> and the <u>DIDMCA</u> had authorized.
- Add more depositor funds and contemporary assets to its balance sheet.
- Create a menu of revenue-generating, non-traditional services.
- Establish a distribution network that could access new, lucrative markets for deposits and loans.
- Make it attractive to investors who could sufficiently augment the bank's capital base in a way that would allow for Erie's essential growth.

We realized, of course, that in order to accomplish these goals, we were going to have to make some painful adjustments that were not without risk.

Nevertheless, prevailing circumstances were telling us, loud and clear, "It is time for a *big* change."

The Phoenix Plan provided the framework for a continuing series of annual plans, each of which would refine, expand, and modify, where necessary, the basic trajectory of the turnaround that management had charted. It was essential that the Plan afford us the *time* necessary to implement the tactics it entailed. History strongly suggested that, ultimately, inflation would subside and that "normalcy" would once again prevail.

My Master's thesis at the University of Buffalo had focused on the historical patterns of economic cycles and I also had studied the interesting phenomena of biorhythms. Both curiosities led me to believe that the inflationary surge of the '70s and '80s was an aberration and that interest rates would eventually cycle down to more accommodating levels. I was convinced that our national economic "organism" would eventually right itself and allow thrifts to gradually repair the damage that interest rate cyclicity had inflicted on their surplus accounts. Historical evidence was on our side, if we could just weather the storm and get some regulatory accommodation in the meantime.

(My presumption concerning the abatement of inflation would eventually be proven correct. The timetable I had forecasted for such denouement – and for achieving the maximum benefits such a remission would provide – was ten years, a span perceived by many economic analysts at the time as too short. Nevertheless, it was, in my opinion, a perfectly reasonable expectation given historical patterns. Coincidentally, it provided a compatible window of opportunity for the implementation of the Phoenix Plan.

My forecast was validated when the desired downturn in interest rates *did* commence only eight years later – which was less than six months after Erie was assimilated by other financial institutions in early 1990. The critical downturn in interest rates I had envisioned turned out to be substantial and protracted, and it would have easily allowed for the survival of Erie… *if* regulatory intervention had been delayed for just one more year.)

## A bigger footprint

The Phoenix Plan was designed to employ our proven strengths and experiences to *work out* our problems. It was not predicated on a *bailout* solution of the kind that was beginning to achieve currency in regulatory circles. The most essential components of our plan were asset and revenue growth through geographic expansion, product and service diversification, and capital acquisition.

Obviously, growth was key.

We had to offset the "drag" of the past by putting more mortgages and other types of credit assets on the books at higher rates of return. This, of course, required increased deposit inflows. In the Phoenix Plan, we estimated that our balance sheet would have to grow to $16 billion in assets in order to throw off the magnitude of revenue necessary to carry the burdens accumulated in the past *and* to move on to a brighter future. This was quite a reach since, at the time the Phoenix plan was being compiled, Erie's total assets amounted to less than $3 billion.

We knew that such growth was not feasible in our existing primary markets. In the City of Buffalo, for example, population had declined dramatically since the 1950s and growth in the metro area had been stagnant for some time. Between 1970 and 1980 alone, there was a 23% decline in the city's population. Local home-building was at a standstill due to inflation, the population falloff, and the rapid rise in overall housing costs. Both loan demand and savings inflows shrunk precipitously. The same conditions prevailed elsewhere in New York State.

Regions in the south and west, on the other hand, were experiencing dramatic population growth and a concomitant demand for housing. Erie couldn't share in this kind of growth because of a long-standing New York State statute that precluded out-of-state lending (with the exception of lending in New York's five contiguous states which, not surprisingly, were also experiencing slow loan growth). Moreover, in the most prosperous regions of the country, new-generation, short-term, adjustable-rate mortgage contracts were in use and readily accepted by borrowers.

Opportunities for *smart* high-yield lending were essential to the Big E's institutional viability in the face of the burgeoning "thrift crisis." A huge number of savings institutions had already been "done in" because they offered competitive – but unaffordable – deposit rates to avoid a "run on the bank." It was clear that such high rates could be sustained only if they were quickly offset by investments in even higher rate loans. For Erie, this meant tapping into new, more rapidly-growing geographic areas where such lending opportunities were available.

Meanwhile, cash-strapped and with limited abilities to actually manage a savings institution should they be forced to take one over and operate it, regulators began to search for well-run shops like Erie that could – with the aid of government sanctioned goodwill and purchase accounting – acquire, rehabilitate, and reinvigorate failing savings institutions. The government hoped to use the purchase accounting technique to minimize the cash that would be otherwise necessary to "subsidize" merger partners who were willing to absorb the swelling pool of swiftly deteriorating thrifts.

In 1981, a precedent was set for such a rescue program. It employed a technique called "supervisory acquisitions." With the assistance of the FSLIC, Citizens Savings FSB, located in a San Francisco, became the first thrift to acquire another thrift (actually, two troubled institutions at once) across state lines, i.e. Westside Federal S&L in New York City and Washington S&L in Miami Beach, Florida. Citizens concomitantly changed its name to First Nationwide Savings.

As our management team analyzed this transaction, we began to see some exciting opportunities that we could constructively exploit. As previously related, we had endeavored in 1978 to use a New York State "leeway" investment power to acquire the Ontario Savings and Loan Association in Southern California. Since that time, we had continued to evaluate the potential benefits of a physical presence outside of New York State.

Despite the disappointing outcome of our earlier initiative, the experience inclined us to a strategy of wide geographic expansion through acquisition. Such an approach gained even more credibility when Citizens Savings completed its mergers *and* received federal cash assistance to abet the process.

Empire of America had a strong management team; a creditworthy portfolio bred of sound, very conservative underwriting practices; and, an employee base that reflected the strong Buffalo work ethic. We had also recently demonstrated our abilities to consummate mergers in remote markets with the acquisition in 1981 of savings and loan associations in Rochester and the Hudson Valley.

We concluded, therefore, that the major thrust of our Phoenix Plan would entail:

- Growth through the acquisition of troubled (in terms of finances or management) savings institutions in out-of-state regions with high potential.
- Receipt of cash assistance *and* special permissions (forbearances) from the federal government for our efforts in subsequently working out the difficulties plaguing those institutions.

To help us in this aspect of our program, we retained a Washington attorney who, ironically, had represented the Federal Home Loan Bank in our previous unsuccessful negotiations to acquire Ontario Savings and Loan Association. Needless to say, we had gained – the hard way – an appreciation of his acumen.

Erie's interest in working with the regulatory establishment at this point was not, of course, occasioned by altruism but, rather, by a strategic estimation of what the bank would need to survive for ten more years... and to thrive thereafter. The market dynamics that were negatively affecting all thrifts were buffeting institutions in the Northeast especially hard, and Erie was one of them. Unless something akin to the growth-focused provisions of our Phoenix Plan was implemented, Erie, we feared, could very well disappear by mid-decade.

Accordingly, it was in the best interests of Erie, its customers, the communities it served, *and* the government to explore an innovative "partnership" with Uncle Sam that would productively address the burgeoning problems the Big E faced.

We decided to approach the Federal Savings and Loan Insurance Corporation (FSLIC) – the government agency holding the bag, so to speak – with a novel proposal patterned after the Ontario Savings and First Nationwide transaction models. In this proposal, we stipulated that Erie would be willing to take one or more emaciated or failing thrifts off the regulators hands if we could receive, in return, permission to grow dramatically by acquiring a presence in a vibrant out-of-state market and, concurrently, obtain the right to convert to a stock institution.

Very importantly, because of the rapid institutional growth entailed in the Phoenix Plan, the deal we envisioned would have to include the receipt by Erie of comprehensive regulatory forbearance from prevailing capital requirements. Such a provision would afford Erie the time necessary to devise and implement enduring solutions for the metastasizing problems that had beset Erie and the institution (s) it would acquire.

We made our proposal to the Federal Home Loan Bank Board in the spring of 1982, and it was well received. Our search for appropriate merger partners began immediately.

Over the course of several months, I, along with a special "acquisition team" of big E specialists, reviewed scores of individual S&L financial statements provided by the government.

We crisscrossed the country visiting numerous imperiled thrift institutions in an effort to find a "problem" that was large enough to concern the FSLIC but small enough for us to manage without compounding our own difficulties.

Not only did we have to find appropriate thrifts, but, in many cases, we had to convince their managers and directors that the merger of their institutions with Erie was in the best, long-term interests of their employees, customers, and the communities they served. Most of these thrifts had not yet been officially taken over by federal authorities, so the voluntary cooperation of those who governed them was essential.

Erie's financial analysts and its outside advisors formulated detailed cost/benefit analyses with respect to each "opportunity" we discovered. We made sure that the projected costs of every envisioned transaction constituted a reasonable burden. This kind of in-depth analyses gave us confidence that any proposed acquisition or merger transaction would result in a successful workout. In this regard, our proposed agreement with the FSLIC was carefully designed to provide appropriate benefits and protections for both Erie and the government.

Eventually, we found a large institution in Detroit, Michigan that had been in dire straits for some time. Its circumstances were a little more daunting than we had hoped for, but it seemed to be the kind of deal the FSLIC would be willing to make... and time was running out on all sides. Furthermore, the market area and demographics of Detroit were similar to Buffalo, so we concluded that we could manage the situation and still limit our downside exposure.

Michigan law also allowed for stock thrift institutions. This meant that, if Erie moved its banking charter to that state as a consequence of a Detroit merger, it could eventually tap private capital markets by converting to a public company.

However, the situs of this deal – Detroit – was even more economically depressed than Buffalo. Clearly, a transaction that included only Detroit thrift would not satisfy our need to tap into a growth market.

Despite this handicap, Erie made a proposal to the FSLIC to acquire the Detroit thrift. However, our proposal was contingent on the FSLIC giving us, in exchange for our agreement to accept the Michigan shop, an opportunity to acquire an additional, struggling thrift institution in each of the states of California, Texas, and Florida. These states, not incidentally, enjoyed the most ebullient growth forecasts in the nation.

The FSLIC agreed that we could search for an ailing thrift in those states but, since a merger in these "hot" regions of the nation was seen as a very valuable "prize" that was coveted by other thrifts, it would be "politically" doable only if no substantial cash assistance were provided by the FSLIC to Erie to facilitate the transactions that we desired. In addition, the FSLIC insisted that Erie agree to the acquisition of other thrifts that were characterized as "troubled" according to the agency's "viability" tests. (Several decades later, these types of viability evaluations would be called "stress tests" by a new generation of regulators.)

Further, we had to personally demonstrate to the Boards of Directors and/or owners of these "target" thrifts that a merger was in the best interests of their institutions. Those principals had to voluntarily agree (with some urging from their regulators) to be acquired since the government still did not have the funds necessary to conduct a takeover.

After weeks of analysis, travel, and negotiation, we made our final proposal to the FSLIC. We proposed to merge with the Michigan thrift – and three small shops we found in Florida, Texas, and California – *if* we could get federal cash assistance and forbearances from certain net worth regulations for a reasonable period of time.

The amount and duration of the assistance we requested had to be sufficient to allow Erie to:

- Right its ship as well as "digest" these troubled thrifts.
- Achieve a reasonable presence in those new markets.
- Cast the entire merged entity into a profitable, self-sustaining institution that could attract capital.

We requested cash assistance that would allow us to hold the projected losses of the merged institutions (including Erie) to "only" $155 million over the five to six years following the merger. In addition, we needed forbearance from FSLIC capital requirements for at least fifteen years in order to build up our surplus to a point where we were self-sufficient and eventually able to comply with future capital requirements.

The forbearances were absolutely essential in order to allow Erie to grow beyond the capital limits that would otherwise constrain it. The kinds of forbearances we requested would make a $16 billion balance sheet achievable within a decade. This was the institutional asset size that we had calculated would be necessary in order to generate the kinds of revenue that would allow us to both carry the merged entities and to take advantage of the growth and diversification opportunities we foresaw.

Despite the fact that regional federal regulators appreciated Erie's demonstrated capacities to function successfully in a market with demographics like those of Detroit, and despite their need to engage a viable institution like Erie in a turnaround of a very troubled S&L in Southfield, Michigan, their "chief honchos" in Washington were less accommodating. There was quite a bit of protracted dithering.

Such reticence on their part was astonishing since Congress had still not provided the Federal Home Loan Bank and the FSLIC with sufficient funds to even initiate a resolution of the burgeoning S&L debacle. Aside from the DIDMCA and the Garn-St. Germain Act, which tardily gave savings institutions a few new powers that somewhat increased their abilities to compete with commercial banks and investment companies, little had been done to structure meaningful responses to the expanding crisis.

To our dismay, none of the top decision-makers in Washington exuded a sense of urgency. Rumor had it that some of the hesitancy to act was caused by the fact that Vice President George H. W. Bush's selection as the "point man" in the Reagan Administration's S&L "cleanup" efforts had occurred just prior to the revelation that one of his sons was thought to have played a role in the ignoble collapse of a thrift in Colorado. Apparently, it was felt that the "optics" associated with this circumstance had to be carefully managed. Regulators did not want it to look as if they were giving a "free pass" to thrift acquirers like Erie. (The Office of Thrift Supervision ultimately concluded that Neil Bush engaged in numerous "breaches of his fiduciary duties involving multiple conflicts of interest.")

Eventually, the government countered our proposed initiative with a "take it or leave it" counter-proposal involving a process known as a "supervisory acquisition." This deal called for only $79 million in federal cash assistance and/or notes (i.e. "income capital certificates") along with limited forbearances.

We would also have to agree to assume another severely troubled thrift in Michigan and two on Long Island. In return, the FHLBB would agree to Erie's pursuit of two merger opportunities that we had identified in Florida and Texas. But, for "political" reasons, no acquisitions would be permitted in California (the home state of many Reagan Administration officials).

After much negotiation, a deal was finalized in July 1982, and it met almost all of the FSLIC's terms and conditions as well as Erie's most pressing needs. We gained a smidgen of additional satisfaction, too. In recognition of our increased geographic spread and our New York State ("The Empire State") heritage – and in deference to our sacrosanct Big E logo – the regulators acceded to our request that Erie be henceforth known as *Empire Savings Bank*.

Shortly thereafter, Erie's final merger agreements were signed and sealed with a flourish that only a great government can inspire. There were, however, some unexpected "difficulties" that had to be overcome on the day of the mergers. (Perhaps these "bumps" should have given us pause to anticipate the possibility of more down-the-line difficulties in our unique public-private relationship.)

First off, on the morning of the closing, the regulatory staff in Washington that was charged with consummating the mergers locked itself out of the only conference room available to it. Once a D.C. locksmith arrived and plied his craft, everyone was able to settle down and take their places. We, thereupon, engaged in a marathon telephone conversation which lasted over ten hours. (Remember, those were the days when office telephones were tethered to "land lines," thus restricting otherwise natural human mobility). Several times during the closing, document-carrying messengers had to be dispatched between Buffalo and Washington.

When it came time to transfer – via the FSLIC – $50 million from Erie in Buffalo to the new Empire entity in Florida (as part of the agreed upon merger process), it was discovered that Erie did not have access to an old-fashioned machine that could emboss, as the government required, an eight digit number on a paper check. Normally, we would have simply wire-transferred the funds to Washington. But, our forward-thinking government required payment via a properly-embossed paper check.

Once an appropriate alternative approach was conceived (i.e. fifty checks in the amount of $1 million each), we were confronted with another issue. We were informed that the contract documents would require the manual application of the bank's corporate seal. The bank hadn't used that antiquated approach in years. (As early as 1932, even the Marx Brothers had poked fun at the absurdity of a corporate "seal" in their movie Horsefeathers.) After all, it was the sworn intent of signatories that conveyed binding substance to documents, not a mechanical embroidery that couldn't, in most cases, be deciphered even with 20/20 vision! In any event, given the fact that Erie's headquarters had moved several times in just a few years, much of its unused paraphernalia of bygone days was still in storage… somewhere. But despite the march of time and technology, the regulators held out for the application of a seal – "any seal" – to the merger documentation before us. After much angst and turmoil, a surrogate "sealing" device was finally found and put to paper.

Late that evening, the final document was executed. Elated, the Empire team was free to attend a long-anticipated closing party. Alas, most of us were too pooped to participate, and we called it an early evening. In this instance, a rousing party wasn't necessary to assure us that we had scored a major accomplishment. Empire had become the third, truly interstate savings institution in the nation with a wider geographic reach than any other thrift.

(Unconditional interstate branching privileges did not become available to savings institutions until 1992 when the Bush administration became tired of waiting for congressional action on the matter and prodded the Office of Thrift Supervision to issue a rule that allowed such branching by healthy thrifts. In 1994, Congress authorized interstate branch banking for commercial banks.)

Of course, no undertaking of this magnitude ever proceeds without multiple hitches. The next one we encountered was a doozy.

Seemingly before the ink on the merger contracts had dried, the newly-constituted Empire Savings Bank was sued by a small financial institution in northern Michigan that happened to bear the name Empire National Bank of Traverse City.

Despite the fact that we would not be operating in its market territory, its lawyers insisted we change the name of our bank in Michigan.

If we were to change our moniker in the Wolverine State while maintaining operations in other states under a different "flag," our future marketing efforts would be severely compromised. Hence, we quickly decided that our name, so briefly borne, would have to be changed.

Rapid action was essential because thousands of signs were on order and regulatory approval for yet another name change would have to be secured. Moreover, we wanted to make sure that there would be no similar legal challenges from competitors in other states. Complicating matters was the fact that we felt it essential to choose a name that allowed us to retain both our valuable "Big E" brand and, at least, a nominal connection to the (Empire) state of our origin.

Over the next few days, we hurriedly contacted several consultants and advertising agencies that specialized in formulating new names for business institutions. We were shocked when we learned that the process of creating a new name, for whatever reasons, required several months and could cost as much as a half-million dollars.

It was clear that the job was going to be up to us.

Since we didn't have time to conduct an internal suggestion process among all employees (probably a blessing because, in the end, all but one of the "suggestors" most likely would have been disappointed by the final choice), we kept deliberations within our senior management team. However, we quickly learned that, when it comes to selecting a name for a new "baby," even as few as seven people can become "uncoordinated."

So, on that weekend, I began my quest for a new name that would accommodate our specific needs... and that would be embraced by all six of my colleagues on Empire's senior management team.

I scoured every thesaurus and dictionary I could find. At the library, I culled business names beginning with an "E." I found, among others, an 1888 listing for Excrement Crematory Company at 122 Franklin Street, Buffalo. (Yes, the name was currently available.)

I went through the archives of banking magazines and newspapers. On Saturday night, I even had an extra cocktail to induce inspiration!

Nothing was working.

But on Sunday, the day that even God doesn't work, He helped by presenting me with a very logical question: "Why not use a name that simply describes where the entire Empire is located without using any geographically provincial trade names that could be challenged?"

*America!*

To me, the combination of Empire *and* America sounded professional, grand, and patriotic. It described the new bank perfectly.

The "Big E" could soldier on.

To my relief, on Monday morning, our management team agreed. I tried not to be the "boss" during the ensuing discussion, but who knows what factors were at work. I think we all were tired and just wanted to get on with our new institutional "life."

So, *Empire of America* it was.

(It took 20 years for me to discover that the appellation Empire of America had been used long before my "inspiration." In the early 1800s, Congress proclaimed war hero Andrew Jackson as "Regent of the Empire of America." I was forced, once again, to acknowledge my ol' Uncle Ollie's long-ago observation, "Kid, there ain't never nothin' new.")

In short order, new signs were going up on buildings in New York, Michigan, Texas, and Florida, and we prepared to kick off an ambitious program of growth and diversification for the new *Empire of America.*

## Benefits

Our supervisory acquisitions were structured to be very beneficial to Empire over the long term. As earlier described, the Erie County Savings Bank's unwavering commitment to its local residential loan markets in a period or accelerating inflation had left it with a significant negative earnings gap. The only feasible way to gradually fill this chasm – and preclude the kind of illiquidity and insolvency it portended – was to book billions of dollars of *new* deposits and *new* loans at current rates.

Such growth, however, required a bigger market footprint; a larger array of customer services for savers and borrowers; and regulatory forbearances from the kinds of capital requirements that would preclude the growth that was necessary. Our contractual agreements with the government in 1982 accommodated all of these needs and more.

Importantly, they afforded Empire a unique multi-state presence in rapidly-growing markets which granted access to millions of new potential savers as well as to the existing depositors of the acquired thrifts. Further, we secured a vast opportunity to originate new loans at adequate rates and in contemporary formats. Our new market territories also allowed us to pursue our vision of creating supplementary revenues via non-traditional banking activities such as securities and real estate brokerage; insurance and mutual fund sales; home relocation support; and, real estate development.

Also, the forbearances from regulatory capital requirements that were provided for in our agreements with the government facilitated the growth that the bank required. Absent forbearances, additional capital would have been required to allow for growth, and such capital supplementation in the open market was well-nigh impossible given the prevailing economic environment.

The forbearances that Empire was granted would expire at various dates through 1992. However, the agreements we executed with our regulators allowed for further extensions of five years, if necessary, to meet basic regulatory capital requirements. The bank was also granted regulatory capital forbearance in connection with the liabilities of the merged bank subsidiaries. This relief would expire on December 31, 1997.

Taking into account these forbearances, it was projected that Empire's regulatory capital on December 31, 1988 would amount to $490 million, or 8.64 % of its total liabilities. This amount exceeded the bank's regulatory capital requirement of $196.5 million by $293 million.

Another great benefit of our agreements was the authority we achieved to establish our legal headquarters in a state where the sale of stock by savings institutions was permitted. It was essential that Empire have the ability to convert to a stock institution and offer shares to the public in order to acquire the additional private capital necessary for growth to a $16 billion asset plateau.

By virtue of our agreements, the government approved a novel organizational structure which would greatly facilitate capital augmentation. Instead of requiring that we merge all of our acquired institutions into Erie Savings Bank in Buffalo, the government provided us with a Federal Savings Association (FSA) charter for an entirely new banking institution in Florida.

That association became the repository for all of the merged S&Ls with the exception of those in Michigan and upstate New York. The latter were merged with the "old" Erie Savings Bank and the resulting amalgamation was converted to a Michigan-based FSA.

The Florida FSA embodied all of our acquired operations in the "Sunshine State" as well as the institutions we joined with in Long Island, New York, and Houston, Texas.

Thus, the new Empire enterprise consisted of two separately-chartered federal savings associations, one based in Southfield, Michigan and the other headquartered in Gainesville, Florida. Each was officially named Empire of America, FSA. (To add to our acronymnal angst, Empire would soon convert – *again* – from an FSA charter to a Federal Savings Bank FSB charter.)

"Empire-North" had its legal headquarters in Southfield, Michigan and corporate headquarters in Buffalo, New York; "Empire-South" maintained legal and corporate headquarters in Gainesville, Florida. The Florida association would operate as a subsidiary of the Michigan institution. The corporate executive offices and headquarters staff of the combined entities would be located in Buffalo, New York.

This configuration afforded Empire the legal and market postures that were absolutely essential to the success of their workout and turnaround efforts.

Given its organizational structure, regulatory forebearances, and funding (which included a $50 million capital injection from the "old" Erie Savings Bank), our southern association possessed, from the get-go, the resources necessary to grow and develop new revenue streams. The profits so generated could be consolidated with those of Empire - North thus helping to carry that institution's impedimenta until routine mortgage payoffs over the next decade would put it on equal footing with the southern operation. (In later years, this would be referred to by regulators as a "good bank; bad bank" strategy. Its popularity as a "solution" grew during the banking crisis of 2008-2009.)

There was another, less obvious benefit from the mergers. The creation of the Empire enterprise provided the time and opportunities necessary to resolve the long-standing earnings problems of the Erie Savings Bank's old portfolios of low-rate mortgages. Because of the spike in interest rates, the liquidation value of Erie's mortgage portfolios at the time of the 1982 mergers was estimated to be $450 million less than their book value. This meant that, in the prevailing high rate environment, Erie was enduring an annual earnings deficiency of more than $50 million. This equated to the difference between the annual income from those mortgages and the *current*, annual cost of the deposits needed to carry them. The 1982 transaction, therefore, facilitated a workout not only for the acquired S&Ls but, also, for the old Erie Savings Bank.

Subsequent to the consummation of its mergers, Empire pursued an aggressive reorganization and amalgamation process that continued for the remainder of 1982. During that time we also acquired – at the government's behest – additional banking operations in Eastern Michigan; Long Island, New York; Fort Worth and Houston, Texas; and Florida.

Empire was blazing new trails nationally with 120 branch offices in four states

Like Erie/Empire, the government managed to walk away with reasonable benefits, too. Absent their merger agreements with Empire, the only "tool" that regulators had at their disposal for dealing with the growing horde of withering or dying thrifts was *hope* for an imminent decline in interest rates. Since economic history suggested that a sufficient diminishment of rates would probably not occur in the immediate future, the best, lowest-cost strategy available to the regulatory establishment entailed a cobbling together of the "drowning" shops with more viable institutions like Erie so that they could mutually form an interim "life preserver" that could carry all merger partners through the turbulence of a turnaround. Such transactions afforded the government a ready opportunity to avoid the political turmoil and public cost entailed in large-scale rescues.

Empire and the FSLIC had great confidence that a sweat-equity workout – with Empire providing the sweat – was eminently achievable over a reasonable period of time. Accordingly, both parties willingly entered into binding contracts to assure it.

As might be expected, the FSLIC had conducted a thorough pre-merger, "viability test" to gauge the ability of the resulting institution to sustain its operations over the long-term while it reinvigorated its income statement and balance sheet. This comprehensive, highly-detailed analysis of Erie's capacities to succeed with such a venture concluded that the its experience, prior performance, extant talent, organizational culture, institutional integrity, technological capabilities, and resources – coupled with the operating and capital enhancements provided by its merger contracts with the government – were adequate to the task of resolving the unique problems of each savings institution that would comprise the new Empire entity.

Perhaps one of the greatest benefits the government accrued by virtue of its transactions with Empire was the validation of a pattern for workout deals it could engineer with other savings institutions. Use of this model in subsequent months enabled the government to off-load soon-to-fail institutions without having to provide a cash-based "rescue." Erie/Empire's reconstitution demonstrated that supervisory acquisition agreements which permitted goodwill amortization and long-term regulatory forbearances could save the day for many worthy institutions while regulators awaited access to the Treasury's coffers and, thereby, to the funds necessary to *buy* itself out of the S&L morass.

## Costs

Empire assumed responsibility for significant costs in exchange for the ability to pursue the growth element of its Phoenix Plan. Of the sixteen mergers consummated in the '80s, thirteen were supervisory mergers with troubled thrifts. The reported marked-to-market book value of the assets held by these S&Ls was $2.68 billion.

Contra-positioned to this $2.68 billion asset value were simultaneously assumed, offsetting liabilities which consisted principally of obligations to the deposit customers *at* the acquired institutions. These totaled $3.52 billion.

After adjustments to reflect cash contributions by Erie and the FSLIC, these two values produced a very significant $926 million balance sheet "gap" between *earning* assets and *costing* liabilities. As previously described in Chapter Six of this book, this gap was "filled" by a non-tangible, non-earning asset called "supervisory goodwill." This approach – referred to by accountants as "purchase accounting" – was contractually sanctioned by the government and was in strict compliance with prevailing accounting standards. (This practice was previously described in detail in Chapter Six.)

As a result of these transactions, $926 million of goodwill was booked by Empire. This goodwill did not directly produce tangible cash income but, nonetheless, represented a supplement to the aggregate *business value* of the acquired savings and loan institutions. Goodwill consisted of the professionally estimated *intangible* value of customer relationships, proprietary technology, employee talents, institutional reputation, brands, geographic locations, etc.

The contracts with the government stipulated that /Empire would have to amortize (i.e. write-off) the resulting goodwill over a period of forty years. (It should be noted that, while this kind of goodwill-creating technique had been in use by nonfinancial corporations for many years, non-banking companies were usually *not* required to amortize the goodwill they created.)

The consequent annual goodwill amortization expense to Empire resulting from the acquired excess of real liabilities over tangible assets would total approximately $23 million per year. This expense was a direct hit to our annually-reported bottom line earnings but, on the plus side, it did not constitute an actual outlay of cash. This ongoing amortization cost was one of the primary reasons that Empire sought forbearances as part of its merger agreements.

In addition, Empire assumed responsibility for paying interest on $926 million of deposits that were conveyed to us in our mergers and that were not accompanied by offsetting tangible earning assets. This annual cost to "carry" goodwill approximated $60 million, but its impact on earnings would gradually diminish as new, higher-yield assets were booked and as overall interest rates (and deposit costs) began their forecasted decline.

Importantly, the negative income impacts that Empire was absorbing were offset, to a great degree, by "purchase accounting" which allowed Empire to book, during the eight years following the transactions, substantial non-cash income in the form of "discount accretion." During the remainder of the 1980s, the aggregate amount of this income helped to partially offset the deposit costs entailed in funding the loans acquired loans through the mergers. Both the FSLIC and Empire reasoned that the income offset which was derived from discount accretion would allow the bank to continue to grow and enhance its portfolios as it self-restructured during that time.

The discount accretion procedure was extremely complex. It took into consideration a value that is generated by virtue of the differential between the original interest rates contractually associated with the loans acquired by Erie/Empire and the prevailing loan rates in the marketplace at the time of the subsequent acquisitions. A portion of that value could be accreted annually by the acquirer as income during a specified number of years.

(It is interesting to note that, had Erie received assistance at the time of its supervisory acquisitions in the form of *tangible* interest-earning assets instead of the $926 million of intangible goodwill, the bank's capital by 1987 – as conservatively estimated and without giving effect to any of our capital forbearances – would have been approximately $1.2 billion, or 10.6 % of our assets, well within regulatory guidelines.)

Unfortunately, some additional, unforeseen costs emerged subsequent to our transactions. They were a consequence of:

- **Increased regulatory scrutiny, oversight, and second-guessing**. As noted elsewhere in this book, the regulators were plagued by a gnawing fear that the kinds of early transactions consummated with Empire and other thrifts might not produce the desired results. This prompted them to introduce a stream of new controls, "standards," and regulations. Indeed, as time passed, many components of our original agreements were unilaterally "re-worked" by virtue of new regulations and legislation. A "CYA" mentality began to emerge within the government as the storm of negative press coverage concerning the industry and its travails continued.

  Further, in 1983, a close friend of Nancy Reagan was appointed Chairman of the FHLBB and, much to the chagrin of the Reagan Administration, he began to reverse many of the significant innovations of the previous Chairman. "One-upmanship" among successive leaders tends to foster changes to extant policies and this, in turn, typically confuses – sometimes paralyzes – those governed by them.

  In addition, the antics of a relatively small number of ne're-do-well investors who had participated in other government resolution attempts ignited major scandals which began to scorch the entire industry. Needless to say, this kind of turmoil discouraged additional legislative and regulatory efforts to innovatively resolve the industry's problems. Distinctions between the "villains" and the "good guys" (like those at Empire) began to blur, thus making our ensuing workout efforts considerably more difficult and costly.

- **Discoveries.** It was determined soon after our mergers that the *actual* fair value of the loan assets we acquired in our mergers was only $2.3 billion, a significant negative deviation of $300 million from the value originally alleged by the government. This unanticipated deficiency significantly diminished the future stream of earnings we had counted on to offset deposit costs. This value shortfall would adversely impact our earnings in every subsequent year.
- **Delayed market growth.** Empire's supervisory acquisitions would eventually give it a presence in fourteen major markets embracing 110 cities and towns in five widely-separated states. Our plan was to consolidate and grow selected segments of this valuable distribution franchise. However, unanticipated regulatory constraints with respect to organic deposit growth and branching were introduced soon after our acquisitions. They significantly delayed the growth we had planned and diminished the cost-offsetting earnings that we had anticipated.
- **Separate charters.** In order to ensure Empire of America's compliance with regulatory capital requirements subsequent to its supervisory acquisitions, it had to hold the acquired savings institutions in separately-chartered banks. We had underestimated the costs associated with achieving operating integrity and efficiencies in such a complex organization. (On December 31, 1987, Empire was authorized to merge the separate charters – which had grown to four by that time – into one, thereby enabling us to realize gradual cost savings.)
- **Follow-on regulatory "recalibration."** In 1986, the bank submitted an application to convert to a stock savings institution, the shares of which would be held by the public. As we shall see in a later Chapter, the regulators imposed, as a condition of their approval,

some unreasonable, costly requirements. The stipulations they extracted increased our goodwill amortization expense by over $6 million annually and added a preferred stock dividend burden in a like amount. Of all the cost-contributing factors cited above, the most damaging was the heightened regulatory oversight the bank endured during the remainder of its workout efforts. It hobbled the bank's ability to fully implement its Phoenix Plan. The innovative, merger-based resolution technique it called for entailed some residual risk, and this exposure troubled our regulators. They feared that the forbearances they had granted Empire might prove to be an embarrassment if a workout wasn't achieved "on schedule." This concern was heightened as newly-minted government officials arrived on the scene and undertook to "protect" themselves by negatively criticizing their predecessors' actions. Such disparagement of previous regulators and Empire persisted for the next six years despite the fact that all of the government's pre-merger evaluations and assessments demonstrated that the residual risks Empire had assumed were reasonable and acceptable. In fact, the regulators had often employed the Big E's "resolution model" as the tactic of choice for resolving subsequent thrift failures.

Ironically, the "embarrassment risk" regulators perceived would ultimately prove to be the Achilles heel in our joint workout plan. As time passed, Congress did provide the FSLIC and the FDIC with ample cash to facilitate once-and-for-all, walk-away deals. Accordingly, the FSLIC was able to structure future mergers and acquisitions with little risk of follow-on transactional "embarrassment." Its only continuing exposure in this regard resided with Empire and a number of other institutions whose early, creative, non-cash deals entailed "strings" that the regulators felt could eventually trip them up. As a consequence, we would be forever on their "radar."

As time passed, regulators became even more worried about the reputational "risk tail" associated with protracted, workout deals like Empire's. Their gradually rising unease about potential, albeit remote, career-tarnishing failures as a consequence of previously-executed, long-term deals like ours made Empire a target of increasing scrutiny and regulatory control. This "tightening up" constituted an unanticipated and cost that the Big E had to carry during the years subsequent to its mergers.

The regulators' fear was unfounded, since Erie's acquisition of the failing thrifts had immediately reduced the FSLIC's caseload and relieved it of the substantial costs that would otherwise have resulted from their liquidation.

The great financial benefit that accrued to the FSLIC because of Empire's involvement becomes obvious when the comparative costs of alternative forms of resolution are considered. Conservative, documented estimates, as described in Chapter Twelve of this book, show that, absent Empire's intervention and workout effort, the liquidation of the thrifts it acquired would have resulted in a resolution cost to the FSLIC of at least $1.5 billion.

In contrast, the true dollar cost of the Empire transaction to the government was relatively small. In return for Empire's assumption of responsibility for the organizational consolidation, re-staffing, systems integration, facilities rehabilitation, and customer re-solicitation, the FSLIC provided Empire with net cash assistance of $79.2 million.

Obviously, with a net cash cost of only $79.2 million, Empire of America's intervention was a very low-cost solution for the financially strapped FSLIC.

**New services for new markets**

In addition to growth through geographic expansion, the Phoenix Plan called for us to exploit another avenue to income growth – *product diversification.* In the years ahead, the broadening of our "product mix" would be given a high priority by the Big E team.

We believed that a wide array of financial services that were neither deposit nor mortgage in nature was essential to customer retention and solicitation as well as to the generation of much-needed supplementary revenue. Importantly, these kinds of activities would not significantly expand the bank's balance sheet and, therefore, not occasion a concomitant need for additional capital.

Further, such non-deposit related revenues promised a return on assets greater than that which could be provided by the traditional deposit/loan intermediation model. By way of illustration, back in the good ol' days, one deposit dollar invested in our traditional real estate loan portfolio would provide about a two percentage point gross margin *before* taking into account operational expenses and the always-present risk of loss. Alternatively, the net return on a dollar deployed in non-bank type financial services businesses like insurance, securities, or real estate brokerage enjoyed significantly higher margins.

Erie's initial forays into service diversification had been enormously successful. Our shared Metroteller point-of-sale banking system was extremely profitable and expanding nationally; our investment in a developer of real estate projects had been highly profitable; and our insurance agency, Shelton Square Agency Inc., was performing beyond expectations.

In early 1982, Erie became the first thrift institution to operate a full service securities brokerage firm by acquiring William Cadden & Co. in White Plains, New York (later renamed Empire National Securities Inc.) In the next two years, the firm became licensed to do business in 30 states. While statutes and regulations prohibited the direct sale of securities by bank employees, we had designed a "sub-subsidiary" configuration which allowed Cadden to lease space in Erie's branches through which its licensed representatives could offer investment services to bank customers.

This in-branch sales arrangement was extended to include our Shelton Square Agency insurance operation (which was renamed Empire Agency Inc.).

To comply with federal law, we had to differentiate these subsidiary functions from traditional bank operations. Accordingly, their in-branch sales activities were collectively housed in separate and distinct service modules which were structurally and cosmetically designed to provide them with a unique, non-banking identity. To reinforce this distinction, these modules were marketed as Moneyplex financial centers.

Empire had the ability to diversify even beyond these early initiatives since Erie's "leeway investment" powers had been "grandfathered" by its S&L acquisition agreements with the government. This meant that Empire retained the ability to utilize up to an aggregate of 2% of its assets to launch or acquire almost any kind of business enterprise (with the exception of insurance companies and commercial banks). Financial service companies were particularly attractive since, as Empire subsidiaries, they could greatly help the bank in its efforts to attract new customers and expand its relationships with existing customers.

The Phoenix Plan called for the eventual investment of all of our available "leeway" dollars in non-traditional ventures as long as they: 1) were related to our basic banking business and markets; 2) were compatible with our established customer base, distribution network, and marketing reach; 3) provided a valuable service to existing and new customers; 4) held great promise of profit generation; 5) had limited downside risk; 6) could be monitored centrally but managed in a decentralized fashion; 7) minimized our exposure to interest rate fluctuations, and; 8) legitimately capitalized on the bank's prevailing financial and tax circumstances.

(During the seven years following its mergers, Empire would invest in over 40 such subsidiary ventures. With only two exceptions, they quickly became profitable and offered substantial returns on investment after their "learning curve" periods.)

By the end of 1982, our Phoenix Plan diversification strategy was in full implementation mode.

**Digesting the outcomes**

Major effort would be required from mid-1982 through 1986 to consolidate our new market presence, compensate for flaws in our original deal with the government, and acquiesce to FSLIC and FHLB pressures to provide them with greater assistance in resolving other failed institutions.

Understandably, our overriding objective was to quickly realize the profit potential of the S&Ls we had acquired.

The projections we originally included in our Phoenix Plan and the "term sheet" that guided our initial contracts with the FSLIC in June 1982 showed that, over the seven years subsequent to our 1982 mergers, Empire would accumulate – as a consequence of those transactions – significant, but continually decreasing, annual net losses before it began to show a positive bottom line in the early '90s.

Over the decade, this pattern of *diminishing annual* losses would gradually and consistently lift the value of the bank and its future shareholders' interests. FSLIC and FHLB officials were fully aware of these anticipations at the time our deal was originally struck and acknowledged them at frequent, subsequent meetings.

Empire's team members moved smartly between 1982 and 1985 to rationalize the eclectic, far-flung organizational structure that had been created by our mergers. Understandably, the management and control problems were enormous.

We moved quickly to achieve improved control of staff and operating departments of the acquired institutions. With respect to staff services, our first efforts involved an enrichment of the audit, accounting, and personnel functions. Our marketing, legal services, and property management functions were addressed immediately thereafter.

Our primary goal, however, was an accelerated generation of higher-yielding mortgages and consumer loans in our new markets. This was a daunting task since safe and sound, high-yielding opportunities were greatly prized in the stressed financial environment of the early 1980s. It was made even more difficult by our (necessary) efforts to simultaneously introduce lending policies, procedures, limits, and criteria that were similar to the proven, conservative guidelines that had been followed by Erie.

The loan origination personnel of the acquired institutions were, understandably, inclined to continue following the lending criteria and policies that had guided their shops prior to their acquisition. The process of reorienting these new team members, acclimating them to new policies and procedures, and, if necessary, helping them "adjust" their career plans was arduous, costly, and time-consuming.

As a consequence, the costs – in dollars and hours – of gaining control of the lending activities of our acquired S&Ls and inculcating their staffs with more productive and less-risky methods of operation went far beyond what we had anticipated at the time of the mergers.

Vexing, too, were the loan portfolio problems that emerged *after* the mergers were completed. Value deficiencies were discovered when Empire managers finally gained the access necessary to conduct detailed, on-site evaluations. Numerous "surprises" were encountered.

They found many portfolio "clunkers" that were not adequately disclosed in the documentation that was provided to Empire by the government prior to its mergers. In one shop, for example, loan agreements were stored in obscure file drawers and packing boxes, not to be found until many months after the initial merger.

The credit quality of many of the portfolios we acquired ranged from "fair" to "poor." After all, those loan portfolios were arguably the primary reasons for the misfortunes of those institutions. These kinds of portfolio problems could not be cured quickly or easily, given prevailing economic conditions and regulatory attitudes.

Unfortunately, there was no going back to the government to renegotiate what was, in its eyes, a done deal. Empire of America had, for all intents and purposes, no legal right to "put back" unsatisfactory assets to the government.

From the time of Empire's original acquisition negotiations with the government, we were always confronted with a "take it (and keep it) or leave it" attitude. We had no bargaining power since the government knew we needed these transactions in order to forge a workout program for the old Erie Savings Bank. As far as the regulators were concerned, if assets acquired by Empire were of less value than the government's initial representations, the resulting gap was Empire's problem, not the government's.

One would have thought that the commitment on the part of Empire to make this all happen would have warranted a degree of tolerance with respect to our subsequent appeals to "put back" some misrepresented assets to the government. But that was not to happen, despite the fact that rigorous ex post facto portfolio analyses – using FSLIC quantitative estimation techniques – revealed that, absent Empire of America's intervention and workout efforts, the liquidation of the thrifts acquired by Empire would have cost FSLIC, in 1982 dollars, *at least* $1.5 billion.

The government's posture didn't actually constitute a "bait and switch" situation, but it sure as heck felt like one. (Interestingly, such re-do options were provided as an avenue of redress in merger deals that were consummated with other S&L acquirers later in the 1980s. Of course, by that time, the regulatory establishment was able to dip, unrestrained, into its new, Congressionally-provided "deep pockets.")

The mergers created other unique issues with which we had to contend throughout the remainder of the 1980s. For example, as mentioned earlier, in order to ensure Empire of America's compliance with regulatory capital requirements subsequent to its transactions with the government, its multitude of acquired institutions had to be managed within four separately-chartered banks, thus creating enormous problems of governance and dis-economies of scale.

As a consequence, the top four officers of Empire of America had to attend five different Board of Directors' meetings each month in four distant and widely separated parts of the country. Each institution had a separate Board of Directors, and the governance of each of them had to be responsive to the unique policies and cultures of those associations and the needs of the communities and markets they served. Since prevailing regulations made Empire executives adhere rigorously to the restrictions governing *separate* institutions (despite the fact that they were all part of the same ownership group), control was diffused, and cost-effective centralization was a mighty challenge. Operating and economic efficiencies were difficult to achieve.

Moreover, as earlier noted, the institutions acquired by Empire of America were quite diverse and included an Hispanic bank in Houston, Texas; an alleged overly-aggressive deposit aggregator in Windsor, California; the nation's first gay-owned thrift in San Francisco; and a Detroit thrift where operating losses had been incurred for forty consecutive months prior to its acquisition by Empire and where prior loans from the government were funding fifty-percent of its balance sheet. These were institutions worthy of our assistance but they presented challenges with respect to appropriate cultural and operational integration. The management team from Erie had scant experience with these kinds of situations. Thankfully, it was able to learn and adapt quickly.

Additionally, the different operating processes, employee policies, advertising requirements, portfolio management techniques, lending criteria, audit procedures, and accounting systems inherited as a result of the mergers created expensive, time-consuming, and productivity-diluting difficulties for the Empire of America management team. Also, there were the administrative issues associated with the transfer of our bank's charter to Michigan in order to take advantage of that state's favorable provisions concerning public stock offerings by thrift institutions.

Subsequent to these mergers, eleven different computer operations existed... and they did not "speak" the same "language." They were supported by six different computer systems. It took several years to consolidate this multi-part, disparate computer platform and re-launch it as a unitary, on-line computer network that could efficiently serve all of our banking operations.

Adding to our difficulties at this time was the fact that regulators occasionally "pressured" us into adding additional weak or failing S&Ls to our organizational mix as the industry continued to deteriorate and as Empire demonstrated success with its restructuring. For example, to preserve our profitable Pacific Thrift and Loan Co. in Los Angeles (the acquisition of which will be addressed in subsequent pages) in the face of a collapsing California depositor insurance fund, we had to agree to acquire two other failing thrifts in the state and absorb the subsequent losses of one of them to the tune of $16 million. Only if Empire agreed to those acquisitions and their associated indemnification terms would the regulators allow our profitable Los Angeles thrift subsidiary to obtain FSLIC insurance coverage.

Given the prevailing difficulties in the industry, the "detachment" of the government in this regard was, to a degree, understandable, but it continually added to the burdens that Empire had originally assumed.

Even with these distressing post-merger "bumps," we did not, at that time, regret our transactions with the government. Without those "deals" – as troublesome as they proved to be – Erie would have, in all likelihood, ceased to exist. And, if the Erie Savings Bank failed, all of Empire's future contributions in the '80s would have been lost too, including: the mortgage loans that made thousands of people homeowners; the savings that taxpayers ultimately realized; the careers that it launched; the innovations it produced, and the hundreds of millions of dollars it pumped into its circumjacent communities.

It bears repeating that the 1982 transactions were Erie/Empire's *only* avenue to securing the time necessary for a workout. So, we had to make the best of a less-than-ideal deal. With our encumbered bargaining power (due to Erie's fragile financial posture at that time), it was the only arrangement we could forge that would provide the bank with the time and opportunity to survive... and *ultimately* thrive.

It was obvious that the regulators used the triage power they possessed to hammer our string of acquisition agreements into a very low-cost way of postponing thirteen enormous problems until a time when a decline in interest rates would bring about a complete and permanent resolution.

But Empire was not just a hapless "survivor." Despite a challenging environment and deteriorating industry circumstances, the bank had struck a critical deal in 1982. Its provisions allowed Empire to enjoy the time and forbearance necessary to employ the kind of "sweat equity" tactics envisioned in its Phoenix Plan.

As the preceding pages illustrate, every opportunity to re-energize, rationalize, and re-direct our newborn enterprise was eagerly seized upon. Gradually, with much trial, error – and some pain – important "lessons" were learned and productive coordination was achieved without compromising the essential integrity of our institution. While it was an arduous and costly reformation, our experiences, we believed, would gradually provide Empire with competitive advantages that could continually increase its value and attractiveness to the government and potential investors.

This kind of integration in the pursuit of improved performance was especially challenging since each Board of Directors in each geographic area was ultimately responsible for the operation of its institution. Directors frequently had different attitudes and expressed different desires based on their personal (pre-Empire) experiences in the thrift business and on their highly-individualistic perceptions of the needs of their staffs and the customers they served.

Fortunately, in the final analysis, an extremely high percentage of the employees and managers inherited by Empire continued as Big E team members, bringing with them important experiential and cultural diversities. To a much greater extent than we had expected, they brought ability, integrity, loyalty, and ambition to their new "home."

A great deal of this is due to the fact that the Big E "veterans" imbued the new Empire with our successful "Buffalo brand" of operating culture. This was not an easy task since many of our new team members had been traumatized by the recent mergers *and* the loss of their previous organizational identities.

Nevertheless, in a relatively short period of time, the Big E had mustered a powerful team that would grow from 400 individuals to over 4,000 in the span of just a few years.

*Chapter eight*

## EXPANSION AND CONSOLIDATION

### Spreading the web

As the four year period subsequent to the Big E's 1982 mergers unfolded, the bank, in furtherance of its Phoenix Plan, expanded its national presence – coast to coast and border to border – and delivered its products and services to over one million households in the five states where 53% of this country's post-1980 growth had occurred. The series of mergers prior to 1986 expanded our interstate branch network to 146 branch offices, allowing us to take advantage of new markets for deposit and lending growth.

The five states in which we enjoyed market access had been carefully selected because of the unique strengths they brought to the Empire network. And they were living up to expectations.

- New York, our state of origin, was the nation's second most populous state. It was home to 17.7 million residents and the site of our nation's money center.
- Michigan, with record domestic auto sales in 1986 of $300 billion, boasted a flourishing industrial economy. Oakland County, site of eleven of the Big E's twenty-one Michigan offices, had one of the highest per capita income levels in the nation.
- Florida was the sixth-largest state and its population was growing at a rate of 5.6% per year. New-home construction was booming with 194,000 single and multi-family units projected for 1987 – a figure that put the Sunshine State second only to California in housing starts.
- Texas, the third-largest state, was adding over 60,000 new residents per year. Economists anticipated that, through 1990, metropolitan Fort Worth – the location

of our southern headquarters – would experience population, income, and economic growth at a rate nearly twice the national average.

- California, the newest jewel in Empire of America's crown, was the undisputed national leader in population growth, housing starts, and potential for economic expansion. It was the country's largest job market and provided immense opportunity for the state-chartered, thirty-year old, Los Angeles-based Pacific Thrift and Loan Association (and its subsidiary, Presidential Mortgage Company) which Empire acquired in 1984.

Our West Coast market territory expanded quickly. In July 1986, Empire, through the auspices of the FSLIC, acquired the assets of Atlas Savings and Loan Association, San Francisco, California (Atlas) and Golden Pacific Savings and Loan Association, Windsor, California (Golden Pacific) and merged them with Empire's wholly-owned subsidiary, Pacific Thrift and Loan Association. This created an FSLIC-insured institution named Empire of America – California FSB. The combined fair value of the total assets acquired was $132.4 million.

Empire had initially applied to the FSLIC for only the acquisition of Atlas Savings as a means of acquiring, through merger, FSLIC deposit insurance for its Pacific Thrift & Loan Company customers. Pacific was a state-chartered institution that was about to lose its deposit insurance due to the failure of the State of California deposit insurance agency.

As a "price" for facilitating Empire's requested merger with Atlas (and the associated coverage of FSLIC insurance), federal regulators stipulated that Empire must also acquire the very distressed Golden Pacific Savings and Loan Association in Windsor, California and one other very troubled FSLIC-insured thrift in the San Francisco area. We took on these two additional weakened institutions and assumed responsibility for up to $16 million in possible losses on their problem assets. Thus, we acquired a new "earnings drag" as we struggled to serve and protect our depositors in our California market.

Adding complexity to the integration issues associated with these new acquisitions in the Golden State was the fact that Atlas Savings was the nation's first gay thrift, established, owned, and operated by the gay community to serve the large population of gay customers in that region. That very close-knit community was legitimately concerned about a "takeover" of an institution that they had started and worked so hard to nurture. It took a considerable amount of time and some major commitments to the community (including sponsorship of the Gay Olympics, which were first organized in 1982) for us to establish trust with understandably skeptical customers in this important market. Ultimately, we were accepted and thrived on the famous Castro Street strip as well as in the city's financial district.

The absorption of these distressed assets further diminished our capital ratios but, on the bright side, the transaction enabled us to procure federal deposit insurance for our existing California customers and acquire fifteen new "windows of opportunity" in Southern California and the San Francisco metropolitan area.

Alert to the growth potential in both the northern and southern markets, we opened additional Big E branch offices in Michigan, New York, and Florida. Each of these new facilities significantly exceeded its opening deposit goals, thus demonstrating the huge potential of our recently acquired markets.

Concurrently, we developed a number of important new savings account formats to take advantage of our expanded branch network, including:

> The Insured Fund Beater: This account category grew to over $1 billion in deposits in the first two months subsequent to its introduction in 1983. A novel savings account, it was the first of its kind to be offered in the banking industry. It gave customers assurance that they would be able to earn an interest rate on their bank savings that was comparable to the

rates offered by money market funds, which were growing in popularity.

The Dollar Doubler: This was a time deposit account that promised to pay an interest rate that would serve to double its initial deposit in less than seven years.

The Convertible Term Account: Debuting in 1984, this was a four-year CD which gave customers a mid-maturity option of maintaining a fixed-rate of interest or converting to a variable rate.

Negotiable Rate Certificates of Deposit: These CD's provided customers with a competitive market rate while simultaneously providing Empire with fixed-rate funds that could be profitably matched with the rates it earned on newly generated loans.

401(k) Savings Accounts: These accounts allowed business firms to provide their employees with tax-sheltered retirement savings opportunities. They enabled the Big E to tap further into the highly-lucrative pension market.

Through the continuous expansion of our retail banking network, we had reached a deposit level of $7.4 billion in 1986. Total assets passed the $9 billion mark.

We had also begun a program of supplementing deposit funds with capital market borrowings. In 1984, we formed a subsidiary, Empire Capital Corp., which tapped the capital markets with a $75 million offering of adjustable-rate preferred stock. The stock offering was rated AAA by both Moody's and Standard & Poor's. Proceeds from the offering were reinvested in variable-rate assets and, thus, provided the Big E with some extremely favorable, flexible interest rate spreads. Also in that year, Empire began to issue letters of credit that backed private purpose, AAA-rated, tax-exempt revenue bonds. In December 1985, Empire entered the European capital markets with a $125 million Euro-Note offering.

## Non-traditional networks

During the first four years of post-merger Phoenix Plan implementation (1983–1986), a number of non-bank subsidiaries were launched or expanded to help us obtain new customers from outside of our traditional markets.

These included:

- **Smartline**

  The Big E became the *"Everywhere Bank"* in 1983 as a consequence of establishing a central telephone call center – dubbed Smartline – through which we could open new accounts, provide general banking information, and accept loan applications from anywhere in the nation. It operated twelve hours a day, seven days a week, and provided (pre-Internet) "online" access to a full range of banking services, including funds transfers, new account openings, and balance inquiries. It also accepted consumer loan and VISA credit card applications. We became the first thrift to operate a telephone call center that possessed this kind of reach and functionality.

  Amazingly, Smartline reduced the cost of handling transactions by 62%. Further, in just two years, the deposit base it created grew to almost $240 million. Nearly 170,000 Big E customers called "1-800-THE BIG E" during the first six months of its opening. In short order, over 40% of our VISA credit cards and consumer loans and 12% of our liability products – i.e. savings, money market, and retirement accounts – were originated in this manner.

  In 1986, Smartline put the finishing touches on a new, state-of-the-art telecommunications computer system, thus enabling its staff of financial consultants to handle a typical inbound transaction in five minutes or less.

  Smartline soon became a turnkey, *outbound* telemarketing operation as well, serving more than a dozen major corporations in addition to the Big E.

193

- **Metroteller**

    During this period, our Metroteller subsidiary became the largest and most profitable shared, retail point-of-sale (POS) banking network in the nation, with 650 facilities in eight states. It served Empire of America and more than seventy-five other financial institutions.

    In July 1985, Metroteller marked its 10th anniversary by processing 1.5 million transactions in a single month. It had proven itself as the first successful, commercially-shared, system of its type.

    By 1986, Metroteller was deriving 80% of its revenue from clients other than the Big E. Transaction volume through its extensive ATM and POS network skyrocketed after Metroteller entered into an agreement to share its facilities with Citibank customers. It became the first electronic network of its kind to be accepted into VISA's new international ATM system. In addition, a reciprocal agreement with Hudson's Bay Company of Toronto, Canada' s largest retail chain, gave Metroteller customers access to their funds at hundreds of Canadian sites.

    Through its ATM links, our Metroteller network enabled Empire depositors to have 24-hour access to their accounts in all fifty states.

- **Moneyplex**

    During the first half of the decade, we expanded the number of branches that hosted Moneyplexes in order to increase our sales of non-deposit products like mutual funds, real estate, and insurance.

    Notwithstanding the Glass-Steagall Act, this initiative was possible because we had carefully designed within each of the selected branches a *virtual* regulatory "wall" between its traditional banking operations and its resident Multiplex "tenant." By creating this "combined-but-separate" customer venue, the big E became the first bank to offer a *complete* array of financial services under one roof.

A Moneyplex presence afforded many of our branches the kinds of electronic communications and video technology that would conveniently expose its customers to a full array of financial services and provide them with an interactive ability to conveniently avail themselves of the ones that met their unique financial needs.

In addition, in order to further expand our geographic reach, we designed and developed a unique type of stand-alone Moneyplex facility that was patterned after the Moneyplexes that had found success within our traditional branches. These highly-automated, stylistic modules – also dubbed Moneyplex – could be located within retail store facilities, airports, and other high traffic venues. Each Moneyplex featured video technology that helped customers to learn about our products and services. Through this kind of remote Moneyplex "non-branch," customers could access our banking staff via telephone and conduct any transaction – including a loan application – without filling out a single paper form.

Moneyplexes soon appeared in the Dallas-Fort Worth airport. In addition, they began operating in a number of Montgomery Ward & Co. retail stores. (At that time, Ward was the nation's sixth largest retailer.)

Our Moneyplex innovation gave true meaning to the term "one-stop financial shopping."

- **Macrotel**

    As early as the beginning of the decade, the bank's technology whizzes were experimenting with television sets and the newly-introduced personal desktop computers to see how they might be employed to give individual customers direct, two-way communication with bank service specialists.

In 1981, Empire established a research and development subsidiary, Macrotel Inc., which was tasked with developing a system that could link, via television or other technologies, consumers at home with financial institutions and retail merchants. This subsidiary's mission was to develop a prototype home banking system that would exploit such emerging technologies as television-based Videotext and the just-introduced personal computer. Called QUIXX, this pre-Internet, pilot program pointed the way to a future in which computer/video technologies could offer banking and shopping opportunities to customers in their own homes or places of work. At this point, we believed that a huge market opportunity would emerge as the personal computer (PC) gained traction and offered advanced, on-line networking capabilities.

We made modest, continuing investments in this new platform (Noteworthy is the fact that Empire launched this initiative thirteen years before the advent of Amazon.com. We had not yet been exposed to the full potential of the "Internet.")

During the course of Macrotel's pioneering activities, it experimented with a wide variety of emerging technologies but, unfortunately, none of them could provide the specific – *affordable* – utility and reliability that would be necessary to launch an aggressive campaign to link home electronic devices with banks. However, these stumbling blocks – which were not unusual in the nascent but rapidly-expanding world of computer technology – did not deter Macrotel, and it produced a number of promising prototypes. Many of these innovations would have proved invaluable if Empire had lived to enter the fast-approaching age of the Internet.

Interestingly, the curiosity of our Board of Trustees with respect to the world of bits and bytes was continually piqued by one of its members who had been an early acquirer of a personal computer and spent countless hours experimenting with it. At Board meetings, he frequently rhapsodized about the incredible future that it portended. (Little did we realize…!)

- **Catalogs**

    In 1984, we introduced a handsome and colorful, forty-eight page, print catalog that very dramatically displayed all of the financial products that the Big E offered. It explained how various bank-based, remote-access technologies could be used to obtain them. The catalog, described by the press as "the first of its kind in the industry," was designed primarily for use in conjunction with our toll-free Smartline telephone banking center and our Moneyplex facilities. In those pre-Internet days, catalogs were the preeminent way of maintaining tangible links with important, remote, customer constituencies.

Our non-banking subsidiaries also helped us solidify and expand our retail presence in the many markets we had begun to serve across the nation. They grew handsomely and, in 1986, contributed $70 million to our revenues.

Among their accomplishments:

- Empire National Securities Inc. opened thirty-two offices in six states. Its in-branch registered representatives expanded their offerings of reduced-commission brokerage services that were tailored to novice and mid-scale investors.
- Empire Agency Inc., our full-line insurance affiliate, offered annuities and insurance plans that provided customers with opportunities to build substantial wealth. By this time, the agency was also offering mortgage protection and credit life insurance policies that dovetailed with our lending activities.
- Brandywine Enterprises Inc., the bank's real estate development company, based in Deland, Florida,

began to focus on the construction of luxury residential developments in Vero Beach and New Smyrna Beach, Florida, and the development of projects in Texas and Long Island, New York.

A number of new subsidiaries further propelled the bank's revenue diversification during the first years of the Phoenix Plan's implementation.

- In 1983, Empire acquired Gallery of Homes, Inc., a national network of franchised real estate sales offices. We also acquired direct ownership of its affiliated real estate brokerage firm in Buffalo, New York. In addition to generating supplementary operating revenue for Empire, Gallery's affiliated franchisees and sales associates in forty-two states and Canada enjoyed access to a potentially endless source of loan applications for our mortgage banking operations.

  In less than two years, Gallery of Homes, Inc., would grow to almost 400 member offices with 4500 sales associates in forty-two states and Canada.

  In conjunction with Empire of America Realty Credit Corp., the Gallery of Homes began to facilitate the distribution of multiple products – including insurance policies and residential mortgage loans – through its franchised outlets.

- At mid-decade, Empire of America enhanced the performance of its real estate sales and home financing networks with the acquisition of the nation's fifth-largest corporate relocation management company. This new subsidiary, which had been a wholly-owned subsidiary of Control Data Corp., was renamed Empire Relocation Services Inc. (ERS). It provided support to large corporations that needed assistance in implementing employee relocations. ERS aided transferred executives by acquiring and selling their homes as they moved to new company locations. It also provided the necessary interim property management services.

In its first year as a subsidiary of the bank, Empire Relocation Services, through regional offices in Orlando, Florida; Norwalk, Connecticut; Minneapolis, Minnesota; and Walnut Creek, California, supervised the moves of 5,000 transferred executives for its extensive list of Fortune 500 corporate clients.

These business endeavors were dramatic manifestations of the benefits associated with geographic and functional diversification, as prescribed in the bank's Phoenix Plan.

## Bolstering the balance sheet

During the first four years of Phoenix Plan implementation, the Big E worked to restructure its portfolios and synchronize the maturities and price sensitivities of its assets and liabilities.

We supplemented our portfolios with top quality, short-term or variable-rate assets that produced contemporary yields which boosted our earnings. In addition, we accelerated the risk management programs that had been put in place to insulate the bank's portfolios from debilitating external impacts.

The biggest challenge we faced – i.e. reinvigorating our asset portfolios with *new* loan product – proved to be more formidable than we expected. But this is not to say that success eluded us.

We diligently pursued asset growth in all of our primary lending categories, including:

- **Mortgage lending**

  In 1983, thanks to recent legislation, we introduced a unique adjustable rate mortgage (ARM) product that was attractive to the bank's customers while still affording it a competitive rate of return *and* opportunities to increase the favorable matching of assets and liabilities in its portfolios. This one-year adjustable rate loan carried an initial 9.75% interest rate and attracted over $1.2 billion in loan applications in just nine months. It was the first single-digit interest rate offered on mortgages since the '70s and received personal praise from President Ronald Reagan, who called it "a bold plan." In the first year of this ARM program, the bank's total mortgage originations rose more than 700%. These new mortgages provided a significant – variable-rate – supplement to portfolio earnings.

To further accelerate the growth of our portfolio of contemporary higher yield mortgages, the Big E purchased, during 1983-84, an additional $380 million of ARMs in the secondary market.

Empire of America also began *selling* other selected mortgages that were already in its portfolios by aggregating them as mortgage securities. These securities represented segmented pools of fixed rate loans having varied rates and maturities. The segmentation of coupons and maturities within these securities resulted in our receiving significantly higher prices for the assets which were sold. Our initial $342 million offering gained recognition as the forerunner of the "collateralized mortgage obligation," which eventually became an industry standard. This offering was one of the largest public offerings of mortgage-backed securities up to that time and it very favorably altered the average maturities within our loan portfolios.

Late in 1984, the Big E completed the consolidation of its residential mortgage lending operations across the country into its recently formed subsidiary, Empire of America Realty Credit Corp. (EAORCC).

This company introduced novel configurations of computer systems in order to lower costs and reduce loan-approval time. It also provided for detailed analyses of portfolio components so that profitable mortgage origination and sales strategies could be implemented. Its computer-based systems were designed to also serve the company's correspondent mortgage loan originators including its own network of loan production offices; third-party savings and loan associations; commercial banks, and mortgage bankers; Gallery of Homes, Inc.; and other independent real estate sales companies.

Together with its various correspondents, EOARCC originated, in 1986, almost $1.2 billion in residential loan product, up from $411 million in 1985.

At this time, EOARCC was also servicing – in return for healthy fees – over $5 billion of mortgages owned by other lenders.

During 1986, the bank sold into the secondary market approximately $1.5 billion of residential loans that it had originated or purchased. In most cases, it retained the income-producing servicing rights that were associated with these assets. Because of origination and sales programs like these, Empire's assets and liabilities that were maturing within one year were – much to the delight of our regulators – seventy-five percent matched... a significant improvement over the less-than-twenty-five percent match that existed five years earlier.

By the end of 1986, Empire of America Realty Credit Corp., which had become the nation's 22nd-largest mortgage banking company, was operating through thirty loan production offices in ten states as well as through Empire of America's extensive network of branch offices.

Empire of America Realty Credit Corp. would eventually become the bank's most profitable subsidiary.

- **Commercial mortgage lending**

For years, the bank had originated commercial mortgages for a wide range of business enterprises and investors. Empire's commercial mortgage loan portfolio – which consisted of adjustable-rate permanent loans for apartment houses, office complexes, and industrial real estate – had grown to $1.7 billion by 1986. In that same year, the bank's commercial mortgage banking subsidiary, Empire of America Realty Funding Corporation, provided $183 million of commercial construction mortgage loans to developers of shopping centers, multi-family apartments, and other commercial ventures.

- **Business lending**

During the early '80s, our commercial lending specialists were striving to expand their capacities to originate floating-rate loans for creditworthy, mid-sized business enterprises. These were "classic" commercial loans that were not secured by real estate. This lending initiative grew slowly since, as a neophyte in this field, Empire had established conservative lending policies that focused on the profitability and viability of borrowers; geographic diversity; and, cautious loan-to-value ratios. Due to our stringent criteria, our ratio of non-performing commercial loans recorded an extraordinarily low level of 1.38% in 1984... a year in which we had a 219% increase in our total commercial loan portfolio – from $73 million to $233 million. This was quite an achievement for a new entrant in the commercial marketplace, especially in light of the conservative lending guidelines it had established.

By mid-1986, only five years after savings institutions were granted commercial business lending powers, Empire of America had become the fifth largest corporate lender in the thrift industry... with a loan portfolio that exceeded a half-billion dollars.

Of course, we were the "new kid on the block" and faced enormous competition from well-entrenched commercial banks. Nevertheless, our pace of lending increased respectably, aided in part by our participation in a number of leveraged buyout transactions (LBOs) which involved large corporations.

LBOs offered a unique opportunity. By virtue of the operating losses Empire had incurred by selling mortgages it acquired from the thrifts with which it merged in the early '80s, it had amassed huge tax loss carry-forwards that could be employed to reduce the taxable profits of partnerships purchasing control of established business entities. Empire served as a partner in these ventures, using its accumulated losses to shelter the earnings of these acquired companies. These techniques maximized the tax-free cash flow which could be used to gradually reduce the leverage associated with the buyout transactions. As compensation for its involvement, the bank participated in the profits generated by the operations of these acquired companies; it also enjoyed a portion of the capital gains created by the subsequent re-sale or recapitalization of those firms. These LBOs constituted a very lucrative niche for Empire and did not require a great expansion of its balance sheet (or of the capital that supported it).

Unfortunately, as Empire moved into the second half of the decade, it encountered major obstacles to continued growth in commercial lending. Because of new regulatory capital constraints, the bank faced significant limitations on the size of its in-house portfolios of mortgage loans and business loans.

Further, a considerable amount of our loan officers' time was still being consumed by the troubled mortgage portfolios of our acquired institutions. The California thrifts, which Empire was "induced" to assume, had brought with them some particularly problematic portfolios.

In addition, our projections for future commercial lending revealed that our in-place operations would soon be inadequate to the task of providing the kind of risk-averse portfolio growth that would be necessary to generate reasonable, consistent profit. Our conservative approach to lending to businesses coupled with intense competition from commercial banks and the slow growth of the Buffalo business community promised only modest profitability in this relatively new field of endeavor.

(After a thorough analysis in mid-1987, Empire's commercial lending operations were scaled back in favor of more profitable leveraged buy-out projects. By then, Empire had acquired equity positions in more than a dozen large operating companies by virtue of restructuring their ownership via management/investor buyouts. These LBOs yielded revenues to the bank of more than $14 million.

Unfortunately, later in the '80s, even LBOs would prove to be a short-lived profit source as new changes in the tax code prohibited the carrying-forward and sharing of tax losses, an accounting procedure that was essential to the viability of LBOs.)

- **Consumer lending**

The immense challenges associated with originating an adequate flow of quality mortgages in a very adverse economic environment served to highlight the relative advantages of *consumer* lending. Accordingly, after it's mergers of 1982, Empire began to devise ways in which an even larger volume of credit card paper and auto loans could be generated for its portfolio, and – very importantly – for packaging and resale.

Empire had been in the consumer loan business for several years. It had accumulated considerable experience and had established a rather sound track record. The challenge in the '80s was to expand the flow of such loans by exploiting the substantial, geographically diverse market presence of the thrift institutions if had acquired. Consumer credit was a rapidly growing sector of lending that Empire could not afford to ignore. Because of the continuing upward march of interest rates and the dearth of worthy mortgage product, we needed short-maturity, high rate asset product like that which consumer lending could produce.

We had been advised by experts in the field that the creation of a consumer loan business of the size and type we envisioned would be expensive in its early stages as we moved along a learning curve and slowly ferreted out the large crew of bad-credit borrowers that traditionally swarm to the "new (lending) kid on the block." Accordingly, we recruited top-notch lending specialists along with the best computer technology and credit scoring systems that were available at the time.

Empire's management team advised the bank's Board of Directors that the operating costs and loan reserves associated with our consumer lending initiative would, in its early years, be higher than those experienced by well-established, seasoned lenders. This inevitable reality was accepted by our Directors as the essential cost of entry into a lending area that would, eventually, provide the kinds of rates, maturities, and asset marketability that Empire needed and that the regulatory agencies had been encouraging. Indeed, there were no other permissible areas of investment that could provide Empire with the kinds of balance sheet and earnings enhancements that were provided by consumer lending.

Fortunately, Empire's existing regulatory forbearances and goodwill-related income accretion would give it the wherewithal to absorb the start-up expenses and charge-off costs associated with entry into the consumer lending business. We would not, therefore, run afoul of prevailing capital requirements.

Nevertheless, since the benefits of accretion would begin to expire in just a few years, it was incumbent upon Empire to build its presence in the consumer loan market as rapidly as possible, absorbing the necessary up-front costs while its "discount income" still offered a cushion to capital.

205

The income accretion associated with the bank's assets that had been "marked-to-market" (i.e. revalued in accordance with current market interest rates at the time of Empire's supervisory acquisitions) would begin to decrease in 1988. This source of bottom-line profit would have to be replaced. For the period 1983-1987, the accretion of these portfolios had provided Empire with a positive enhancement to income of approximately $209.7 million, more than offsetting the drag of goodwill. However, projections showed that accretion would produce much less income supplementation during 1988-1992. As a consequence, the loan portfolios of Empire would have to pick up considerable additional responsibility for earnings generation as our deal-based accretion benefits phased out.

We reasoned that, once we passed the costly start-up phase, our new consumer lending initiative would provide Empire with a stable, high-volume earnings stream that would contribute much more to the bank's financial welfare than did the forbearances and the purchase accounting treatment that we currently enjoyed. It would facilitate a shift from acquisition-facilitated earnings to more classical – and durable – operating profits.

Abetting our decision to enter this market was the fact that almost all professional economic forecasts to which the bank subscribed called for a drop in interest rates during the last years of the 1980s and into the 1990s. Traditionally, consumer loan rates do not closely track mortgage rates during interest rate down-cycles and remain comparatively high for an extended period, thus increasing the relative market value of an institution's consumer loan portfolio. As rates declined, this would give our bank some wonderful opportunities for sustaining relatively high income streams and for realizing gains through the sale of its accumulated consumer loan portfolios.

Of equal importance, a prominent presence in the consumer loan business would enable Empire of America to acquire new capital supplementations through future securities offerings or the sale of all or part of its consumer loan line of business.

Therefore, consumer lending, while still a secondary line of business for commercial banks. – seemed like one of the major solutions to our long-standing earnings challenge.

Fortunately, Empire of America's entry into consumer lending was met with extremely favorable market response. Not only did the lending volume expand vigorously, but the balances associated with outstanding loans also burgeoned.

The response of the marketplace to our new consumer loan marketing initiatives was far stronger than we had anticipated, so we quickly augmented our extant staff talents and experience in that area.

It didn't take long for Empire to become a major player in the consumer loan business.

Accelerated generation of consumer and commercial loans during this period enabled Empire to increase its portfolio yields significantly and to even more profitably contra-position the interest rates and the maturities of its loan assets and deposit liabilities. By year-end 1984, Empire of America had quadrupled the dollar amount of its assets and liabilities with matched maturities, from 10% of all assets in 1981 to 41%. It was another encouraging milestone for the Big E team (and its regulators).

Between 1983 and 1987, the Big E worked diligently to exploit a variety of measures to expand its consumer loan portfolio. We entered into arrangements with non-bank venues – including automobile dealers, boat dealers, and insurance agents – to generate consumer loans for us. Some 64% of Empire's loan originations during the first year of the expanded consumer lending initiative came from these indirect sources.

In addition, we introduced a new home equity line of credit program to provide consumers with a continuing credit capacity tied to collateral in their homes.

Student loans also continued to be a significant portion of our consumer loan portfolio.

By 1985, our consumer lending activity was growing steadily and our portfolio boasted well over $500 million of loans, with a yield of 12.7%. That amounted to a 235% increase in just three years.

Our VISA credit card operation, which was established 1981, was serving more than 80,000 customers nationwide.

In 1985, Syracuse, New York – a city in which there were no Big E bank branches – became the site of our first dedicated consumer loan office.

By the end of 1986, Empire had built a $1.1 billion consumer loan portfolio. It served more than 100,000 VISA cardholders; it was a major lender to mobile home buyers; and its automobile loans accounted for $307.3 million of the bank's total consumer loan portfolio.

Noteworthy was the fact that, in 1986, Empire was able to *profitably* sell $190 million of auto loans in the secondary market – the largest transaction of its kind ever consummated by a thrift institution.

**Speaking up**

With a sprawling geographic marketplace and a huge bundle of service offerings, it was important for Empire to assure that existing and prospective customers enjoyed informed access to the benefits the bank provided. It was equally important for our team members to have an in-depth understanding of the products they were offering.

These needs, plus the growing complexity of the financial services industry in general, spurred us to develop new ways to communicate with our most important publics, i.e. more than one-million customers; over four thousand employees; and – looking ahead – thousands of shareholders.

In 1986, with assistance and inspiration from, its Macrotel Inc. subsidiary, Empire became the first bank in the nation to acquire a mobile ku-band satellite videoconferencing system. It would be used for interstate employee video communication and would "ride" on the same range of frequencies that were used by NASA for space shuttle and International Space Station communications.

We used this two-way teleconferencing capability to communicate frequently with our employees across the country. It enabled us to provide financial updates, product information, and employee news to Empire team members. The system also allowed the bank to offer specialized training programs to selected groups of employees wherever they were. This capacity advanced the cohesion and camaraderie that was so important in an institution with far-flung, disparate operations.

It also became a source of supplementary income for the bank. For example, shortly after its inception, the system – which was managed by Sherwin-Greenberg Productions, the bank's film and video production subsidiary – was leased to such corporate clients as Amoco, Chrysler Corporation, Ford Motor Company, and Dunlop Tire Corporation, as well as to commercial television network affiliates and Public Broadcasting System television stations.

Macrotel, Inc., in a joint venture with Sherwin-Greenberg Productions Inc., created a series of interactive, laser-read, video disc training programs for bank employees. These programs served both the Big E's needs and – on a fee basis – those of other, non-competing, financial institutions.

In addition, Empire acquired a controlling interest in Levy, King & White Companies (LK&W), Buffalo's second-largest advertising and public relations agency, which, through its

Pearson Thomas/Levy King & White Division, also maintained offices in Tampa and West Palm Beach, Florida. At year-end, LK&W had capitalized billings of $43 million, $8 million of it consisting of work from Empire. The bank channeled bank and subsidiary advertising through LK&W, thereby maximizing the Big E's access to creative talent and greatly reducing its marketing costs. Additionally, we shared in the income generated by LK&W's other accounts.

This kind of expanded communication capacity enhanced the bank's performance while increasing its revenues and decreasing its operating expenses.

**Converting for capital**

As Empire approached the midpoint of 1986, the Big E team was taking a measure of satisfaction from its ongoing implementation of the Phoenix Plan. But, despite many achievements, it remained apparent that in order to attain a reasonable level of consistent and sustainable profitability, our rate of institutional growth would have to be accelerated.

While the mergers of 1982-85 contributed to a dramatic, non-organic spurt of expansion for Empire, much more growth was needed. Additional profitable asset and deposit combinations were necessary to fuel the "new" Empires in Florida, Texas, and California while simultaneously carrying the poorly-contributing mortgage portfolios of the old Erie Savings Bank and the acquired S&Ls.

As previously noted, it was conservatively estimated that Empire would have to grow to approximately $16 billion in assets by the end of 1992 in order to generate a stream of net interest income that was sufficient to compensate for the past *and* to allow us to take full advantage of our new future in the national marketplace.

Current market conditions would make the attainment of a $16 billion asset base difficult; but an insufficiency of institutional capital necessary to support such growth would make such attainment impossible. Alas, Empire of America was suffering the legendary "Siberian dilemma." The bank would be a continual "loser" if it didn't add profit-generating new assets to its balance sheet, *but* it would be in violation of government regulations if it grew assets without concomitantly expanding its capital base.

(The "Siberian Dilemma" refers to the legendary observation which says, "If you fall in the water in Siberia and remain there, you'll freeze to death in thirty seconds; if you get out of the water, you'll freeze in twenty seconds.")

Therefore, by 1986, the need to raise additional capital to fuel sustained organic growth became our primary focus. Funds from outside investors were absolutely essential since they constituted the kind cash injection that is free from a corresponding liability. In contrast, funds solicited through deposit-taking and borrowing occasion liabilities to savers or other lending institutions and, thus, they did not constitute leverageable capital.

Such *unencumbered* capital was necessary to support deposit growth since federal regulations required a measure of "free" capital for every new deposit-dollar generated. At different times, as federal and state regulations changed, anywhere from two cents to five cents of capital was required to "support" a dollar of assets. In these troubling times, regulators were suggesting even higher capital ratios, some as high as 10%.

We had long anticipated the need for capital supplementation, and we knew that the most efficacious way to raise such capital was for Empire to convert to a public company which could, through an IPO (i.e. initial public offering), sell shares to institutional investors and the general public. As you will recall, one of the reasons for our Michigan mergers and the relocation of our charter to that state was to gain an ability to convert to a publicly-owned entity.

In 1983, when economic conditions favored initial public offerings of thrift stock, we had submitted our first stock conversion application to the FHLBB. But that application to convert and raise outside capital did not fare well. Despite the

211

fact that we were being strongly urged by regulators to seek fresh capital, differences almost immediately emerged with the FHLBB staff over the accounting treatment necessary to accommodate the goodwill amortization provisions that they had included in our S&L acquisition contracts. They also had questions with respect to the treatment of the cash "given" to Empire at that time.

In essence, our regulators didn't want us to calculate our existing capital in a manner consistent with the terms of the agreements that we had consummated with them at the time of our merger transactions.

Protracted negotiations concerning these issues shelved our conversion application for months. Unfortunately, during that delay, the market for initial public offerings (IPOs) declined dramatically and the window of opportunity for a successful offering closed before we could convert. The delay was unfortunate since interest rates moderated in 1983 and 1984, and Empire's resulting net interest margin would have justified a substantial capital raise at that time. Further, our operating losses in this period turned out to be less than earlier anticipated. It would have been a good time for a public offering.

So, in the spring of 1986, when the stock market again looked promising for the sale of thrift stock, we quickly submitted a renewed stock conversion application to the FHLBB. Investment banks and independent valuation experts had earlier opined that an offering in the range of $275 to $350 million was feasible. A capital raise in this range would be more than sufficient to get us to our $16 billion asset goal.

Notwithstanding this favorable market opportunity, the regulators' accounting "concerns" of 1983 immediately resurfaced and the application languished. Eventually, to avoid the type of protracted delay experienced in 1983, we acquiesced to the expensive accounting provisions proposed by our regulators.

As a condition of conversion, the amortization period of our goodwill was reset to 28 years, down from the originally agreed-upon 40 years. This meant that, even though we had written off almost $100 million of goodwill to date, our future *annual* write-offs would increase by $10 million.

Furthermore, to secure permission to convert, we were required to issue market-rate preferred stock to the FSLIC in place of a regulatory capital instrument we had given them at the time of our supervisory acquisitions. This added an average annual dividend expense of approximately $6 million.

These new costs were certainly not envisioned in our initial supervisory transactions with the FSLIC.

Notwithstanding these difficulties, the bank was optimistic about successfully completing a public offering of shares in late 1986. We were well-positioned to execute such an offering since, in March of that year, the Big E had reported a 1985 operating profit (calculated according to the new regulatory goodwill amortization standards demanded by the regulators) of $17.8 million.

With respect to our stock offering, we proposed to give first subscription rights to our customers, borrowers, and employees. Once that round of sales was wrapped up, we intended to offer the remaining unsold shares exclusively to the residents of the communities we served in New York, Michigan, Florida, California, and Texas.

During the pre-offering period, I was informed that, in order for our underwriters to proceed, the bank would be required to enter into employment contracts with its top officers. They wanted to be able to assure investors that the leadership team that brought Empire to this point would continue to serve after the bank became a public institution.

Since the bank had never utilized employment contracts before, this was the first time we had ever been asked to contractually commit to service with our employer. We knew that such agreements would preclude our future acceptance of the kinds of lucrative employment offers that had been coming our way of late from other banks and financial service companies.

A highly-regarded human resources consulting firm was retained to recommend compensation alternatives to our Board. After due deliberation, the involved officers and our Board members concluded that the salary, benefits, and termination allowances that were finally recommended by the firm far exceeded what the bank could afford in light of its continuing efforts to increase profitability. Accordingly, we agreed on a remuneration structure that, at the time, ranked in the bottom twenty-five percent of compensation packages offered by the thirty-five thrift institutions in the nation that were comparable in size and scope to Empire.

Nevertheless, we all felt that our decision was entirely appropriate under the circumstances. "Pay for performance" had long been the bank's guiding compensation principle; but "fair pay *and* profitability" were now its dominant priorities. We all confidently looked forward to better profit *and pay* in the near future.

We all signed on the dotted line, straightaway.

Empire of America began its actual conversion to public company status in the second half of 1986. We hoped to raise as much as $150 million in fresh capital. This, however, turned out to be an unattainable aspiration.

Since the most recent third-party valuation of the bank in 1983 – which concluded that a capital raise of up to $350 million was feasible – quite a few other savings institutions had converted and the current prevailing market for new thrift shares had contracted considerably. As a consequence, a revised appraisal conducted by outside professionals indicated that capital raise in the range of $115 million to $175 million was more realistic.

Despite this disappointment, ninety-eight percent of our voting depositors approved the sale of stock; and by August, we were accepting subscriptions for shares at a $10 price point. By the end of the month, 18,000 subscribers had subscribed to purchase $50 million of stock. It wasn't the kind of response we had hoped for, but the large number of subscribers that emerged indicated that our loyal customers had considerable faith... if not investable funds.

We then had forty-five days to raise, at least, an additional $65 million through a nationwide offering conducted by a syndicate of securities broker-dealers.

The response from that source was disheartening. By the end of September, it was evident that the proposed capital raise was a no-go and that we'd have to scrap our initial offering terms and reconsider the goals of our entire capital acquisition program.

The appetite for thrift stocks had diminished far more than we expected. One of the major causes of this disillusionment had emerged at mid-decade with the almost total collapse of the economy in the southwest. By 1986, a precipitous decline in oil prices hit Texas and began to rapidly – and negatively– impact the state's burgeoning real estate market which, in recent years, had been based, to a great extent, upon oil profits.

In late 1986, Congress was mulling a revision in the tax code which would make investments in commercial buildings and residential multi-family properties far less attractive than they had been. Such a change would make thrifts' *existing* real estate loan portfolios more risky and less valuable than they had been under the tax provisions that prevailed when the mortgages were originally booked. Under these circumstances, it was very likely that some property owners would simply walk away from their "underwater" properties and the mortgages that financed them.

The number of bank and thrift failures began to accelerate and cast a pall on the entire industry. Especially harmful was an investigative report on the much-watched 60 Minutes television program about the disgraceful failure of Empire Savings and Loan Association in Mesquite, Texas. That shop was not related to Empire of America in any way, but the distinction was lost on many potential investors.

All of these factors – not to mention continuing high interest rates and a recent decline in the stock market – contributed to a glum outlook for new stock offerings by savings institutions. (The Dow Jones Industrial Average dropped from the 1900s in

July to 1790 in early October, including a two-day decline in mid-September which cost the DJIA almost 121 points... a drop of more than 5%. Understandably, these events dampened the enthusiasm of prospective Empire of America stock purchasers.)

Notwithstanding these hurdles, we decided, after considerable analysis and soul-searching, to move ahead with a revised stock offering. Our decision was abetted by the fact that almost every prominent economist was forecasting lower interest rates, which would help Empire of America's earnings prospects considerably. Importantly, even after its conversion, Empire would still enjoy the support of its government forbearances and extant goodwill.

In the opinion of the bank's senior managers and Directors, a change in corporate legal status (from private company to publicly-owned company) was as important to our future as the amount of dollars raised by our proposed initial stock offering. Once converted, Empire would be able to quickly come to the market again for additional capital as economic conditions improved.

We believed that a subsequent, second offering of stock was eminently doable once Empire's track record was more widely appreciated and after its first-round stock purchasers had enjoyed some enhancement in share value. Then too, by that time we would be more familiar with the process of guiding a stock offering proposal through the regulatory approval maze.

We were confident that, when circumstances were again favorable for a supplementary stock offering, an additional capital raise could be accomplished... if we moved quickly to finalize our *initial* stock offering.

Accordingly, in early October, we modified our stock offering plan and recruited a prestigious investment firm to underwrite a revised stock sale. Those who had previously subscribed for shares could cancel their purchase offer or re-up for the new offering. All interested purchasers would be required to subscribe according to the revised terms and conditions.

Our proposed, reconstituted stock sale would consisted of 15 million shares, with an offering price between $5.61 and $7.59 per share

The logic of moving forward with this revised offering was emphasized by our financial advisors. They claimed that it was reasonable to achieve an annual return on assets in the thrift business of .40%. Indeed, history showed that .40% was on the low side of actual performance in the industry. Therefore, it was reasonable to assume that, as Empire's turnaround progressed and interest rates moderated, the bank could generate forty basis points (i.e. .40%) of earnings on its assets. With a $16 billion asset base, its annual earnings could easily approximate $64 million.

Further, the stocks of already-converted thrifts were selling anywhere from six to fourteen times earnings. That meant that, if the stock price multiples prevailing at the time of the offering persisted, our bank's per share price could move up smartly as its workout proceeded.

Here's the math. Using the above earnings' estimates, if the bank were to sell 15 million shares at $6 a share in its initial offering, each share could conceivably reflect annual earnings-per-share of $4.27 in the relatively near-term future.

Assuming a price/earnings multiple of only six, the stock price could reach almost $26 dollars per share as the bank's Phoenix Plan wrapped up. Presumably, there would be dividend income also.

In other words, it was not unreasonable to anticipate that an Empire share of stock could quadruple in value in the next five years.

Of course, we could not share these kinds of calculations with prospective shareholders since they were based on subjective assumptions and anticipations. Nevertheless, we believed that the scenario that the numbers suggested more than justified moving ahead with a down-scaled stock offering. We hoped that prospective stock purchasers would be able to come to the same conclusion.

I was a believer and tapped my IRA to buy a very large block of stock, making me the largest non-institutional shareholder in Empire of America at the time of its public offering. (I was humbled, however, by the fact that the amount of my investment was almost equal to what my father had earned during his entire fifty-year banking career.)

Originally we had anticipated only a limited "community offering" of the stock but, encouragingly, a major Wall Street firm – Kidder Peabody & Co. – stepped forward and offered to execute a traditional, full-scale underwriting.

In October, the sales process began once again.

We had previously received regulatory permission to use the bank's extensive satellite video broadcasting network to inform our depositors and other interested investors nationwide about our stock offering. The use of a proprietary video network to facilitate a public stock offering had never before been attempted. It allowed groups of potential stock purchasers to assemble simultaneously around the country for several rounds of teleconferencing. This afforded bank officers an opportunity to personally communicate with our prospective owners and answer their questions directly, in real time. Very importantly, it allowed us to clearly emphasize the distinction between riskless deposit accounts and publicly-traded stock.

But our rollout did not perform as expected. Unfortunately, the media continued to focus on bad news about the prospects for the thrift industry. Accordingly, investors became increasingly wary of financial institution stocks.

We were told by some securities experts that we were too aggressive in warning our depositors about the risks of stock as contrasted to savings accounts. But many of our depositors were elderly and lived on a fixed income; others had limited experience with the stock market. Consequently, we believed it was essential for us to remind them that our stock was not a reasonable place to put *savings*. Insured deposit accounts were better suited for that purpose.

From the beginning of our conversion efforts, we strongly felt that there was a need for a clear description of exactly what was being offered. It was entirely possible that this candid forewarning dissuaded some prospective shareholders. Nevertheless, we were confident that it was a prudent action.

Bottom Line: We didn't want our savers' loyalty to the bank and to our community to prompt them to ill-advised investment decisions.

Finally, after six months of effort, on November 27th, we were able to announce that 5.8 million shares had been sold to our depositors and that Kidder Peabody & Co. had sold an additional 9.2 million shares in the open market. The price of the stock was initially pegged at $5.625 per share, and the net proceeds to Empire were $69 million... less than we had hoped for, but still enough to fund a successful implementation of our plans.

Considering the discouraging environment, the number of people who purchased stock was astounding. Empire's offering created more shareholders than any previous offering on the American Exchange by a company of our size.

Obviously, there was a desire to participate, but, unfortunately, not enough investors saw the kind of profit potential that would justify a large investment. Our offering netted, on average, about $4,000 per investor... one of the smallest average investment figures in recent Exchange history.

Despite the fact that our capital raise produced a lesser amount of funds than we desired, Empire was on its way, and we were determined to complete a turnaround that would reward the investors who had the confidence and wherewithal to join us.

Even if further stock offerings were precluded in the short run by economic events, Empire of America had become a stock company and its prospects for raising more capital at a later date – or for an eventual acquisition of the bank by another financial institution at an attractive price – were expanded tremendously.

Indeed, we believed that, once Empire became better known in the nation's financial marketplaces, institutional acquirers would eventually be attracted by its many unique "pluses," viz. its extraordinary geographic market penetration (which was denied almost all other thrifts at that time); its profitable array of non-banking services; and its innovative portfolio management techniques.

It was reasonable to assume that these attributes would make Empire, at the very least, an attractive acquisition candidate for a larger financial services firm or for a non-banking company that wanted to enter the financial services industry.

Under every scenario we envisioned, Empire's initial shareholders were well-positioned to eventually realize significant gains on their investments.

Very importantly, the anticipated capital infusion provided by the stock offering would facilitate institutional asset growth to almost $16 billion.

By New Year's Eve 1986, our management team was able to deservedly celebrate the amazing growth of its diverse financial enterprise, which boasted assets of over $9 billion. It offered its customers access to their accounts at 150-plus branch offices and 48,000 other locations in all fifty states and six foreign countries.

Not incidentally, we – and our regulators – were justifiably pleased that our balance sheet's "sensitivity index" passed the fifty-percent mark. This was an extremely significant milestone in our turnaround effort.

The first phase of our Phoenix Plan was completed, and we were more than $240 million ahead of the earnings target we had set for ourselves in 1981.

To add icing to our cake, a 1985 study compiled by the London-based PA Consulting Group for the World Forum on Consumer Financial Services included Empire of America as one of four US enterprises (including Merrill Lynch) on an international list of twelve "Crème de la Crème" financial service innovators. Empire was cited because of its "breakthrough innovations," including its Moneyplex facility and its platform for providing stock brokerage, insurance, and real estate services in one location.

## Governing

Empire's experienced and dedicated Trustees and Directors provided invaluable assistance and oversight as our management team implemented the Phoenix Plan and pursued the expansion and diversification it entailed.

The bank's cash flow during the years immediately following its mergers was enormous. The Board monitored the investment of at least $4 billion of cash each year. When such a gigantic torrent of cash is being invested in a hostile economic environment, concern for the integrity of the asset acquisition process is paramount.

The Board beefed up our audit department and created a separate department to monitor the bank's loan production process and its compliance with prudent loan standards and criteria. This department was staffed, in part, with former government regulators and bank examiners. A special committee of our Board of Directors reviewed the department's activity on a bi-weekly basis.

The Board also participated in the formulation of new, comprehensive lending policies that would guide the bank's far-flung asset origination activities. While we were committed to rapidly increasing the volume of loans we generated, we were equally dedicated to preserving the quality of the bank's portfolios. As ol' uncle Ollie used to advise, "You never want to lose on the bananas what you make on the apples."

In late 1986, McKinsey & Co., a well-respected management consulting firm, was retained by our Board of Directors to evaluate our system of institutional governance. Given our rapid geographic, asset, and functional growth, we wanted to be sure that we were employing the best techniques for Board oversight and involvement. Further, as a public company, we needed new types of information and reports for our Board of Directors, shareholders, and the public at large. This necessitated reporting procedures that were in strict accordance with public company regulations, accounting protocols, and stock exchange requirements. Disclosures of information had to be managed very carefully.

McKinsey & Co. studied our Board meeting agendas and procedures; the information that our Directors received; and, the structure, functioning, agendas, and manning of our Directors' Committees. One of their early observations was that we were already providing too much information and going into too much detail at Board and Committee meetings. They suggested streamlining both the informational flows and the nature and composition of our Directors' committees. McKinsey specialists met with each Director individually to gain insight. (The final McKinsey report was submitted directly to the Board in January 1987. Shortly afterward, the Board formulated a host of new governance policies including both those recommended by McKinsey and additional initiatives formulated by the Board in conjunction with management.)

## Managing

In keeping with Empire's growing size and scope – and the demands of operating as a public company – the bank effected a reorganization of its executive cadre in 1986. I had served as Chief Executive Officer since 1983 and in 1986 I was elected Chairman of the Board & CEO.

At the same time, three experienced Presidents were elected to oversee the operational Groups that comprised all of the bank's activities. Additionally, a skilled Chief Financial Officer (CFO) was recruited to our team.

All of these executives, along with our planning director and chief legal counsel / director of governmental affairs, were appointed to an "Office of the Chief Executive" (OCE) to oversee the national operations of Empire.

All staff and administrative functions were gathered under one President, who also assumed responsibility for the bank's non-bank subsidiaries. Our huge, rapidly-growing mortgage banking functions were assigned to another President. The third

President assumed responsibility for all deposit and lending operations.

The OCE met several times weekly, and its efforts were supported by a Fiscal Management Committee of senior officers.

This technique for sharing responsibility and authority proved to be ideally suited to the very complex and far-flung activities of Empire of America.

We were confident that we had a team that was ready to capitalize on our conversion and keep us on track until a complete turnaround was accomplished within the next three to six years.

**Follow-on planning**

The post-Phoenix Plan course of growth and transformation that was envisioned by our team necessitated a sophisticated planning, measurement, and review process. The strategic and operating plans required by such a process had to be dynamic and perpetual, and provide for *annual* iterations.

Empire's senior management promptly established a "Planned Action Program" (PAP) to accommodate this task. (Interestingly, the planning methodology of the PAP was, essentially, an expanded and more sophisticated version of the very first plan configuration I foisted upon the bank in 1968.)

According to the PAP regimen, the bank's Board of Directors set broad five-year objectives while managers of the bank, at every level, would prepare more specific annual plans that they felt were appropriate to the mission. Each plan that resulted was presented to the bank's Board of Directors for approval. Any interim plan modifications were also reviewed by the Board.

Importantly, every Empire team member was involved in the undertaking. An experienced planning director had been recruited from a large commercial bank to coordinate the process.

Our planning was assisted by newfangled desktop computers that were linked to a central "plan-in-progress" repository on a mainline computer. The planning progressed in stages, producing sequential goals and detailed action programs for achieving them.

Once this annual plan was engaged, progress reports were solicited and examined *quarterly*. Board members evaluated these reports in conjunction with their monthly reviews of financial and operating statements.

# Chapter nine

## SUNNY WITH A CHANCE OF.....

### The midpoint

As 1987 began, we prepared to cross the mid-point in our Phoenix Plan's ten-year repositioning effort. We seemed to be well situated to successfully complete our "workout" on schedule. Empire of America had become a major force on the national financial scene as it expanded in five roles of growing significance, i.e. investment manager; lender to consumers; retailer of a wide range of savings and investment products; mortgage banker; and thrift rehabilitator. Since the beginning of the decade, Empire nearly quadrupled in size.

By using distinct merchandising and pricing strategies for each of our fourteen major markets, we had developed a unique ability to generate funds on a least-cost, as-needed basis. Our novel multi-market presence allowed us to reduce our interest expense/deposit costs by continually targeting geographic areas that featured the lowest cost funds. This capacity – along with our proven ability to structure low-cost capital market borrowings and novel asset securitizations and sales – enabled us to expand our funding alternatives and control our weighted average cost of funds despite interest rate volatility and severe competitive pressures.

Empire had a sophisticated system for pricing (i.e. setting rates) on its deposits. Each week, a senior officer in each of Empire's primary market areas would report our competitors' apparent rate structures to Empire's Treasurer in Buffalo. Through a telephone conference system, the high, low, and medium rate levels in each market would be discussed and, depending on Empire's cash needs at that time, a deposit-generating, marketing push would be launched in our geographic service areas where savings dollars could be generated at least cost.

This selective, regional approach to deposit garnering was extremely helpful in our management of overall deposit costs but it would have been even more beneficial if the individual banks in the Empire system were able to actually transfer deposits to one another. Such funds-shifting would have improved our overall ability to take advantage of loan and investment opportunities in areas of the nation were deposits were prohibitively expensive. Unfortunately, in the time since our mergers were consummated, new regulations emerged concerning "brokered deposits" and they precluded such reallocation of funds even in banks, like Empire, that were part of a single ownership group. Thus, one of the important benefits we anticipated as a consequence of a multiple market presence was unexpectedly denied us.

Nevertheless, thanks to the bank's unique geographical presence and its regionalized rate-setting strategies, it was still able to reduce its overall total weighted average cost of funds – during an extremely volatile year – to 7.18%, down from 7.7% the year before and from 9.2% in 1985.

Our market footprint grew dramatically as we added real estate sales offices and loan production offices in thirty-eight additional states. Further, Empire's distribution prowess was being enhanced by the expansion of its Moneyplex concept into additional Montgomery Ward Department Stores in Texas, Illinois, and New York. These Moneyplex facilities were being upgraded to include technology which allowed the bank's financial service subsidiaries to communicate directly with customers via telephone and dedicated access terminals. They featured on-line video presentations that provided financial planning information, stock quotations, and listings of available residential real estate.

In early 1987, federal regulators strongly "urged" Empire to acquire the $78.3 million Equitable Savings and Loan Association in San Mateo, California, a costly transaction that would expand our market coverage but would not substantially benefit our ongoing work-out program.

The productivity of our distribution network was enhanced during this period by the launching of *USA Direct,* one of the first "branchless banks" in the nation. *USA Direct* was, in reality, a separately-chartered Houston, Texas S&L that we had acquired in early 1984. We closed all of its branches but retained its operating charter. This bank eschewed bricks-and-mortar branches in favor of employing mail, fax, and telephone communications to penetrate deposit and consumer lending markets in which Empire had no physical presence. We believed that this stand-alone bank would, eventually, become the hub for activity generated through personal computers and television sets, a concept that, heretofore, gained attention only from "futurists" writing in publications such as the American Banker, a daily newspaper, and Popular Mechanics magazine (both pretty reliable oracles of "things to come"). Our Macrotel Inc. subsidiary was one of the few enterprises that were seriously exploring the business application of these new functionalities in the banking industry

The simple, stripped-down, operating premise of *USA Direct* allowed Empire to minimize operating expenses, selectively tap into underserved markets and, thus, pay savers attractive rates of interest. All of this helped boost the current profitability of the bank while it experimented with a futuristic business model for branchless banking.

We were learning a great deal from Smartline and our other involvements in the non-banking corporate world. For example, we had developed an innovative employee sales training and compensation system that enhanced the ability of the service representatives in our "stores" to sell our profitable *non-banking* products like securities, real estate, and insurance. The marketing knowledge we were gaining contributed to the increased success of our traditional, established products as well.

A major new product initiative was unveiled in 1987. The Big E Pathfinder Family of Mutual Funds, a contemporary package of equity and bond mutual funds, was the first of its kind in the thrift industry. Up until this time, only two commercial banks – Citibank and Wells Fargo – offered their own mutual funds. Our family of funds included the <u>Government Plus Fund</u>, <u>Tax-Free Income Fund</u>, <u>New York Tax-Free Income Fund</u>, and the <u>Total Return Fund</u>, the latter a balanced fund that invested in debt securities and in common and preferred stock.

The funds were managed by outside investment advisors who were retained by a newly-formed bank subsidiary, Empire of America Advisory Services Inc. They were sold through the bank's securities brokerage subsidiary, Empire National Securities Inc., which, by that time, had sales representatives in many Empire branches. A minimum initial investment of only $1,000 was established to make the funds affordable to Empire's customers. Our Pathfinder subsidiary had an independent board of directors and retained an outside firm as a sub-advisor.

Other profitable synergies between our financial service subsidiaries and our traditional banks were forming. For example, Empire of America Realty Credit Corp. (EOARCC), our full-service mortgage banking company, structured an on-line transaction conduit using telephone and facsimile transmissions that enabled our real estate brokerage subsidiary, Gallery of Homes Inc., to initiate home-buyer loan applications for the bank. This linkage offered great potential since the Gallery was brokering the sale of more than 30,000 homes annually. The aggregate value of the homes sold each year totaled more than $2.5 billion.

The Gallery's national market presence abetted the growth of EOARCC which achieved loan closings of almost $2 billion in 1987. According to a cost survey conducted by Peat Marwick Main & Co., EOARCC ranked third among the nation's largest fifteen mortgage bankers in terms of residential loan servicing efficiency.

At the same time, the Big E expanded the mortgage loan services it was offering to the thousands of executives being served by Empire Relocation Services, Inc.

Unfortunately, because of intense competition for quality loans in both the residential and commercial mortgage markets, good mortgage product was only available at extremely narrow interest spreads. We were faced with the choice of seeking high yields and getting high-risk loans (which in our estimation – given our first hand observations in Texas – were going to become even more risky as real estate markets continued to deteriorate ) or make moderate-risk loans with relatively paltry contributions to net interest income.

Confronted with this Hobson's Choice, we chose the lower risk course.

Alas, so did the pension funds and insurance companies which were also looking for good quality investment paper. They became strong competitors since the nature of their businesses (which featured low-cost funding and an ability to buy and hold assets at fixed rates) allowed them to all-too-frequently underbid us.

In 1987, Congress revised the provisions of the Economic Recovery Tax Act of 1981 and increased the tax rate on capital gains from 20% to 28%. As a consequence, the demand by real estate investors for commercial mortgage loans decreased dramatically. The 1987 action sharply reduced investor interest in new building projects since it also eliminated significant tax advantages associated with real estate ownership. It, therefore, negatively impacted Empire's ability to generate new commercial mortgages, and it increased the risks associated with its previously-booked loans.

In addition, an oil glut hit the Southwest and, as a consequence, the value of the collateral supporting many already-booked real estate deals was shrinking.

At the same time, the quality of the new loans that were being presented to Empire's underwriters for consideration was deteriorating.

Since we were loath to lower our standards, we were having difficulty meeting our loan origination goals. Prudently, we retrenched in the area of commercial loan origination, cutting back our loan production offices in cities in which we did not have a branch presence.

Given this downward turn in the mortgage market, Empire accelerated its efforts to seek other types of mortgage-like assets for its portfolio. As a consequence of open-market bulk purchases, the bank's mortgage-backed securities (MBS) portfolio grew to $1.5 billion. This accomplishment was made possible by our proprietary system for conducting customized computer analyses of mortgage-based securities available for purchase. This sophisticated system enabled Empire of America to quickly analyze loans and manage its MBS purchase and sale activities with precision. The bank was able to identify distinct investment opportunities and, at the same time, rapidly adjust its investment mix to reflect changing economic conditions. (The lack of this kind of analytical capacity in some large banks was a major reason for their MBS losses in 2008 which, in turn, contributed to a massive financial industry meltdown.)

Investment in mortgage backed securities would not, however, totally offset the deterioration of the commercial mortgage markets and the slump in demand for residential mortgages. In fact, in our estimation, the real estate crisis was going to get worse before it got better.

This put our Phoenix Plan in jeopardy since it was predicated on continued asset growth at positive interest rate spreads. Accordingly, we decided to turn even more to consumer loans for the balance sheet growth we required.

Consumer loans were especially beneficial to Empire at this time since they offered high yields; were compatible with prevailing regulations concerning balance sheet composition; and provided an opportunity for re-sale profits in the secondary market.

Empire's consumer loan strategy was already paying off in 1987, as the portfolio grew 13% to $1.7 billion, representing almost 18% of the bank's interest earning assets. Encouragingly, between March and December 1987, consumer loan delinquencies dropped steadily.

Empire of America had become the nation's fourth-largest thrift consumer lender. We had invested heavily in building the loan generation capacity of our 150-plus full-service branches, fourteen loan production offices (LPOs), nineteen affinity credit card affiliations, and an indirect lending network of more than 1,900 auto dealers around the country. Through our Smartline telemarketing affiliate, we processed more than 30,000 loan applications by phone, generally completing actions on applications within 24 hours. We also expanded our credit card program by contracting to serve the members of large affinity groups like the National Academy of Television Arts and Sciences (the home of the "Emmy" awards).

We were well along the learning curve, and the profit potential associated with this type of lending was expanding nicely.

There was an additional benefit, too. In just a few short years, the growth of Empire's consumer loan portfolios had enabled it to comply substantively with new government mandates which required savings institution portfolios to be more "interest rate sensitive," i.e. featuring assets with short maturities and adjustable rates. At the end of 1981, less than 25% of Empire's assets were maturing within one year. By the beginning of 1987, Empire's match of assets and liabilities had grown to 75%.

Based on that performance, Empire's Board of Directors, in late 1987, approved a three-year plan that would see the consumer loan portfolio expanded to $6 billion.

In order to prudently track the quality of such growth, Empire adopted sophisticated, computerized formulae (that years later gained fame as "algorithms") to assist in the projection of consumer loan loss potentials and aid in the estimation of necessary loan loss reserves.

The growth of Empire of America's consumer loan portfolio in 1987 was spurred by a number of developments. Most notably, changes in the tax law made the home equity line of credit (HELOC) an extremely attractive product. HELOCs enabled customers, in most circumstances, to fully deduct interest

231

payments when computing their taxes. Through a joint venture initiated in 1987 with the Mutual Life Insurance Company of New York (MONY), a private-label version of the Big E's HELOC loan was sold through MONY's nationwide sales force of some 5,000 sales representatives. Through an assortment of such aggressive marketing efforts, the Big E was able to expand its HELOC portfolio more than five-fold in 1987 to $107.6 million.

Indirect auto loan origination – i.e. the purchase of loans from automobile dealers – became another important thrust of the Big E's consumer loan program in 1987. Through a network of more than 1,900 automobile dealers, Empire of America generated $742.6 million of auto loans in 1987. And, in response to the increased demand for leasing, the bank added vehicle leasing finance to its menu of services.

CoinLink, a computerized network that allowed automobile dealerships nationwide to electronically receive, process, and transmit automobile financing information, was introduced by the bank's Metroteller subsidiary in concert with a joint venture partner. By connecting auto dealers and financial institutions around the country, this system revolutionized on-the-spot auto financing and created tremendous value-added revenue potential for the Big E.

It was this kind of loan origination capacity that enabled the Big E to profitably sell in October 1987 – in the largest transaction of its kind by a thrift institution – $262.2 million of securities backed by auto loans. In addition to producing immediate profit and continuing servicing income, this transaction – and other ensuing similar transactions – gave Empire of America a self-renewing source of funds for future lending activity. We had developed a practical origination/sale model that we believed would serve us well – and safely – in the future.

There was also good news as far as expenses were concerned. For the previous five years, Empire had been burdened with sizeable costs associated with the necessity of maintaining four separate bank charters. The benefits originally accrued by virtue of by maintaining separate charters had been eliminated by recently introduced regulations. Therefore, after receiving regulatory approval in 1987, we were able to undertake the merger of all of our of bank charters, an action that would result in significant expense reductions.

At the same time, we completed the *final* conversion and consolidation of most of the separate computer systems the bank had inherited by virtue of its mergers. There was cause for celebration as 615,000 accounts were logged into the central processor at the bank's new computer center in Amherst, New York. This tremendous achievement would result in ongoing annual cost savings of approximately $4.5 million.

Other Empire endeavors – in addition to deposit and loan generation – also began to show exceptional promise in 1987. Some of these bright lights of accomplishment are reviewed in the following paragraphs.

- In order to achieve an even greater reduction in its cost of funds, Empire of America carefully nurtured an ability to structure low-cost, non-deposit borrowings in the capital markets. By the end of 1987, the Big E had put together seven borrowings, generating a total of $536.5 million of funds for the bank. Many of these low-cost borrowings were the result of innovative, first-of-a-kind transactions which set promising patterns for the future.

- Empire's equity positions in seventeen companies acquired through previous leveraged buyout financings were contributing revenues of $15.6 million annually.

- Asset Management & Disposition, Inc., a Big E subsidiary formed to assist less-practiced financial institutions in the fine art of working out non-performing loans was also enjoying great success.

- Mutual fund sales by Empire National Securities Inc. hit $110 million in 1987 and suggested great future success for our proprietary Big E Pathfinder Family of Mutual Funds.

- Empire Agency, the bank's insurance subsidiary, generated $2.2 million in paid premiums which were associated with approximately $50 million of annuity sales. Supported by this steady stream of income, the company began to broaden its product mix, offering a complete line of life, accident, health, homeowners, and auto insurance in Empire's five-state network. (Incredibly, in a few short years Empire Agency would become the largest business of its kind in Western New York.)
- Brandywine Enterprises, a bank subsidiary in Deland, Florida, was contributing nicely to Empire's profits in 1987 by developing and building attractive "up-scale" and "lifestyle" homes, shopping centers, and apartments. It was recognized nationally for its attention to environmental preservation and enhancement. The company's production schedule included projects in New Smyrna Beach, Vero Beach, Tampa, and Merritt Island, Florida.

The bank had big growth plans for its infrastructure, also. In 1987, Empire announced that it had initiated plans to construct an $80 million, 600,000 sq. ft. national headquarters facility in Amherst, New York and shift many jobs to New York from other areas of the country. Its specially-designed campus setting would facilitate organizational and operational improvements as bank activities from across the country were consolidated in one location. It was estimated that the project would considerably reduce the bank's operating costs by eliminating duplication in its national support staffs and far-flung administration centers.

Sixty-four acres of land, neighboring the Amherst campus of the State University of New York at Buffalo, was purchased for $2.4 million. It was estimated that, within five years, 500 bank employees would work there, with 3,000 more jobs possible in ten years. The campus would host a 100,000 sq. ft. national headquarters building, a 50,000 sq. ft. training and conference center, and up to five additional buildings.

Given the unpredictable economic conditions that prevailed and the stresses that Empire was encountering, this initiative was considered a long-term project that would not require significant capital expenditures until Empire's turn-around was approaching completion. Early on, it had been decided that construction would not commence quickly since there remained a great deal of work to be done with land owners, developers, and municipalities. Thus, a definite timetable for groundbreaking and construction was not set.

It was anticipated that, upon completion of this project, the bank's extant Main Place office tower in downtown Buffalo would continue to be headquarters for Empire's operations in the Western New York region and that no reduction of employment in the city would occur.

All in all, from a "bottom-line" perspective, the bank could claim a measure of success in 1987 in that it earned a profit of $12.7 million or $.46 per share for the year. We had succeeded in originating and booking large quantities of quality assets featuring higher yields and shorter maturities. The bank had also increased its net interest income (which reduced its dependency on profits from asset sales) and decreased in the bank's provision for loan losses.

Our shareholders benefited from this success as our Board of Directors declared a cash dividend of $.26 per share.

**The tipping point**

Despite all of its progress in 1987, the principal, long-standing threats to Empire's vitality were not significantly diminished. Events continued to impede our progress toward classically-defined operating profitability. Like the proverbial "mice and men," even the best laid plans of bankers sometimes go awry. Economic turbulence, intense competition, an increasingly distressed financial industry, and shifting accounting and regulatory standards prompted our team to regroup and re-think some elements of our Phoenix Plan strategy.

The first obstacle we encountered was an April 1987 spike in interest rates. In a three-day span, rates increased 1½ percentage points, wreaking havoc for the entire financial community.

As a result, our mortgage banking affiliate, Empire of America Realty Credit Corp., like its industry counterparts, incurred losses on loans it held for sale. In EOARCC's case, this charge was $6.3 million. Fortunately, the company had a sophisticated hedging program in place. Without it, the losses would have been much more. Compared to many of its counterparts, EOARCC came through this rate spike relatively well.

A month later, the government's General Accounting Office determined that the Federal Savings and Loan Insurance Corporation's secondary reserve fund had to be eliminated, producing a one-time charge to most FSLIC-insured institutions. This hit to our earnings amounted to $5 million.

Perhaps of most importance to Empire as the year drew to a close was the economic uncertainty engendered by the greatest one-day stock market collapse in U.S. history. On October 19th – "Black Monday" – the Dow Jones industrial average plunged 508 points – 22.68% – sending shockwaves through the economy. This contributed to a record 36% point dive in less than two months and created additional pain for Empire as it nicked the bank's equity portfolio market value by $7 million. It also cast a pall on Empire's shares and created great alarm among our new stockholders.

Another challenge loomed. In recent years, a portion of our bottom-line gains had been due to the sale of higher-than-market-rate mortgage loans from our portfolios. In fact, such gains-on-sales had constituted a significant part of Empire's income since it's mergers in 1982. By 1987, however, Empire's supply of "above water," "marked-to-market" loans that were acquired through our mergers had dwindled significantly. That meant that, in succeeding years, traditional *operating* profits – exclusive of these kinds of gains – would have to expand greatly to make up the difference. Fortunately, gains from the sale of packages of consumer loans we originated would continue to supplement, our earnings. But, we knew that other, relatively- new sources of earnings would have to be assiduously cultivated as we approached the end of the decade.

Alarms were sounded in the summer of 1987 when Congress approved a $10.8 billion capital infusion for the FSLIC. The agency immediately began working to "bail out" some of the largest and most troubled thrifts in Texas by aggressively soliciting bids from interested acquirers.

This was only a drop in the bucket compared to the widening hole in the industry's aggregate net worth, but it provided the government with an "activist" image and muted, to slight degree, public criticism of its policies with regard to savings institutions.

Unfortunately, as we feared, most of the resulting 150 bids for failing thrifts came from highly-opportunistic investors, including large non-bank corporations (many of which had strong political connections). All of the bids were predicated on substantial government subsidies. As a consequence, quite a few "sweetheart" deals were consummated which, not surprisingly, created more (government-subsidized) deposit rate competition for the struggling thrifts – like Empire – that could not participate in such deals. Moreover, this new form of generous government assistance changed the paradigm by which investors structured acquisitions and capital investments within the thrift industry.

As a consequence, these events reduced the value inherent in Empire's once novel post-merger configuration. Not only would the competitive landscape be challenged by new, subsidized competitors, but Empire's fundamental appeal to investors and other capital providers would be significantly diminished in the face of the abnormal profit potential now promised by other savings institutions that were being generously subsidized by the federal government.

These government-led deals constituted only a short-term, cosmetic resolution to an industry-wide affliction that would continue to metastasize. Nevertheless, to investors and acquirers, the attractiveness of this type of subsidized investment far overshadowed the promise associated with a long-term turnaround situation like Empire's.

Moreover, these quick, "cronyesque" deals signaled that the government was losing interest in constructive approaches which would provide limited capital and forbearances to troubled – but not "terminal" – thrifts so that they could gradually, over time, *work* their way out of difficulty by using sweat equity and entrepreneurial initiatives, i.e. *the Empire approach.*

To make matters worse, "institutional shrinkage" and "balance sheet downsizing" were now being advocated in regulatory circles as the "school solution" to the thrift "problem." New regulations and regulatory jawboning began to push thrifts in the direction of becoming *smaller.* Apparently, according to regulatory reasoning, a smaller thrift would ensure a smaller future governmental bailout.

To abet this strategy, severe percentage growth limitations were imposed on all thrifts in order to limit potential future "damage" to the Treasury's coffers.

These tacks, obviously, were inimical to the interests of Empire whose turnaround depended upon growth. This approach and other similar proposals were arguably reasonable remedies when applied in the cases of the "buccaneer" investors who had only recently entered the industry and rapidly reconfigured their acquired thrifts as personal piggy banks to support their high-risk ventures. But this "medicine" was poison to thrifts like Empire which were burdened with problems not of their making. For many of these, responsible growth was their only avenue to survival.

The "downsizing" line of attack did, however, provide a measure of comfort to queasy, increasingly-fearful regulators. After all, in their estimation, it would be "safer" for them to immediately pay-up and "solve" a thrift failure at any *current* cost than it would be to continue to laboriously cooperate with industrious, struggling managers who were engaged in sweat-equity workouts which could not *guarantee* a zero future cost to the government. It was becoming apparent to us that the effort and "reputational risk" associated with the latter – wiser – workout approach had little appeal to harried legislators and regulatory bureaucrats who wanted to get away from the perceived "tar baby" as quickly as possible.

As might be expected, commercial bankers also liked the regulators' approach since it improved their chances of gaining market share via thrifts' failures and their subsequent, subsidized liquidation. It was becoming increasingly apparent that much of the pressure in Congress for a comprehensive "bailout bill" which entailed the liquidation of thrifts came from the commercial bank industry.

Many commercial bankers were salivating at the prospect of a once-in-a-lifetime opportunity to gain subsidized market presence through the annexation of customers displaced by thrift institutions that were "closed" by the government. (As we shall see in later pages, their "dreams" would be realized in 1989 with the enactment of the Financial Institutions Reform, Recovery and Enforcement Act - FIRREA.)

All of these events constituted a significant threat to Empire's workout. They meant that offsetting cuts in our non-interest expenses were essential. A reduction in operating costs was the only way we could hope to offset the rising deposit interest costs that were resulting from the new spate of "reregulation."

As a consequence, we began an aggressive program of overall expense containment which entailed divestitures of selected business lines, subsidiary companies, and bank branches that no longer fit our refocused plan or the increasingly stringent expectations of our regulators. Our employee count was also frozen at the then current levels.

Cost-containment would be the current "order of the day" until our long-term initiatives matured to the point where they generated the kind of revenue necessary to facilitate Empire's turnaround program.

However, we were not going to forsake all of our important long-term growth and diversification undertakings, since we firmly believed that they would provide us with a firm foundation for increased and sustained profitability – and enhanced institutional value – in the future. The challenge would be *surviving* until the future arrived.

All in all, by the end of 1987, it was becoming very clear that the economic and political environment in which we were operating would make Empire's long-term "workout" process significantly more arduous than we had originally anticipated.

# Chapter ten

# TURBULENCE

### Enemies at the gate

Contrary to the sanguine forecasts of most analysts, economic conditions in 1988 caused the rates paid on deposits to move up smartly... *once again.* For the year, Empire's deposit costs would increase $68 million, thus decreasing the bank's net interest income substantially. With the economy weakening – abetted primarily by an oil glut and continuing deterioration within real estate markets – it had been believed that interest rates would decline.

The major uptick in rates that actually occurred was a surprise and was not good news for Empire. Interest rates paid on deposits had an enormous impact on Empire's well-being. Every one-half percentage point increase in interest rates cost the bank at least $50 million. Interest costs at Empire were to jump over $30 million above our budget for 1988 due to overall interest rate spikes which were being exacerbated by the "panic mentality" that was spreading among savers. Interest paid on deposits in 1987 amounted to $657 million; in 1988, it would total $780 million. This constituted a 19% jump of $123 million.

Interest rates were poised to create a "perfect storm." On one hand, rates charged on real estate loans began to soften, reflecting a fear of protracted deterioration in that economic sector. On the other hand, interest costs associated with deposits were increasing at a faster clip than were interest rates in general thanks to a large number of cash-starved thrifts that were chasing deposits at any cost and to depositors who wanted to earn rates comparable to those being paid by subsidized thrifts.

Further, as the thrift industry garnered increasingly negative publicity, and as thrift failures continued to escalate, managers of hundreds of teetering institutions were forced to stanch deposit outflows – and institutional collapse – by offering savers ridiculously high interest rates on their accounts... rates that responsible thrifts like Empire had to match in order to maintain a reasonable measure of liquidity.

Even many of the institutions that had already been seized by the government and were operating under the control of regulators were attempting to stem their deposit outflows by offering above-market rates that other, still-independent shops couldn't afford to match. At this point, the regulators who were controlling failing or failed thrifts were sanctioning the payment of virtually any interest rate to avoid a "run" on the institutions which they were nursing pending liquidation.

Then too, a large number of other thrifts had already been taken over by the government and sold to investors with generous financial assistance packages that afforded these re-born shops the opportunity to be extremely competitive with their subsidized deposit rate offerings.

Even in our Buffalo market, where we had so ably served customers for over a century and a quarter, we began to feel heightened depositor concern about the safety of their deposits.

As a consequence, deposit outflows became a major problem. Empire suffered an unprecedented $500 million outflow in the last five months of 1988. If nothing else, this change in deposit patterns was a portent of even more difficult days ahead.

Despite its huge late-year deposit outflow, the bank's total deposits showed an increase of $300 million for the full year. Nevertheless, as a result of the surge in late-year outflows, Empire had to borrow $450 million from other, more expensive, non-deposit sources simply to facilitate depositor demands. This necessary tactic, alone, increased our cost of funds for the year by $35 million... another direct hit to our bottom line.

Empire was further disadvantaged in its Buffalo market by the predatory actions of some of its competitors, especially commercial banks. As an example, the pension services representatives of one commercial bank would frequently contact Empire's pension plan customers with frightening rumors and conjecture about Empire's financial condition and its prospects for survival... *and* the survival of pensioners' savings. (Apparently, Bedford Falls wasn't the only town with a Henry Potter!) A great deal of time and effort was expended by Empire team members in dispelling such scurrilous innuendo.

Nationally, the number of thrift failures increased dramatically as the year wore on. Overworked regulators were beginning to wilt as the regulatory system was engulfed by panic. As might be expected, additional rules and regulations were promulgated in Washington to forestall a collapse of the industry. Unfortunately, most of these "decrees" harbored a potential to hurt Empire rather than to help it.

Our regulators and the makers of public policy in Washington began to see "causes" for the thrift debacle everywhere. Growth was the cause. Fixed rates were the cause. Real estate was the cause. Brokered deposits were the cause. Non-traditional investments were the cause. Inadequate capital was the cause. Inept thrift managers were the cause. In short order, all of these causes were attacked with new "remedial" regulations.

Hard-working thrift managers had neither the time nor credibility to publicly place the blame where it belonged... on the legislators and bureaucrats who had, for generations, tinkered with an industry to make it serve their collective will. In their zeal to make housing affordable and available in a hyper-inflated economy – *which they created* – our nation's lawmakers had deliberately laid the seeds for the demise of an economic institution that had been – and still was – critical to the economic welfare of the nation.

Even this late in the game, legislators and regulators sought to escape blame for their egregious missteps, they decided to "tinker on" and introduce yet another "too-late-to-the-party" spate of re-regulation. These efforts only served to further confuse an already traumatized industry. It was impossible to plan from day to day because the ground rules were constantly changing. What was good and acceptable one day, became bad and prohibited the next.

Regulators began to pressure thrifts to "downsize" and "rationalize" with maneuvers that they should have realized were inimical to the welfare of the industry. This was especially true in Empire's case, where growth and prudent management of opportunity were the only strategies of merit.

On the positive side, the bank's consumer loan initiative was moving along smartly, and customer response was beyond what had been initially expected. As previously noted, in late 1987, Empire's Directors had approved a 1988-91 strategic plan which called for growing the consumer loan portfolio – through both direct and indirect sources – to $6 billion. They specifically authorized a 35% increase for 1988. It was, once again, agreed that consumer loans offered the best hope for developing the income and balance sheet dynamics that Empire needed over the long haul. Empire's recent profitable sales of consumer loans into the secondary market served to validate our Board's belief that this line of business was essential to Empire's survival.

Encouragingly, reasonable projections showed that by 1990 Empire's consumer loan portfolios would be adequately "seasoned" and, thus, able to begin demonstrating more industry-typical expense levels, reserve requirements... and profit. (Empire's confidence in this kind of lending was ultimately validated in 1989 and 1990 when it was able to sell, as per regulatory "encouragement," substantial portions of its consumer loan portfolio – *at a profit* – despite adverse market conditions.)

In the interim, however, doubts were blooming among regulators concerning Empire's staying power for this line of business. They preferred to focus on *their* beliefs that portfolio growth meant new upfront expenses, expanded loan loss reserves, and more risk despite the fact that all of these were natural corollaries to consumer lending. They were not willing to accept the fact that such loan growth was the only reasonable avenue by which Empire could achieve enhanced profitability in the near-term future.

Compounding our problems at this time was the fact that investment analysts were beginning to question the durability of the government's pledges to stand by the capital forbearances it had granted to Empire. These pledges were necessary to facilitate continued growth. If a traumatized government was to renege on these important commitments, Empire would fall significantly below required capital levels and its consumer loan initiative would be brought to a screeching halt at the very time that its portfolios were becoming seasoned and profitable.

Given these circumstances, Empire's management team began to consider other possible options for enhancing profitability in the short-run. The sale of parts of our branch network was considered early on. Depending on the market geography involved, some revenue could be created by the sale of selected branches – and their deposits – to other thrifts and commercial banks. Four percent to six percent premiums on "sold deposits" had become commonplace in the industry.

But Empire faced two obstacles in this regard. First, the bank had to be liquid enough to transfer, to an acquirer, cash in an amount that was equal to the depositor liabilities of the branch being purchased. With the deposit outflows we were experiencing, such liquidity was extremely expensive to realize.

The second and most important problem was goodwill (again!). Prevailing accounting practice called for the value basis of a branch to be increased upon sale by the amount of goodwill that was ascribed to it at the time Empire attained the benefits associated with it (i.e. at the time of its related merger). Accordingly, a significant amount of goodwill would have to be written off immediately by Empire if some of its branches were sold. In almost every case, the negative impact of such write-offs would exceed, by millions of dollars, the profit and the cost savings realized on the transaction. In effect, we were "damned if we didn't; and even more damned if we did."

Fortunately, we were eventually able to identify several constellations of branches that could be sold within our goodwill constraints, and sales were promptly effected.

At mid-year, we also decided – after considerable regulatory prompting – to explore the sale of the indirect auto loan portion of our consumer loan business. While this had been a difficult area to manage, it was profitable and would be much more so once the portfolio had been fully "seasoned" and the dealer origination network pruned on the basis of experience. But, notwithstanding all this positive potential, we reluctantly decided, at the strong urging of our regulatory wardens, to eschew growth in both indirect auto lending and credit card lending, and to seek a sale of existing portfolios.

## The Southwest Plan

The most aggressive response by the federal government to the thrift crisis in 1988 was its Southwest Plan which facilitated generously-subsidized mergers and acquisitions of thrifts. The Plan, while helpful to some institutions, proved very costly to shops like Empire of America. As a consequence of the Southwest Plan, our bank's interest margin was squeezed by frantic – often federally-subsidized – competition for deposits from the thrifts that the feds were trying to resuscitate. The benefits of forbearances and intangible goodwill we received at the time of our mergers were now beginning to pale in comparison to the huge slugs of hard currency that the government was literally *giving* to investors in the thrifts that were being" sold" under the auspices of the Plan. Many of the aided institutions were, in our opinion, far less worthy of such assistance than was Empire.

We concluded, therefore, "If you can't beat 'em... join 'em." Accordingly, we began to prepare an application to participate in the Southwest Plan.

Our Directors and management team reckoned that the deleterious economic circumstances in the southwest were not really different from the difficulties we faced in Buffalo and Detroit. If tax dollars from the northeast were being used to subsidize initiatives in the southwest, wasn't it fair to expect that a similarly afflicted institution in the north would be afforded some of these benefits also?

It should be noted that Empire had made a similar request – which was not directly related to the <u>Southwest Plan</u> – to the Federal Home Loan Bank of Dallas early in 1988. According to that proposal, Empire would provide some valuable, low-cost, failed-thrift workout services to the FSLIC in return for some recompense for Empire. We proposed to facilitate a limited number of mergers which would give Empire greater presence – and economies of scale – in its existing markets. Under this arrangement, the bank would share with the FSLIC, on a 50-50 basis, any earnings from tax advantages that were realized as a consequence the mergers in which it participated. Most importantly, we requested that Empire receive some additional forbearances.

This seemed to be a reasonable avenue to pursue. After all, we concluded, "we're in this thing together."

Much to our dismay, we quickly learned that the government was not interested in an initiative that entailed work, patience, and a modicum of risk. It would rather spend its newfound cash to quickly *buy* its way out of the thrift industry's problems and, thereby, minimize its reputational jeopardy.

The government's dismissal of our earlier proposal did not, however, deter the Empire team from submitting a subsequent application for formal inclusion in the <u>Southwest Plan</u>.

We submitted our formal request for participation in the Plan on early 1988... and heard nothing in response.

Time passed.

More time passed.

Still nothing.

Since time was of the essence, we requested a face-to-face meeting with top federal regulators. An appointment was arranged for me to meet with senior officials of the FHLBB in Washington. The conference was chaired by Roger F. Martin one of the three Members of the Federal Home Loan Bank Board and the person spearheading the Southwest Plan for the Bush Administration. You simply couldn't go any higher.

On the appointed day, I trekked to Washington and offered an analysis of our situation and asked for some guidelines that we might follow in order to be considered for inclusion in the Southwest Plan or something similar to it. Alas, after several hours of discussion – and no small measure of pleading – I was shocked by the rejoinder I received.

I was given by the Board Member a single-page, Xeroxed copy of some sentence fragments that he referred to as "guidelines" that would be used by the regulatory establishment in evaluating an institution's worthiness for participation in the federal government's resolution efforts.

I knew we were in trouble when I read the "guidelines" which are reproduced on the facing page as **Exhibit 1**. They are displayed in the same disjointed, spelling-deficient, ungrammatical form in which they were imparted to me.

As you can see, these "guidelines" called for management "compentence" (sic) to be displayed within a thrift before it could be considered for assistance.

Obviously, we were not dealing with a well-oiled machine and this experience suggested that whatever cooperation we received would probably be inadequate to Empire's complex needs even if we provided the regulators with the "warrents" (sic) they greedily sought.

Needless to say, such a slapdash approach by the government to a critical regulatory and policy issue did not inspire confidence within the Empire delegation. It was apparent that the agency's list of particulars was merely a last minute, token effort on the part of the FHLBB to temporary mollify the visiting Empire contingent

Nevertheless, we resolved to continue to press for a formal response to our initial application. Despite the dismay occasioned by our meeting, we returned to Buffalo more determined than ever to get the "powers that be" to, *at least,* sustain the strategy that was shaped by the agreements that they had already forged with Empire.

**Exhibit 1**

## <u>WHAT WE SHOULD LOOK FOR</u>

Management

 Honesty/integrity

 Compentence

Reduce Duplication

Reduction in operating expenses

That we do not take a small problem and make it a major catastrophe

No cash, or cash over time

The net worth target after 3 years of X%

what does a corporation look like immediately after, and 3 years later

FSLIC to share in "the action" – warrents, stock, etc.


TEXAS PACKAGE
Focus on capital, management and contraction.
Package of regulatory and supervisory cases and MCPs

Ultimately, our application for participation in the Southwest Plan went nowhere. Despite our considerable presence in the southwestern portion of the nation, we were not granted participation.

To say the least, were disheartened by the outcome of our meeting in Washington and the follow-up response we received. For the first time, I began to critically reassess my conviction that the government would not abandon the allegiance it had contractually proclaimed to Empire in the early '80s.

At this point, Empire's Board of Directors made one of the most difficult decisions it had ever deliberated. It authorized its management team to engage Morgan Stanley, a leading Wall Street investment bank, to solicit additional capital for Empire in the private money market. A realistic deal package and a term sheet were prepared. They included numerous options, including the sale of all or part of Empire.

Our goals in this effort to raise additional capital were to provide a margin of current protection and future upside potential for our shareholders; continue the heritage of a venerable institution; ensure that the Herculean efforts of our team would ultimately accomplish the workout it envisioned; and mollify the agitation of our regulators. This was an emotional as well as a business issue and required quite a bit of soul-searching on the part of our Directors.

Morgan Stanley subsequently conducted an exhaustive canvass of potential capital providers but, after considerable effort, it concluded that a complete or segmented sale of Empire's operations was not feasible. The generous deals that the government was then making with potential acquirers of troubled thrifts offered returns that greatly exceeded that which we could demonstrate to investors. The government, in fact, had become our principal competitor in the capital market, offering investors the kind of advantages we could never muster. Empire's dependence on capital forbearances was perceived as a worrisome negative by qualified investors who were concerned about our vulnerability should the regulatory establishment attempt to forcibly renegotiate or nullify its previous contractual arrangements with the bank (which, in the long run, proved to be a valid concern).

In sum, potential investors perceived other federally-assisted investment opportunities that were currently being offered through the FHLBB's Southwest Plan to be more attractive than the unassisted investment opportunity that was presented by Empire of America. Once again, the deteriorating image of the thrift industry overall was a major contaminant of our efforts to lure private investment.

Prospective investors were discouraged by another troubling obstacle, i.e. the recent proposal by the Federal Home Loan Bank Board to levy even more stringent risk-based capital regulations on thrifts. This proposal, if enacted, would force *all* thrifts – including Empire – to meet new, extremely rigorous minimum capital requirements... another alarming "change in the rules."

In order to comply with such requirements, Empire would have to reconfigure its asset portfolio to include lower-yielding asset components. I presented testimony at an FHLBB public hearing in opposition to the application of this proposal since it would negatively impact our goodwill and capital forbearances. My pleadings had little effect. As expected, in December 1988 the net worth requirement for thrift institutions was raised to seven percent.

To offset these and other negative events that were exploding onto the scene with regularity – and to re-invigorate its Phoenix Plan – Empire began to implement a host of newly-formulated operational improvements with the goal of having them all effective by mid-1989.

Another aggressive expense containment program was launched and quickly produced significant results. By December 31, 1988, there were 300 fewer Empire team members, and our "general and administrative expense" ratio declined by more than 8%.

Empire's subsidiaries were analyzed with respect to their current income contributions and the gains they might generate it sold. Ultimately, Levy, King, and White Companies, Inc. and Empire Gallery of Homes, Inc. were scheduled for divestiture in 1989. Sale negotiations were also initiated with respect to Smartline Corporation and Sherwin-Greenberg Productions, Inc. (All were sold by the end of 1989.)

Our indirect auto lending program was scaled back as we systematically pruned our loan production offices and dealer network.

Despite all of our efforts, the net benefits realized were constrained by persistent offsetting factors including: the continued run-up in interest rates; the early-stage costs associated with building a consumer loan portfolio; abrupt portfolio restructurings occasioned by new regulation; competition from thrifts that were advantaged by the Southwest Plan; and depositor disaffection that was induced by waves of negative publicity. Empire's yield spread (i.e. net interest margin) dropped to 2.72% from 3.11 % in 1986.

As a consequence, Empire incurred a loss of over $57 million in 1988. Even a gain of $35 million on the sale of loans and investments could not push Empire into a profit.

Amidst these developments it was hard to find justification for optimism with respect to future earnings. Empire's shareholders obviously shared this feeling, and the bank's anemic stock price reflected their concern.

We were, however, able to take a small degree of comfort in the fact that, despite all of these difficulties, Empire of America managed to eke out respectable financial performance for the period 1983 through 1988, i.e. a cumulative net loss of only $17.4 million. This was a significant improvement over the projections formulated – and acknowledged and accepted by the regulators – at the time of our mergers in 1982.

But historical performance can carry an institution only so far. The economic and regulatory climate at the close of 1988 threatened the kind of work-out in which innovation and moderate risk-taking were essential.

An atmosphere of panic surged within the thrift industry and it was greatly influencing the federal regulatory establishment, Congress, and the Executive Branch. These fears were stoked by the press which, all too often, had faulty facts and a predisposition to the kind of bad news that attracted readers and viewers. The constant stream of bad news and allegations of misdeeds and incompetence in the thrift industry fed the anger of taxpaying citizens who rightfully feared, at the very least, an enormous cleanup bill. Of course, there was no shortage of critics who had been historically predisposed to abhor "greedy bankers."

Meanwhile, the government continued to make it difficult for banks like Empire. By the late '80s, the regulatory establishment seemed to have concluded that it was time to "bury" the results of some of the early initiatives it had undertaken in the name of resolving the thrift crisis. So, in addition to its less-than-ingenious Southwest Plan, the regulators devised an aggressive initiative to simply liquidate many, large, struggling thrifts whose prospects were in doubt. The sprawling regulatory "rug" would soon have many more victims swept under it.

Under this new "son of Southwest Plan" program – part of a George H.W. Bush Administration initiative – the Federal Home Loan Bank Board would use now-abundant federal cash to attract "big name" outside investors to the savings industry. A number of prominent national corporations stepped forward to take advantage of this "fire sale." These potential acquirers were motivated to act quickly since crucial tax advantages for thrift buyers were scheduled to expire on January 1, 1989. Consequently, many thrift acquisitions were completed in a very short span of time.

Most of the "sales" that were conducted under this plan involved generous – arguably "sweetheart" – deals with private investors. The favorable terms of these deals caused the relative institutional value of Empire to private investors to decline precipitously. It appeared that the FHLBB's efforts were designed to rapidly rid it of involvements and obligations that could be criticized by the news media and Congress. At this point, financial propriety gave way to political pressure and a fear of reproach.

Many of the deals that were being consummated in accordance with this new initiative provided immoderate tax credits which afforded the acquiring enterprises opportunities to use any follow-on losses on their thrift investments as offsets to tax liabilities incurred in their other, non-banking pursuits. Amazingly, many of the acquirers of these newly-constituted thrifts were granted *guarantees* that the government would offset *any* losses that they might incur. The press reported that one investment group turned a quick 100% return on its acquisition of The Bowery Savings Bank in New York City.

A Fort Worth, Texas billionaire formed a group that bought American Savings and Loan of Stockton, California, a $16 billion thrift which was the nation's largest at the time. The group reportedly provided $100 million cash and $250 million in debt and received about $2.7 billion in federal assistance. It proved to be a very sweet deal since the thrift earned $214.2 million the next year (and $179 million in the first nine months of the following year).

A takeover artist from New York acquired five Texas institutions with assets of $12.2 billion and a negative net worth of $800 million. It was reported that his investment group put up $315 million. In return, the government gave his group an $866 million promissory note to wipe out the negative net worth of the acquired institution. The FSLIC further agreed to pay the group an annual subsidy that guaranteed it a profit on all assets covered in the deal *plus* a guarantee against loss if the assets were sold. Government payments on the note were to be tax-free to the investors, and the subsidy payments would also be tax-free. Moreover, the investors could use paper losses generated by the deals to reduce or wipe out tax liabilities generated by other, profitable operations.

Colorado's Silverado Savings – a failed thrift in which one of Vice President Bush's sons was involved – was merged with another thrift, and renamed Columbia Savings. It, in turn, was sold to First Nationwide Bank of San Francisco. The government subsidies provided to First Nationwide were projected to cost the federal government over $500 million and included a "yield maintenance agreement" which guaranteed that all of the money-losing assets taken over by the new thrift's operators would be kept profitable (at a declining rate) for ten years through direct federal subsidies. A second safety net required that the feds compensate First Nationwide for any loss in the capital value of its bad assets as those holdings were sold off over the next decade. Those subsidies, combined with special tax advantages, allowed Columbia to generate a $48 million profit in 1990 – a roughly 50%, one-year return on First Nationwide's $96 million investment.

A number of House and Senate Banking Committees subsequently looked into the efficacy of these deals but it was clear that, by then, "the horse was out of the barn," and there was little that could be done to correct the situation in the time available.

(In early 1991, the Resolution Trust Corp. announced that it would seek to renegotiate the American Savings transaction as well as ninety-six other deals made as part of the 220 "rescues" under the Southwest Plan in the 1980s. No report of the RTC's success can be found.)

These sweetheart deals severely impacted Empire's plans for working its way out of its difficulties. Asset growth was the primary key to the bank's workout. After its recent public offering – and before the introduction of the Southwest Plan – Empire was well situated to facilitate such growth. But skyrocketing interest rates – fueled to a great degree by competition from subsidized, floundering thrifts – were severely impinging upon the profitability of the growth that Empire was striving to achieve… and sustained profitability was essential to the expansion of the bank's capital base. If these abnormal margin-pinching circumstances continued, the growth of Empire's capital base would decelerate and, perhaps, even stall significantly. This was because the profit generated through the favorable intermediation of new deposits and new loans would be insufficient to make adequate contributions to the bank's capital accumulation. As a consequence, Empire would require additional capital inputs from new shareholders or private investors.

Up until the Southwest Plan was launched, such capital acquisition was feasible. We had been confident that that the bank's size, unique geographic spread, and product diversification would make it an attractive investment opportunity for individuals or institutions. In fact, it had been reasonable to speculate that the bank would soon become an alluring acquisition target for other financial enterprises or corporations that wished to have entry to the national financial services marketplace.

But the superior investment deals that were being offered to prospective thrift investors by the government's Southwest Plan – along with the continuing deterioration of the national economy – squelched the idea of any additional capital acquisition through supplementary, near-term stock offerings. The deals offered by the Federal Home Loan Bank Board to acquirers of failing S&Ls were so generous that the value of Empire to potential shareholders and investors declined sharply.

In its panic to quell the burgeoning S&L crisis, the Federal Home Loan Bank Board was, in effect, conducting a buyer-friendly "fire sale" in hopes that it could rapidly rid itself of any evidence of poor oversight on its part that might be criticized by the news media and Congress. As a consequence, Empire now looked "expensive" to potential investors.

The Southwest Plan's radical new paradigm for capital acquisition in the financial industry practically eliminated the possibility of Empire attracting additional capital funds from corporate acquirers or through additional public offerings.

While our regulators hadn't (yet) overtly changed the terms of the contracts we had originally signed with them in the early 1980s, they had changed the playing field. Their actions greatly altered the mechanism for capital flows, thus making fresh capital virtually inaccessible to Empire.

Indeed, the government's actions were beginning to suggest that it would eventually call into question the legally-binding (we thought) contracts that it had previously entered into with Empire.

In addition to dramatically decreasing Empire's institutional value, these deals detrimentally impacted Empire in another important way. The thrifts that were newly constituted under the Southwest Plan were, as a result, well-capitalized and their owners had guarantees of government offsets for any losses they might incur. As a consequence, these S&Ls became very aggressive deposit seekers, offering extremely high rates of interest. Their forays into the national marketplace constituted, along with inflation, one of the main reasons savings deposits were flowing out of traditional savings banks and savings and loan associations. This attempt by government to quickly resolve one set of problems created an even bigger and less survivable challenge for a thousand other disadvantaged thrifts, which represented 33% of the industry.

Meanwhile, the nation's savings and loan associations were rocked by ten months of deposit outflows caused by: negative publicity over the thrift industry "crisis;" a federal proposal – subsequently withdrawn – to make depositors pay for deposit insurance; intense competition from newly-acquired and recapitalized thrifts; and, higher interest rates being offered on short-term Treasury securities and money market funds. In 1988, the industry suffered a net deposit outflow of $8.6 billion. Empire shared in this hemorrhaging of deposits. As described earlier in this Chapter, over $500 million in deposit withdrawals occurred during the last five months of the year, putting a severe crimp in Empire's efforts to grow and return to profitability.

**The regulatory attitude**

It was evident to Empire's management team that the aggressive, growth-based, sometimes unorthodox turnaround plan of Empire – which constituted the only strategy that had a chance of working – was now in danger of being estopped by the actions and pronouncements of an increasingly risk-averse regulatory apparatus.

The regulators who were there at the beginning of the Empire venture now were being required to adhere to *new* policies, enforcement directives, and statutes that were evolving. Their jobs and careers depended upon their compliance with a *new* approach to "problem resolution" in the thrift industry. Also, the many novice regulators who had just come onto the scene had no sense of history relative to Empire, its origins, and the unique but essential regulatory accommodations it had been granted.

The emerging regulatory attitude was, to say the least, hard to accept. After all, our structure, turnaround strategies, goals, growth and risk policies, and operating tactics were all carefully examined by the regulatory establishment at the time we negotiated our supervisory acquisitions. Our long-term needs for accommodation had been explicitly articulated to our regulatory agencies and had been *contractually* accepted by them at the time we consummated our mergers. Empire's frequent progress reports and its formal responses concerning issues that arose by virtue of periodic government Examinations demonstrated our continuing adherence to the "rules" established by our earlier agreements with the government.

Throughout the years of our "joint venture" with the government, all of Empire's accounting treatments were in strict compliance with prevailing regulatory requirements. All of our accounting responsibilities as a public company were conducted in accordance with the Regulatory Accounting Principles and the Generally Accepted Accounting Principles of the time. There had been no deviations from our original agreements, save for those occasioned by government-mandates and efforts to comply with "suggestions" from our regulators.

Every recommendation or criticism advanced by regulators as a consequence of their periodic Examinations of Empire was promptly and thoroughly analyzed, and complete responses were forged by management and Empire's Board of Directors in order to insure compliance or, where a reasonable difference of opinion emerged, to seek appropriate resolution.

At no time were any directions by the regulators defied or ignored. None of the government's routine bank Examinations had levied harsh criticism of the bank's managers or Directors. There were no allegations of negligence, mismanagement, or carelessness. (Indeed, in a press interview following the seizure of Empire, a senior regulator opined that Empire was a "noble experiment that just didn't work out.")

To be sure, ours had been an aggressive strategy that depended upon some unorthodox, unusually-sophisticated operating tactics. But this strategy had been understood, accepted, consistently monitored, and clearly accepted – repeatedly – by the regulatory establishment... until the "doo doo" overwhelmed the "fan" and started to get "deep."

As a consequence, while the substance of our "deal" with the feds never changed; its appeal to the regulators *did*. The unimaginable prospect of the federal government reneging on its contractual commitments was gradually becoming less unimaginable.

Moreover, it was becoming increasingly clear that the fundamental rules of the game would soon be further distorted by comprehensive legislation that was winding its way through Congress. In anticipation of this legislation, our regulators began to call into question the heretofore sacrosanct policies and procedures that were essential to Empire's continued welfare. The regulators themselves had been relegated to the receiving end of scathing criticism from both Congress and the press; and it became "pass-it-along" time.

To their credit, the in-field regulators were trying to do the best they could to implement the dictates of their superiors. But they, too, were being caught up in the vortex of panic-induced "reformation" that was being fostered by members of Congress and top-level regulatory bureaucrats who had, for too long, neglected the *real* problem and avoided facing the music.

The regulatory establishment was becoming increasingly aware of the probable impacts of game-changing Congressional mandates that were in the making. Accordingly, in the interests of market order – as well as self-preservation – they were now contemplating policies and procedures that were in direct opposition to the contracts and understandings that Empire had honored for over seven years.

One-by-one, our survival initiatives had to be scaled down to inconsequence or scrapped altogether because of new regulatory decrees and "interpretations." Many of the programs that we had implemented to squeeze the last dollar of earnings from our available assets were now candidates for extermination. Extremely intricate in their design, they had taken great effort to put into place. Nevertheless, the regulatory establishment was now in a great rush to disassemble them, despite the fact that a great deal of unnecessary monetary loss would be occasioned as a consequence.

Needless to say, the Empire team deeply resented not being been given the time to salvage what it had already accomplished through unceasing sacrifice and hard work. After all, our shareholders and employees – who stood to lose their investments in Empire – were taxpayers, too. They deserved to have their monetary interests protected to the greatest extent possible. But the Congressional winds were blowing ill, and everyone was being pushed to trim the sails... and scuttle if necessary.

During the latter half of 1988, Congress began to assemble the specific legislation designed to "once and for all" resolve the thrift crisis. After all, no Member of that august body wanted to be tarred by an imbroglio that had been too long overlooked and too frequently manipulated. Public opinion was turning testy and 1989 was going to be an election year in which the chief of the former task force charged with addressing the metastasizing thrift crisis (i.e. Vice President Bush) was running for the top office in the land. (It didn't help that his son had been caught up in some nasty thrift issues in Colorado.)

Given the trend of current regulation, the attitude of the public, and the scandals that had emerged in the industry, it was clear that sweeping Congressional action would be forthcoming and that, if history were a guide, nothing that emerged would be beneficial to Empire.

To make matters worse, additional Machiavellian forces were at work, and they would greatly influence the ultimate fate of Empire. According to reports I received during this period, a number of commercial banks were putting enormous pressure on federal regulators and Members of Congress to "*do something* about Empire and Goldome" (the other major savings bank headquartered in Buffalo). To these commercial banks, Empire's persistent and still powerful presence in *their* marketplaces constituted both an irritant and an opportunity. If tackled "properly" this irritant could be extinguished through a governmentally-sponsored confiscation and subsequent "fire sale" of our customer base and assets – *to them* – at bargain prices. (I was informed by several sources that a considerable amount of lobbying, unfounded scandal mongering, and arm-twisting was employed in what eventually would be a successful effort to prompt legislators and regulators to disassemble both Empire and Goldome and convey their valuable pieces – at bargain prices and with taxpayer subsidization – to preying commercial banks.)

In light of the turbulence in the thrift industry in 1988, an October meeting between regulators and Empire's senior managers was convened in Buffalo. As a consequence of that gathering, Empire was directed to prepare *two* new strategic plans for 1989. One was to be constructed with strict adherence to FHLBB assumptions and projections, using the FHLBB plan

261

model as a guide for content. The other plan was to be used to direct the *actual* day-to-day operations of the bank in the "real world."

Once the plans were formulated and approved by Empire's Board of Directors, any differences in outcomes between the plans during their implementation in 1989 was to be reported to the bank's Directors *and* to the staff of the FHLBB in New York. It quickly became obvious that, despite the Herculean efforts of the Empire team over the past ten years, the government's "model" would be the one the regulators would use to guide the future of Empire.

This unusual, bifurcated planning process was a game-changer. During the six years since its initial mergers, Empire had been able to enjoy a measure of plan-making independence by virtue of the "iron-clad" contract it had forged with the federal government. The operating latitudes and forbearances contained in that agreement had provided assurance that Empire would have adequate opportunity to accomplish the turnaround via its Phoenix Plan.

Now, as a consequence of growing discomfiture in "high places," a new, far less suitable "plan" would take precedence.

**A control mindset**

The public policy-makers' strategy for "resolving" the Empire situation was becoming clear. According to their "reasoning," if the government *controlled* Empire, it could control the risks to which the government was exposed. It made no difference to politicians that the risks we bore were natural business risks which the federal government had previously agreed to accept. It made no difference that the nation's interests had been well-served by capable and dedicated professionals at Empire who were still working valiantly to minimize the government's exposure to risk.

As proven by subsequent events, regulators wanted a type of control that would be sufficient to *force* a downsizing of Empire and, therefore, – according to their convoluted reasoning – a downsizing of the government's perceived exposure to risk. What they apparently failed to realize was that the psychic comfort they gained by virtue of shrinking Empire would produce immense follow-on costs when the bank's assets were later precipitously dumped into a frenzied "buyers' market." Piranha-like buyers were already swimming gleefully in a flood of assets being disgorged by other hopelessly-afflicted thrifts. Nevertheless, regulators continued to suggest that the bank's growth – especially in its consumer loan portfolio – created unreasonable risk.

It had long been our opinion that a dramatic downsizing of our consumer loan portfolio was neither necessary nor wise. In fact, the credit quality of that portfolio – even taking into account early-on delinquency rates – was *above* average for the consumer credit industry as a whole. Further, the loans we had previously packaged and sold provided a unique fillip to our earnings. Empire had, in fact, built one of the largest – and potentially most profitable – consumer loan generating capacities in the nation.

Unfortunately, consumer lending was an industry sector with which the regulators of savings institutions had little familiarity. As a consequence, despite their inability to find egregious consumer lending transgressions on the part of the bank, they blithely deemed "consumer credit" the "Achilles heel" of Empire.

That's not to say that the bank did not suffer some lending problems at the time. An extremely thorough bank Examination in 1988 highlighted various concerns on the part of regulators. However, all of those criticisms, save one, were addressed by bank management in its formal reply to the Examination.

The one exception was Empire's cost of deposits and the squeeze it created on its net interest margin. While consumer credit issues were the only criticisms that were eventually cited publicly by the regulators, it was clear from the Examination report that the bank's inability to widen its net interest margin – the difference between its cost of funds and its earnings on investments and loans – was also of major concern to our regulators.

They worried that, if parts of the bank's credit portfolios soured, there would be insufficient income to support our cost of deposits and, as a consequence, losses would ensue. To their great alarm, that meant that the Federal Savings and Loan Insurance Corporation would be left holding the bag. True enough. But, with the effort that the Empire team was expending, it could be argued that, even under the direst scenario, the regulators efforts to avoid the "bag" would constitute an even more costly proposition. Staying the course was, indeed the most prudent path of action because time was on our side; interest rates would soon decline.

But, it was becoming increasingly obvious that the government wanted to get the "target" that Empire constituted off of its back at any cost... *posthaste.*

It should be noted that implicit in the concerns voiced in our 1988 Examination was another worry. The government had begun to doubt the ability of a small staff in Buffalo, New York to manage a huge, nationwide, diversified, highly-complex enterprise like Empire. Our principal regulators, based in New York City and Washington, appeared to view the Empire team as unsophisticated and inexperienced in "big city" operations. (To my knowledge, there was only one Harvard graduate in our officer ranks and many who didn't boast a college education. In Empire's culture, a gilt-edged education and an ability to "walk the walk of Wall Street" were not as important as real-world experience and on-the-job performance.)

Apparently, regulators who lived and worked in more rarefied environs had doubts about our ability to drive the horses we had harnessed. This was ironic in light of the fact that regulatory agencies had routinely sent staff examiners to Buffalo to learn about new industry processes and products from Empire's team members. Indeed, the beneficiaries of those "lessons" frequently praised the understanding and abilities that individual Empire officers possessed with respect to the complex areas of practice that were emerging in the banking industry.

But, at the end of the day, our regulators just could not seem to accept the fact that Empire's turnaround success to date could be sustained in a troubled economic environment without an occurrence of expensive "flubs" that would negatively impact the federal treasury and a lot of bureaucrats' resumes. There was little appreciation for the fact that, while the thrift crisis had plagued America for years, Empire had survived and was reliably executing a reasonable plan for success. In the final analysis, this accomplishment wasn't enough to impress the legislators and regulators who were increasingly obsessed with *possible* losses and *possible* reputational damage.

Much to the relief of our regulatory establishment, Congress was putting the final touches on what would soon become the Financial Institutions Reform, Recovery, and. Enforcement Act, better known as FIRREA. It was to be "THE ANSWER" as far as regulators were concerned. It would enable them to virtually eliminate the risk of loss in the *future* by incurring an arguably larger loss in the *present*. It seemed illogical; but in the world of regulatory and legislative oversight, it was "safe."

Not surprisingly, it was the declared intention of Congress that the *primary* purpose of FIRREA was to ensure that thrifts keep at least 70% of their assets in housing-related investments. Once again, economic reality was being ignored in favor of the always elusive Holy Grail of home ownership.

As indicated previously in this book, ubiquitous homeownership was a worthy national goal. However, given structural changes in the American economy over many decades, the thrift industry could no longer survive if it attempted to function as *the* primary facilitator of that ownership goal. Thrifts had been consistently denied – by Congress and regulatory establishment – the new powers and authorizations that they desperately needed in order to generate the earnings necessary to support contemporary, socially-desirable home lending practices.

Like it or not, savings institutions had, in the face of an increasingly competitive environment, become market-driven businesses that could not survive manipulation by public policy that was contrary to prevailing economic realities. (Even the *public* institutions that were created by government to facilitate homeownership had proven inadequate to the task.) A torrent of laws and regulations could not twist savings institutions into willing and productive of commentators of a government dream without those institutions being strangled in the process. It was becoming obvious that the framers of FIRREA did not take this logic into account.

Reports we received from Capitol Hill suggested that the folks in Congress were simply lunging at a "quick fix" for a chronic problem. To their way of impatient thinking, a *risk* of loss was now more onerous than a *certainty* of loss.

Over the years, in meetings and correspondence with regulators, I often referred to them as "partners." I tried to keep fresh in their minds the responsibility *they* had assumed as they collaborated with us on the implementation of the Phoenix Plan.

This all became "ancient history," however, when troubles in the industry intensified and personal "legacy" fears among legislators and regulators deepened. Increasingly, our "partners" in Washington began to engage in "blame shifting" as they attempted to engineer a quick way out of the mess they helped create.

As Congressional legislation advanced, regulators intensified their aggressive scrutinization and criticism of Empire's interest margin; the size of its consumer credit portfolios; and its geographic scope and diversity. *Any* mistakes or shortcomings on our part were being tagged as evidence that could warrant a quick dissolution of our "partnership" with the government.

To the relief of the regulatory establishment, Congress was moving quickly to enact radical legislation which would give it a convenient "rug" under which Empire's erstwhile "partners" could sweep their partnership responsibilities... *and Empire.*

*Chapter eleven*

## STOLEN PROMISE

### A bad start

Nineteen-eighty-nine did not get off to a good start. Interest rates continued to move up beyond the bank's projections, thus pushing it off the trajectory set by its "dual business plans." This was nothing new. During the late 1980s, the persistent fluctuations in interest rates repeatedly threw the bank off-blueprint. But now these fluctuations were taking on increasing importance. Regulators were vigilantly watching Empire's deposit interest costs and net interest margin as indicators of overall bank health and of management's ability to plan and execute properly. If "reality" and "plan" were not congruent as they evolved, Empire's credibility suffered with the people who counted.

At this point, even the trade group representing the thrift industry began to discriminate in favor of what it termed its "good" thrift members. The U. S. League of Savings Institutions, which had for many decades failed to stem the stream of bad legislation and regulation affecting its members, abandoned its efforts to obtain forbearances for marginally-healthy institutions, leaving such efforts to regional trade groups.

Needless to say, Empire was now facing a huge challenge in a volatile economy. If interest rates edged up just one-half of one percent from where they were projected, the bank's annual interest costs increased to the tune of more than $50 million dollars. A one percent shift produced an earnings hit of $100 million!

Despite the fact that we had no control over interest rates – much less the ability to forecast them with precision twelve months out – our regulators became more and more agitated over what they perceived as "their exposure" and our inability to

267

forecast more accurately. The fact that other reputable forecasters were erring similarly didn't assuage the regulators anxiety. As 1989 began to unfold, this became a *big* factor in the treatment afforded Empire by the regulatory establishment.

On the national scene, with matters still out of control and showing every sign of becoming even more so, Congressional leaders finally cobbled together the <u>Financial Institutions Reform Recovery and Enforcement Act</u> (FIRREA) for formal consideration by the House of Representatives and the Senate.

Its major provisions constituted an enormous threat to the thrift industry. It was becoming apparent that, absent provisions for exemption, the enactment of this bill would annihilate any chance for Empire's survival.

The bill's major provisions:

- Gave the government $50 billion of new borrowing authority to "resolve" troubled thrifts, with most financed from general revenues and the rest from the industry.
- Abolished the Federal Home Loan Bank Board and the FSLIC, our principal regulators, and shifted oversight and enforcement authority to the newly-established Office of Thrift Supervision (OTS) within the U.S. Treasury Department.
- Transferred Responsibility for deposit insurance in the savings industry from the FSLIC to the newly-created Savings Association Insurance Fund (SAIF) which was to be administered by the Federal Deposit Insurance Corporation (FDIC).
- Imposed higher net worth requirements and more stringent regulation by the OTS and the FDIC.
- Created the Federal Housing Finance Board (FHFB) as an independent agency to take the place of the FHLBB as overseer of the twelve Federal Home Loan Banks (also called district banks).

- Established the Resolution Trust Corporation (RTC) to dispose of failed thrift institutions taken over by regulators after January 1, 1989.
- Allocated funds to the Justice Department to help finance prosecution of the wrongdoers within the industry.

Of course, as I had long anticipated, the bill also *allowed bank holding companies to acquire thrifts*. No surprise there!

These proposed changes were of great consequence to Empire since they would allow – in some instances, require – federal regulators to take actions that would negate the assistance contracts they had previously entered into with savings institutions – like Empire – that had acquired failing thrifts.

FIRREA would be particularly devastating to Empire since it prevented regulatory authorities from recognizing forbearances and goodwill in calculating capital ratios after December 8, 1989.

The Act did allow for "open bank assistance" but it left such action solely to the discretion of the regulators. They were given an "option" – not a "mandate" – to help thrifts like Empire.

In fact, FIRREA even precluded the grandfathering of supervisory goodwill. Absent this legislation, Empire's regulatory net worth (RAP) would stand safely above the established regulatory minimum. But this Act would, overnight, wipe out all of the positive regulatory capital Empire could heretofore claim. Empire's destiny was becoming obvious. The Big E would, for all intents and purposes, become hopelessly insolvent on the day FIERRA became effective. This circumstance, of course, made an imminent seizure and liquidation of the bank highly probable.

Once this bill was passed, the regulatory establishment would be focused on funding "burials" of thrifts as quickly as possible.

In early February, in an effort to "stay above the grass," I visited the White House to meet with Richard C. Breeden, the Assistant to the President for Issues Analysis, and one of President George H. W. Bush's most senior economic advisors. He was a major contributor during the drafting of FIRREA.

I asked for the meeting in order to request that the Bush Administration petition Congress to amend FIRREA in a way that would *require* regulators to grant "open bank" assistance to thrifts that had previously collaborated in good faith with the government. I insisted that a bill without such a provision would be grossly unfair to Empire. After some discussion, his concluding response was, "Tell me, Mr. Willax, where is it written that things have to be fair?"

Needless to say, his dismaying interpretation of the federal government's guiding principles – as he "articulated" them just a short distance from America's seat of all power – put Empire's management team on high alert.

At this disheartening time, I called to mind once again the observation of President Ronald Reagan: "If you go to bed with government, you can expect more than a good night's sleep!" The Empire team immediately began to formulate a new proposal which would allow, we believed, the melding of government and

Empire interests in a way that would reduce the cash drain on the public and facilitate the continuation of Empire's workout. On February 27, 1989, Empire of America filed an <u>Application for the Substitution of Regulatory Assistance</u> (Application) with the FSLIC. Our intent was to get ahead of an emerging catastrophe.

We believed that the strategy outlined in this Application would enable Empire to comply with the emerging regulatory standards for the thrift industry. Importantly, it would also equitably accommodate the interests of Empire's shareholders. It was the first application of its kind ever filed.

In the application, we asked the FSLIC to provide Empire with approximately $905 million of "cash or equivalents" in partial exchange for the goodwill asset that the bank acquired and the regulatory forbearances it had received from the FSLIC in connection with its twelve supervisory acquisitions completed since 1981. The "equivalents" that we were willing to accept as an asset "substitution" included non-cash assets like notes and mortgages that the FSLIC had accumulated through its string of S&L closings.

We felt strongly that such a request was warranted given the fact that Congress was preparing to substantially change the terms of the original contractual agreements relating to our acquisitions. Without such an accommodation, the enactment of FIRREA would constitute a unilateral abrogation of our contracts. In our opinion, it constituted an illegal act. Our proposal was designed as a survival strategy for Empire and as a means for the government to avoid the lawsuits that we believed would emerge from many quarters as a consequence of its actions under FIRREA.

Indeed, we were hopeful that the FDIC would act favorably upon our application because the proposed language of FIRREA specifically granted the FDIC the leeway to provide "open assistance" to thrifts despite the other provisions of the Act. Our proposal was designed to qualify under the principle of open assistance.

Importantly, Drexel Burnham, a national investment banking firm, had given Empire strong assurances that if the FSLIC agreed to the kind of substitution we were requesting, it would be able to garner approximately $675 million of private capital for Empire of America. A private infusion of capital of this magnitude would equate to seventy-five cents for every dollar of substituted assistance provided by the FSLIC in response to this Application. This level of private sector investment was greater than that provided by investors in any prior, federally-assisted supervisory acquisition.

In return for the requested "substitution," we proposed – subject to shareholder approval – that the FSLIC would receive entitlement to an equity position in Empire of America which could be converted to cash over time. Further, if Empire were to be subsequently acquired by private investors, the government's stake would be cashed-out immediately.

The combination of substituted assistance and a private capital infusion would bring Empire of America into immediate compliance with the new minimum regulatory capital requirements – without the need to rely on capital forbearances. Furthermore, the investment banking firm's financial projections indicated that a recapitalized Empire of America would immediately begin to produce sustainable operating earnings.

According to this substitution plan, Empire would sell the non-cash assets acquired from the FSLIC to a newly-formed, self-liquidating trust. The trust, financed by the sale of participations or units to institutional investors, would then liquidate the real estate over a three-to-ten year period. This liquidating trust would be managed by an Empire subsidiary set up specifically to administer such transactions.

Once Empire received cash from the sale of real estate to the trust, it would use that cash and part of the $675 million third-party capital injection to offset the negative capital impacts of a write-off the $926 million of remaining goodwill. The bank would also discontinue its reliance on forbearances.

While goodwill and forbearances provided by the government were originally intended to be quasi-assets of substance, they had, in fact, become "Confederate currency" in just seven years. Our proposal would convert those soon-to-be worthless assets to the status of valuable real property.

The improvement in Empire's balance sheet occasioned by our proposed "substitution," coupled with an infusion of $675 million in fresh private capital, would restore health to Empire and enable it to quickly and effectively complete its Phoenix Plan work-out. As a consequence, Empire's regulatory net worth would equal more than 6%, putting the bank in compliance with any of the higher mandatory capital requirements that were then under discussion.

We believed that "substitution" was an equitable arrangement since, as the next Chapter demonstrates, our contracts with the government had already saved taxpayers approximately $1.5 billion. Therefore, the FDIC would enjoy net savings of approximately $695 million, even after it provided the asset substitution we proposed. In addition, the government's perceived risk of future financial liability with respect to Empire would be virtually eliminated.

*Repeat*: Even after providing the $905 million infusion of non-cash capital that Empire was requesting, the government was almost $700 million ahead of the game by virtue of Empire's participation in previous S&L workouts!

This proposed transaction would constitute the largest single investment of outside capital in any FSLIC assisted recapitalization to date.

Our message to the Washington elite was: "If the federal government is going to change the rules, it should at least allow some relief for our shareholders who bought stock under different expectations." The bank's approach to capital acquisition in 1986 would have been quite different if the government had made apparent – or even intimated – a belief that it could eventually renege. By executing official documents and contracts, and by providing subsequent affirmations, the authorized representatives of the federal government had made it clear to Empire and to the professionals who served it that, from the time of its S&L acquisitions, the bank had an ironclad contract with the government. Based on this, Empire had entered into compacts with its investors.

We pointed out that this proposal for "substitution" had been approved by our Board of Directors, and that we fully anticipated that our shareholders would approve it also. (All negotiations of this type by a public company were subject to final approval by its shareholders. Since the primary objective of our Board in preparing this Application to the FDIC was to ensure that the value of our shareholders' interests in the bank was neither unduly nor unfairly diminished, we felt confident that, upon presenting a government-accepted proposal such as this to our shareholders, their approval would be forthcoming.)

This innovative and cost-effective workout proposal was well received within the thrift industry and by the media. Many felt that our proposal, if applied to Empire and other similarly afflicted thrifts, would preclude a further drain on the financially strapped insurance fund and help the FSLIC get rid of some of the billions of dollars of real estate received in the takeover of insolvent savings institutions.

The National Thrift News supported the concept as a blueprint for cost-effective workouts that could reduce the burden on taxpayers resulting from of an industry-wide bailout. The newspaper noted that new private capital investment in struggling thrifts, like that proposed by Drexel Burnham, had become, up until the Empire deal, virtually impossible to obtain given the popularity of the FSLIC's Southwest Plan.

Unfortunately, less than one month after our Application was presented in Washington, the Federal Home Loan Bank Board indicated that it did not plan to act on it. The Bank Board chairman, M. Danny Wall, did, however, tell reporters, "It is helpful for Congress to see that goodwill is not some ethereal thing on the balance sheet of thrift institutions."

The FSLIC decision was perplexing since FIRREA clearly empowered the government to provide "open assistance." Such aid would have enabled Empire to offset the deleterious impacts of the Act and to continue functioning.

However, we soon learned that the FDIC's internally-formulated guidelines called for a "least cost" approach when aiding a thrift institution. Unfortunately, the FDIC signaled that it believed that a *liquidation* of Empire was its least costly option. It reached that conclusion despite the fact that our Application clearly demonstrated that the FDIC would, in actuality, incur *less* cost by helping Empire than it would incur by liquidating it. (Post-liquidation, our assertion was proven to be true; the facts supporting our claim are offered in Chapter Twelve of this book.)

In essence, our plea got lost in the turmoil of the time. Economic conditions were still adverse, more thrifts were being added to the "death watch," and a new President and Administration wanted to demonstrate rapid, uncomplicated progress. In contrast, our proposal required some thought and deliberation, not to mention a tolerance for something new and different. None of these conditions were palatable to a reeling regulatory establishment and a fledgling Administration.

The Financial Institutions Reform Recovery and Enforcement Act was introduced in the House of Representatives on March 6th. It passed there on June 15th and was approved by voice vote in the Senate five days later. The bill was agreed to jointly by the House and Senate in early August and was signed into law by President George H.W. Bush on August 9, 1989.

## Sturm and drang

The remainder of 1989 would consist of a string of stressful days for every Empire team member. The passage of FIRREA introduced a cloud of economic uncertainty; an inability to communicate meaningfully with regulators; funereal press coverage; and, even more undulation in financial markets. For the Big E, strategy was difficult to formulate; plans were of necessity in constant flux; and constructive initiatives, no matter how quickly and prudently they were conceived, often became obsolete before they were stillborn.

It was difficult to communicate our status and prospects to important constituencies because circumstances changed rapidly. Frustration and a stressful urge to "get it fixed" dogged the Big E team. However, we still believed that we could plot a course to a workable solution... if only we could nail down reality for 24 hours. But an unending stream of interruptions foiled almost every sincere intention. A good example is provided by a situation that emerged on the afternoon of the bank's annual shareholders' meeting.

Upon returning to their offices after that gathering, the members of our senior management team were informed by a trusted "source" in the Washington bureaucracy that a regulatory enforcement group was on its way to Buffalo to take possession of Empire. We had just done our best to explain the bank's future to its shareholders, and now we were faced with an uncertainty that could put the lie to what we had said in good faith. Our three

275

bank Presidents and I gathered in a conference room to have a sandwich and commiserate. To say the least, after the fatiguing morning, this was becoming a depressing afternoon.

We examined our alternatives. There were few, since all that we could propose had already been put forth in documents, reports, pleas, applications, and public statements. One attending soul offered a suggestion which gave us some fleeting pleasure. He suggested, "Let's just give 'em the keys and go home. If they believe they can do a better job than we can, let's give them the chance to prove it."

In our angry guts this tactic offered some relief. The chuckles and respite were short, however, since we knew we had a moral and legal obligation to our shareholders to do our best to preserve the bank and their investments. We all were convinced that we could "make magic" better than could some inexperienced "suits" in Washington. Therefore, we would sit and wait and continue to "fight the good fight." (1 Timothy 6:12)

For several hours we sat and waited with increasing apprehension and a palpable inability to do anything else.

No one arrived from Washington.

It was just another day in our world of uncertainty.

We went home, the worse for wear, and returned the next day to do our best.

## It hits the fan

In March 1989, the Federal Loan Bank Board conducted a formal Examination of Empire. Empire's senior management team was provided with a draft of the Examination Report at mid-year. While the final report would not be officially delivered until December, this confidential, preliminary preview gave us some interim insight into the regulators' thought processes and concerns.

The report opined that financial recovery could not be achieved without significant financial assistance and/or a recapitalization.

This was not good news. It also wasn't new news. It simply described the circumstance we envisioned when we submitted our <u>Application for the Substitution of Regulatory Assistance</u> earlier in the year. Without the continuance of our package of goodwill and forbearances – or some form of "open assistance," – it would be impossible for Empire to survive the mandates of FIRREA.

The Examination Report forecasted significant continuing losses given our increasing cost of deposits (which was being occasioned by a nationwide, panic-like, run-up in deposit interest rates). This up-tick – and a surge in interest rates in general – exceeded the projections of all reliable economic advisors. The Report also noted continuing deposit outflows (because of spiraling interest rates); and, a persistent, unfavorable ratio of earning assets to non-earning assets. (In reality, this negative gap in our balance sheet had been previously addressed by purchase accounting and had decreased each year since our mergers.)

Of additional concern to our regulators was the rapid growth of Empire's consumer loan portfolio (which should have been expected since it was called for in the bank's strategic plan, which they had acknowledged and accepted on numerous earlier occasions.)

But the negative publicity attendant to the "thrift crisis," coupled with the continued deterioration of the nation's real estate markets, was causing more damage than anyone had envisaged. Empire lost $209 million in the first nine months of 1989. More than 60% of it was occasioned by the sale – at a loss – of assets that were earning below-market rates. These loss sales were necessary to raise the cash needed to fund deposit outflows. This sub-par performance was due primarily to an environment in which interest rates continued to rise; quality loans at reasonable yields were difficult to find; government-subsidized S&L competition was growing; and, deposit outflows were accelerating as the public image of the thrift industry deteriorated. Depressingly, these prevailing conditions seemed to presage "more of the same."

Following the 1989 Examination of Empire, the government retained an appraisal firm to value Empire's balance sheet. Its report would enable the feds to gauge the seriousness of Empire's problems (and their problems) in the wake of the passage of FIRREA.

While the report was never officially made available to the bank or the public, I was later informed by senior bank officers operating under the control of the Resolution Trust Company (the agency that eventually managed the liquidation of Empire) that the final report showed that Empire carried a negative tangible net worth of $758 million. (This number coincides with a subsequent FDIC disclosure which will be examined in the next Chapter.)

That number reflected a big balance sheet "hole;" but it was not dug by Empire team members.

Here's the explanation. As a consequence of its mergers with thirteen S&Ls, Empire's tangible liabilities increased by $926 million more than its tangible assets increased. In addition, Erie Savings Bank brought with it an additional $450 million negative gap between tangible assets and liabilities when it was assumed by the Empire enterprise in 1982.

It was heartening, therefore, that – despite these merger-driven additions of intangible assets; all of the turmoil in the market place; the growing regulatory burden; subsidized competition; bad publicity; bad luck; and interim, *tangible* goodwill carry costs totaling $300 million – the 1989 Examination revealed a tangible net worth gap of "only" $758 million.

In reality, during the course of six trying years, Empire had assumed, on behalf of the government, a burden of at least $1.5 billion and performed in a manner that should have earned it kudos instead of criticisms.

Our regulators put a different spin on it.

The Examination Report cited two principal underlying reasons for the bank's condition: (1) its unsuccessful attempt to translate its significant goodwill position into a profitable investment overall; and (2) its unsuccessful and costly attempt to overcome the goodwill burden by aggressive generation of high-yield, high-risk consumer loans.

The examiners' disparaging citation of "causes" was an overly simplistic conclusion given the formidable turnaround effort the bank undertook in an increasingly hostile economic and regulatory climate. Indeed, the bank had made great progress ... just not enough to assuage anxieties in high places.

With respect to the regulators' allegation concerning "translating goodwill into a profitable investment," it should be noted that Empire never attempted such hopeless alchemy. Its goodwill was a *non-earning* asset that simply afforded Empire an intangible – but legal (in both regulatory and conventional "generally accepted" accounting contexts) – capital position that provided the *time* necessary to do other things that could produce needed revenue. Goodwill per se was an *intangible* paper entry that levied *real* expenses, and it would never be anything but that.

Empire's principal job, right from the beginning, was to use the time afforded by this paper asset to do what had to be done to generate adequate revenues. So far, it had used this time widely. But more time was needed. Indeed, that is why the expected durations for goodwill and forbearance – as originally envisioned in our merger contracts with the government – extended far beyond the date of the last Examination. In this Report, the examiners were attempting to call the game in five innings!

The Examiners' first conclusion apparently lead them to their second allegation, which was that the bank conducted an unsuccessful and costly attempt to generate high-yield, high-risk assets.

This criticism was directed at a consumer loan initiative that had been discussed and reevaluated with our regulators numerous times in past years. There was ample evidence and industry experience to substantiate a belief that our high-rate, short-maturity consumer loan portfolios would ripen and mature profitably over a reasonable period of time. Again, more than "five innings" would be required!

In fact, in the months immediately preceding the Examination, Empire had responded to similar regulatory criticisms by significantly reducing the size of its consumer loan portfolios and offering many loan packages for sale to institutional investors. We did this reluctantly since these loan portfolios were our best hope for increased future earnings.

The implication of this second criticism was that Empire actually erred by aggressively seeking the only type of asset that could provide the earnings enhancements that the bank desperately needed.

The question that is begged is: Absent that approach, what should – or could – have been done that would have been "successful?" No examples of what was *proper,* and no prescriptions for what was *necessary,* were presented by the government at the time we entered into our contracts. No standards were set for "costly," "aggressive," or "unsuccessful."

Since no one, including all of the regulators who were in constant contact with us, had been able to provide a "better idea," Empire had logically and prudently concluded that the most reasonable course of action possible was the origination of consumer loans.

Certainly the times called for forceful behavior. No one was offering help, accommodation, or capital. We had to aggressively pursue the most promising tactical opportunities available to us in order to sustain viability and protect our shareholders' interests. The markets were hostile and competition was intense. It was not the time for timidity.

The kinds of high-return consumer loans, which were disparaged in the Examination Report, were, in reality, essential to Empire's turnaround. The structural earnings problems of Empire demanded them. With a balance sheet that was constrained in size and composition, and with statutes and regulations that precluded almost all other avenues but real estate and consumer lending, the only practical avenue to the kinds of earnings Empire required was through the origination of higher-yield, "non-mortgage" assets. The industry events of the 1980s had clearly demonstrated that "traditional" practices simply didn't cut it.

Under the plans forged with our regulators in the early '80s, it was apparent that Empire needed an asset base of at least $16 billion of well-paying assets to become self-sustaining. If, however, ultra-conservative, low-yield assets were to become the order of the day (as regulators now seemed to insinuate), a size of $25 billion or more would be required for an Empire turnaround. That was clearly not practical given the condition of the asset markets, our prevailing capital base, and the regulatory restrictions that were in place.

Nevertheless, given the import of the allegations contained in the Examination, Empire spent the remainder of 1989 constructing a tactical plan that would demonstrate to our regulators a very significant curtailment of consumer lending while, concurrently, squeezing-out as much income as possible from a diminishing portfolio.

The bank's activities that had been called "high risk" by "Monday morning quarterbacks," were, indeed *higher* risk than Empire's management might have opted for in normal circumstances. But such lending activities had become essential in a highly dysfunctional economic environment.

In fact, it can be reasonably argued that Empire's entry into consumer lending would have paid off handsomely *over time…* had it been allowed to continue. Our bootstrap operation had paid its dues, moved nicely along the learning curve, received encouraging market acceptance, acquired all of the necessary systems and technology necessary to minimize losses and expenses, and had been able to put together a management team that functioned very well (a fact that was even acknowledged by our regulators). There was no reason to suspect that, with time and patience, this new line of endeavor would have not paid off for Empire like all of its other undertakings had over the years.

Relatively high-rate consumer loans, coupled with lower deposit costs, would have made Empire adequately profitable as the '90s unfolded. Unfortunately, this worthy product initiative was aborted before the costs realized in inception could be translated into a reliable stream of consistent revenue. (Indeed, the downturn of interest rates in 1990 and beyond demonstrated that consumer loan portfolios, with their rather unique rate and fee structures, would have been extremely profitable components of our balance sheet, had the bank been allowed to continue its workout.)

In fact, years after the bank's liquidation, Empire's tolerance for slightly higher risk was vindicated. A report re-surfaced which revealed that a major portion of the troublesome portfolios that had been alluded to in the Examination Report had been sold... "at a small but reasonable *profit*."

Nevertheless, the public comments made by the regulators concerning the causes of Empire's failure focused on the risk associated with "rapid growth in consumer loan portfolios." (Perhaps, some measure of satisfaction should be taken from the fact that this was the *only* public criticism ever made by the regulators during the final "resolution" of Empire's situation.)

The aspersions cast by our Examination Report prompted me to revisit my concept of risk. In my view, risk was everywhere. In a complex, fast-paced world, it is virtually impossible to act without taking a chance that entails some downside peril. The "safe" things we routinely do – downing a doughnut, navigating an expressway, stepping into an elevator, walking in a thunderstorm, meeting a disgruntled customer – all entail "the possibility of loss, injury, disadvantage, or destruction," i.e. Webster's definition of risk.

Risk, in my opinion, was simply the circumstance attendant to actions taken when the perpetrator has less than 100% foreknowledge of the outcome. The savings industry was founded on the premise of risk, i.e. liquidity risk, credit risk, intermediation risk, and economic risk. Without arbitraging (i.e. the inherently "risky" attempt to offset the costs of deposits with the earnings from slightly-higher risk investments and loans), there would be no positive "earnings spread" with which a savings institution could finance its operations, provide meaningful services (especially to homebuyers)... and contribute to a capital cushion.

The necessity of risk tolerance has been convincingly conveyed by University of Chicago Professor H. Edward Wrapp: "Management is a risk-taking job. In most situations, there is absolutely no way you can take out the unknowns and avoid risk unless you don't make any decisions."

Of course, knowledge, experience, prototyping, focused analyses, limited testing, and prayer can all help to mitigate the possible negative impacts of actions taken without 20-20 foresight. I took comfort that all of these had been duly employed at Empire. That is to say, I was comfortable with what we had done... not with what was happening.

Disappointingly, the 1989 Examination Report didn't even allude to the fact that the loan-risk parameters it was criticizing were, for years, accepted by the regulatory establishment when it was in the best interests of the government to do so. Furthermore, at each stage of Empire's workout at which reasonable regulatory accommodation or assistance could have been provided (thereby reducing Empire's alleged proclivity to risk), none was forthcoming. In every instance, the government bargained forcefully to *minimize* any assistance that would have aided Empire. The regulatory establishment's "power of triage," coupled with the "old" Erie's legacy-burden of less-than-market-rate residential mortgages, forced Empire to acquiesce, at each turn, to the "take-it-or-leave-it" posture of the government.

Most galling, was the fact that nowhere in the Examination Report did the government acknowledge the fact that the alleged "higher risk" ventures of Empire greatly reduced the government's final resolution costs. The loan portfolios that were eventually sold at a profit; the operating subsidiaries that were divested at significant gains; the leveraged buyout transactions that produced substantial profits; the highly sophisticated and successful money management techniques that minimized losses and squeezed the last dollar of revenue from available assets; and the capital finance subsidiaries that made assets do double duty as income generators, all required the assumption of a higher degree of risk at their inception. But, in the final analysis, after reasonable time, they paid off abundantly. None of these accomplishments were even alluded to in the bank's final Examination Report. The theme of the Examination seemed to be "what have you done for us – or to us – lately."

There is good reason to suspect that many of our positive accomplishments were not even known to our regulators. In a legal proceeding in which I was involved years later, a representative of the government asked me some questions concerning Empire's "poor portfolios." In response, I asked why the detailed final report that Empire submitted to the regulators about the positive aspects of its consumer loan experience hadn't mitigated their destructive approach to "resolving" Empire. I was told that there was no recollection of receiving that report nor could they find a copy of it in their files. In fact, the questioner said that he was led to believe that Empire's files had been shipped, early on, to a warehouse in Louisiana where, because of delinquent rent, they were "disposed of."

Indeed.

Then too, it was never recognized that there were positive outcomes from Empire's non-banking initiatives. Many of its ventures were highly successful and evolved according to a pattern that featured: low initial capitalization; a novel market entry that had not previously been attempted by a thrift; managers with unique credentials; a capacity for hard work; integrity and honesty; prudent risk tolerance; and, an ability to learn and adapt as the job progressed. All of this took considerable time, money, and patience... but it had begun to pay off.

Given our capital and regulatory constraints, our actions constituted the only approach that had a reasonable chance for success. We did not have the kinds of resources that the goodwill-free giants of the industry had at their disposal. Sweat equity was the name of our game, and it required patience, hard work, prudent risk-taking, an ability to learn and adapt over time.

Apparently, none of this was appreciated.

## It's time to go

In early April 1989, Empire's principal regulators in New York City requested a visit by our senior management team. They gave no indication as to the purpose of the meeting, but we had speculated, in advance, on a number of possible scenarios in order to be as prepared as possible. Quite frankly, we did not expect a difficult encounter since we had achieved a great deal of progress with the operational refocusing that we had introduced – as per their implorations – into our strategic and tactical plans for 1989.

We prepared several reports which detailed the specific progress made in eleven substantive areas. The only thing that had negatively impacted our refocusing efforts was a strong upturn in interest rates which further squeezed our net interest margin. With the exception of this uncontrollable adversity, we were basically on target with our forecast for the year.

Since interest rates were essentially out of our control, we didn't expect an especially critical review of our performance but rather some strong admonitions as to the need to continue to adhere to our program of consolidation, downsizing, and re-focusing.

In mid-April, we met with the senior executives of the Federal Home Loan Bank of New York who had responsibility at that time for overseeing thrift institutions whose primary operations were in New York State. At our meeting, we attempted to get right down to business but were immediately informed that the purpose of the meeting was to present us with a Supervisory Agreement (Agreement) which they wanted Empire's management and Board of Directors to accept. We knew that an agreement of this type was designed to give regulators greatly expanded influence over an institution's operations.

We hurriedly examined the Agreement they proffered and, even with just a cursory review, it appeared that the intent of the Agreement was, indeed, to severely circumscribe the operational discretion of Empire's management team and its Directors. I quickly concluded that the actions proposed therein were not in the interests of enhancing the profitability and soundness of Empire. Neither were they designed to protect the value of our shareholders' interests. It was obvious that the government's intent was simply to preclude *any* risk of loss to the federal coffers.

While our immediate reflex response was to ask some very pointed questions and to resist such imposition, we, instead, tactfully suggested an adjournment which would enable us to study the document in a less stressful atmosphere, confer with the bank's Directors, and meet again with our regulators a few weeks hence.

Our suggestion was accepted and a follow-up meeting was scheduled.

At that point, I alone was asked to remain for an executive session. Thereupon, the regulators who were assembled explained to me that the future of Empire was going to be dramatically different than its past and, as a result, a different management approach would be required to guide the organization. They had concluded that my forte had been building and developing the organization; they did not believe that that kind of entrepreneurial approach was compatible with the direction they wished Empire to take. They believed that it would be prohibitively difficult for me to sufficiently reorient my skills and talents in a manner that would allow me to do the kind of major downscaling and pruning job they wanted done.

It was clear. They had *their* plan; they wanted *their* man. They were seeking "new blood" to lead a charge in a different – governmentally-sanctioned – direction.

I'm not sure if they were expecting me to argue to the contrary, metamorphose on the spot, throw a tantrum, or call my lawyer. But, I knew they were right. It would have been virtually impossible for me to sincerely and heartily lead the bank in a direction that I thought was unwise.

I calmly replied that I believed the bank had made great recent progress with respect to its operational refocusing, resizing, and cost cutting, and that those initiatives had borne fruit under my direction. Nevertheless, I agreed that neither my mind nor heart could enthusiastically embrace the path they were prescribing for the future. I felt that it would be extremely difficult for me to lead, in good conscience, the Empire team in a direction that I believed to be one of emaciation and regression... a direction that, in my opinion, would result in ultimate failure and disservice to shareholders, employees, and the community.

Thereupon, it was agreed that a selection of a new CEO for Empire was appropriate and should be accomplished as soon as possible.

I indicated that I would ask the bank's Directors to immediately launch a search for a capable successor who would be willing and able to implement the regulators' desired strategies and tactics with fervor. They agreed but reserved the right of final approval.

I hoped that the prospect of a pair of fresh eyes and abilities just might induce the regulators to accept yet another bank initiative that would obviate a Supervisory Agreement and possibly work to preserve the bank and its shareholders' interests.

To my surprise, the assembled regulators stated that it was their wish that I remain with the bank in a highly-visible capacity. They were clearly concerned about a depositor run on the bank when a change in Empire's operating-independence occurred. They indicated that a continuation of my long and highly-visible association with the bank might provide some calming reassurance to depositors and shareholders who could be spooked by expanded government intervention in the bank's affairs.

After some discussion, we finally agreed that I should remain with the bank and serve as non-executive Chairman of the Board with primary responsibility for depositor, employee, shareholder, and other external relations. It was understood that I would also work to quickly find, for consideration by our Directors and the OTS, a talented and experienced financial institution executive who would accept the role of President, Chief Executive Officer, and member of the Board of Directors.

Deep in my heart, I still believed the bank had a future given its legal entitlements under the contracts that had been signed with the regulators as a consequence of our supervisory acquisitions. Also in our favor was Drexel Burnham's continuing willingness to come to the table with substantial private capital. Moreover, the bank still was – in the professional opinion of Peat Marwick, its accounting firm of record, – a "going concern."

Needless to say, I personally felt that I was being deprived of seeing our mission through to a successful conclusion and that I was being shortchanged of the psychic and material benefits that would result from such success. However, I satisfied myself with the conviction that a leadership change was a necessary prerequisite to the continuation of any efforts to achieve an eventual workout. Any attempt on my part to stay on and fight the good fight would have hindered the bank's chances for getting the kind of capital substitution it had requested. Further, and of more immediate concern, it would jeopardize any efforts on the bank's part to convince the regulators that a Supervisory Agreement was not necessary.

I suspected that the aggressive profile that the bank had recently been forced to assume with respect to its Application for Substitution of Assistance had rankled the regulators. I knew all along that being "scrappy" entailed downside risks in the prevailing environment, but I had believed that, as the thrift crisis escalated and the government decided to play a more determinative role, it was essential for the bank to publicly and forcefully seek its entitlements lest it be lumped together with all of the other troubled thrifts and disposed of in an unfair manner.

Upon my return to Buffalo, our management team and Directors carefully scrutinized the proposed Supervisory Agreement. The acceptance of it would force Empire to eschew growth; discontinue several profitable lines of business; virtually eliminate reasonable credit and interest rate risk; pare expenses even more than it already had; and incur some significant additional expenses to hire outside consultants to "monitor" its efforts. In sum, it appeared to me that the proposed Agreement, in reality, would require the bank to forego any reasonable efforts to improve its profitability and secure the kind of new capital that would enable it to continue operations.

Empire's management team believed that the acceptance of a Supervisory Agreement at that point in time would be extremely detrimental to the bank's relationships in the capital and depositor marketplaces, making it almost impossible for Empire to do business. We felt obliged to convince the regulators that a formal agreement was not needed. If, however, it was ultimately decided that some type of "control" document was necessary, we strongly wanted it to be something other than the standard, onerous Supervisory Agreement. We felt it was important to pursue an agreement which would not include the extremely restrictive provisions that were being imposed on other, less promising – and less deserving – thrifts in the industry.

As a consequence of these concerns, I was even more convinced that my personal separation as an employee and officer of the bank should be handled with dispatch. I wanted to be sure that the regulators knew that I would be working solely for the benefit of the bank and that my personal convictions and disappointments would not hamper their "resolution" efforts.

I personally decided that, in the immediate future, my energies at the bank would be focused primarily on carrying out my new responsibilities as Chairman; proving that the proposed Supervisory Agreement was not necessary; and, advancing Empire's requests for needed accommodations under FIREEA.

On May 11th, a special meeting of the Board of Directors was held to inform them of the conclusions of the regulators concerning my status. At that time it was agreed that, at a subsequent meeting of the Board on May 18th, the Directors would be offered, for their deliberation, a specific proposal concerning my retirement as an active officer and employee of the bank.

289

Empire's Directors voted to grant my retirement according to my employment contract at its regularly scheduled Board meeting on May 25th.

On that day – the day before my 50th birthday – I concluded my management duties with Empire of America.

Thereupon, I immediately launched an aggressive recruiting effort to find the best possible leader for Empire. This was accomplished in six weeks. An intelligent, proven leader who was highly experienced with respect to thrift institutions and their interaction with the government was recruited to take up the cudgel.

Empire was off to a new start ... *again.*

But it was to be a perilous course.

In June 1989 – despite all of our efforts – Empire of America was forced to enter into a <u>Supervisory Agreement</u> with the Federal Home Loan Bank of New York, its principal regulator. From then on, *all* the activities of Empire were directed or significantly conditioned by government officials. The Agreement also required Empire to retain outside consultants to evaluate Empire's exposure to interest rate changes, overall asset quality, and the adequacy of its reserves for potentially problematic loans.

A few months later, the <u>Financial Institutions Reform, Recovery and Enforcement Act</u> (FIRREA) was finally approved by Congress, and higher hurdles were erected for Empire.

In my opinion, a self-righteous Congress, which was incensed by the outcome of the programs that it fostered for decades, had produced a bill that was – as described by Ted Roberts, CEO of a large and negatively-impacted savings and loan association in Chicago – "ill considered, thoughtless, and arbitrary." Roberts claimed that the day of the bill's passage was the "Pearl Harbor Day of the industry."

A partner in one of Washington's most prestigious law firms openly called it "the worst piece of banking legislation ever conceived of." (Alas, it didn't hold that title for long!)

Essentially, this new bill offered a good place to hide for Congresspersons who had not done their jobs and were afraid of losing them.

Interestingly, most regulatory agencies had neither protested nor praised this bill as it wound its way through Congress. In the final analysis, it was the Treasury Department that convinced Congress that the goodwill on many savings institutions' balance sheets was an "accounting fiction" and that it was being used by thrift managers to avoid putting their own institutions' money at risk.

The allegation that thrifts were using goodwill as an "accounting gimmick" to extend their survival was a criticism that had previously been employed by regulators in attempts to disparage thrift industry efforts to forestall legislation like FIRREA. However, the Treasury's vilification of goodwill was the kind of validation that Congress needed to stumble ahead with its ill-founded legislation. But, that validation was, in reality, *invalid* because, for decades, prevailing accounting standards allowed goodwill to be legitimately carried on the books of a company *forever* as an asset, albeit not as a capital component. Purchase accounting had been employed with increased frequency over the years. Eventually, as the dollar amounts of corporate buyouts soared during the 1960s, the members of the Federal Accounting Standards Board – the "accountants behind the curtain" who formulated the nation's Generally Accepted Accounting Principles – decided that goodwill should henceforth be written off against net earnings for a period of no more than forty years. At the time, critics assailed such write-offs as encumbrances that would discourage salutary mergers. But the accountants insisted on a forty-year write-off period and, ultimately, they got their way.

Alas, with the passage of FIRREA, thrift institutions were called upon to write-off *all* of their goodwill… *immediately.*

Those who really understood the implications of FIRREA realized that it allowed insufficient time for most thrifts to prudently implement the massive changes in structure, policy,

291

capital base, and customer relations that the Act called for. For too many savings institutions, it was going to be just a matter of time before the regulators would appear at the door and ask for the keys.

As a consequence of this new legislation and the regulations that would flow from it, fully 45% of savings institutions, holding 60% of the industry's $1.3 trillion of assets, would immediately fail to meet the new standards. Eventually, over one thousand thrifty institutions "disappeared."

The Thrift and Mortgage News opined that FIRREA was, in reality, self-defeating as far as the federal government was concerned. "It would result in almost certain destruction of many institutions – many of which entered into good-faith agreements with the regulators – and it comes at a time when the government needs an enormous infusion of private capital from existing owners of thrifts and from potential new owners."

This esteemed trade paper concluded by saying that "the Congress has broken the word of the federal government which encouraged acquirers of failed thrifts to take less assistance in exchange for accounting forbearances and goodwill."

Much of the Act's 155 pages of dense "bureaucratese" was wasted on diatribes about how con men, rogue owners, high-rollers, and bumbling managers should be punished for their deeds. (Fact of the matter was that later studies of the so-called "savings and loan debacle" confirmed that only a very small percentage of the damage done to thrift institutions by private parties constituted fraud or malfeasance of any type.)

Nevertheless, as might be expected, the regulatory enforcements that emerged as a consequence of the FIRREA revolved around "mismanagement," a nebulous accusation that was widely applied and almost impossible to define by either the alleged perpetrators or the regulatory punishers.

Given the impact of this misguided legislation, it was clear that that it would be virtually impossible for Empire to obtain a capital infusion from private sources since confusion and panic

reigned supreme among thrift managers, owners, and investors...
*and* the regulators who would condition the fate of the industry.

Things would be forever different. Indeed, apprehension about the passage of FIRREA created widespread public unease which exacerbated deposit outflows and further diminished thrifts' earnings. In the second quarter of 1989, Empire lost a record $54.2 million.

As regulators moved to tighten their control of the industry, a torrent of examinations, investigations, allegations, suspicions, recriminations, and accusations began to flow in a rapidly widening river of doom.

### They take the keys

The Big E team struggled valiantly in the last half of 1989 to satisfy a now dominant regulatory apparatus. Despite the bank's recruitment of a qualified and cooperative CEO, regulatory pressure for downsizing and destructing continued unabated.

Asset sales, branch closings, and restrained deposit generation were the order of the day as the government tried to minimize its exposure. But, in the end, not even all those extreme measures satisfied the regulators. Once FIRREA was enacted, they pushed for an immediate write-off of our $706 million of remaining goodwill

Finally, conceding that they were no longer in control of their own destiny, the officers and Directors of the bank decided that they would execute such a write-off at the bank's January 1990, Board meeting. The agenda for the meeting called for the bank's Directors to, in accordance with the FIRREA mandates, approve an immediate write-off of all of Empire's remaining goodwill.

But, regrettably, our Directors were not even allowed this reluctant act of compliance.

Apparently, in order to cloak the horrific consequences of such a mandated misdeed – or perhaps to preclude a last minute act of resistance by the bank – Empire's new principal regulator, the Office of Thrift Supervision, put the bank into

293

conservatorship immediately prior to the scheduled meeting, and the Board was instantly dissolved by fiat before its members could convene and vote on the write-off.

The process of conservatorship that followed vitiated all shareholder entitlements and provided for the complete assumption of bank ownership by the federal government.

The government now had absolute control of the bank's affairs. A "Supervisory Agent" was designated as the Conservator of Empire and he served as the ultimate on-site manager of its operations. For nine months thereafter, the bank functioned under the leadership of an apparently competent, reliable, and caring (to the extent allowed) government administrator. However, since his prior experience consisted of running a bank the size of our Transit Road Branch in Buffalo, it was evident that his job was not to find new, promising paths to growth and salvation but, rather, to oversee the rapid – if not economically sound – *diminishment* and *dissolution* of Empire.

Once Empire of America was placed into conservatorship, thus turning over full control of the institution to the government, the RTC quickly wrote off the bank's goodwill and, in conjunction with the FDIC, positioned it for liquidation.

In September 1990, Empire of America – the bank that had served proudly for 136 years and had struggled valiantly for more than a dozen years – was turned over to the RTC for an immediate liquidation. A number of commercial banks from the Buffalo area and across the country were selected as preferred acquirers. Some of them had aggressively jockeyed for this privilege for years. The final turnover of all properties and assets of the Big E took place on a warm September evening in 1990.

The clock had run out, and what was once a workable workout became just another painful bailout.

*Chapter twelve*

## THE AFTERMATH

### After the fall

In the months and years following the government seizure of Empire of America – and before a decision by the United States Supreme Court that vindicated Empire (which is semi-happily described in the next Chapter) – there was continuing public, regulatory, and press scrutiny of the downfall of the bank.

In an orgy of acronyms, investigators from the FBI, IRS, RTC, OTS, FDIC and the New York Banking Department scoured every document they could find and interviewed every employee who they believed might have knowledge of events that could have precipitated the "failure" of the institution. Based on the continuing feedback I received from the former officers and staff members who were drawn into the probe, it was clear that the goal of most inquiries was to find and prosecute the "bad guys." Interviewed bank team members were intimidated with accusative inquiries like "why didn't you do something to stop it." The "it" was never really defined.

Throughout the long and tortuous seizure and liquidation, and their aftermath, the only "it" that was identified publicly was the government's belief that the bank had been overly aggressive in expanding its consumer loan portfolio. To this day, that was the only substantive public allegation ever made. Indeed, there was no public criticism of the *quality* of our consumer credit extensions or the means by which the portfolio was aggregated and managed.

Apparently, in the minds of our regulators, size was equated with risk, and risk put government careers and coffers on the line.

**Timing is everything**

It didn't take long for the evisceration of Empire to be proven premature. Interest rates began to decline in the early '90s, making the favorable turn just a few months later than our original Phoenix Plan had forecasted. The Federal Reserve System's benchmark interest rate dropped from over 8% in 1989 to approximately 3% three years later.

If Empire had been allowed to maintain its goodwill and enjoy the protection of its forbearances for *just one more year*, it would have found itself in an environment conducive to the satisfactory generation of operating earnings from both its high-rate consumer loan portfolios and its mortgage assets. In addition, the hundreds of millions of dollars of fixed-rate investments that resided for so long in Erie's and Empire's portfolios could have been sold at a profit, or at worst, a break-even price as interest rates declined.

Empire's shareholders and the government would have been spared the trauma and cost of the bank's liquidation.

History tells us that, had Empire's self-workout been allowed to proceed, the decline in interest rates that commenced soon after the beginning of the decade would have ensured the bank's solvency and enhanced its profitability. Once again, it was proven that "timing is everything."

My ol' uncle Ollie used to say that the words most frequently associated with the causes of disappointments in human affairs are "too slow," too careful," "too reckless," "too selfish," "too risky," "too greedy," and "too stupid." But in this circumstance, "too late" was the most appropriate of all.

An improved economic climate with lower interest rates came "too late" to save Empire.

Uncle Ollie's views were echoed, not long after the government grabbed the keys, by the principal resident manager who was installed at Empire by the Resolution Trust Company (RTC), the agency responsible for wrapping up the affairs of the bank. He conceded over lunch (we each paid for our own) that he and his staff were surprised at the integrity and soundness of Empire's operations and felt that the government created a bigger problem by taking us over than they *might* have suffered if they had chosen to ride out the storm with the bank intact.

His opinion is corroborated in the following Section of this Chapter – **The taxpayers' tab** – which lays bare the true financial impact of Empire's demise on American taxpayers. That Section offers an in-depth analysis of the liquidation cost that was ultimately alleged by the FDIC, and it demonstrates the extent to which that cost was overstated... and unnecessary. In fact, it shows that the cost could have been avoided altogether and that taxpayers could have actually *profited* significantly from Empire's continued operation. It reveals that, by 1989, taxpayers had already enjoyed, at least, a $1.5 billion *positive financial benefit* by virtue of Empire's assumption of thirteen failing thrifts earlier in the decade. Moreover, it illustrates how that benefit would have continued to grow... *if* Empire had been permitted to maintain its operations.

The Section subsequent to that – **The rest of the story: Responsibility for the "loss"** – examines in detail the costly actions the government took in 1989 and 1990 that, in effect, wiped out most of the $1.5 billion benefit that Empire had previously provided Uncle Sam. The pointless liquidation of Empire at that time imposed enormous, *unnecessary* costs on the public sector and the taxpayers who funded it. These costs were suffered because of a bureaucracy's furtive efforts to avoid *possible* future recrimination and *possible* loss by summarily eliminating *all* of the reasonable business risks that were essential to Empire's eventual success.

Importantly, that Section of this book also confirms that the ultimate price tag associated with the Empire tragedy was not caused by poor past performance on the part of Empire's capable and industrious team members. Indeed, the facts examined in that Section show that Empire's efforts served shareholders and taxpayers commendably during a perilous period and, absent its liquidation, the bank could have continued to serve productively, if government intervention had been stayed.

Since the government is bashed enthusiastically in the rest of this Chapter, it is important to make a distinction between the two elements of government that most determinatively affected thrift industry affairs in the late 1980s.

Up until the passage of the Financial Institutions Reform, Recovery and Enforcement Act, most of the less-than-enlightened public policies and practices that emerged were initiated by the actions of high-level regulators in various government agencies. Congress, itself, was seemingly impotent and generally unable do anything...either bad or good. However, once Congress passed FIRREA in 1989, most of the hurt in the thrift industry was prompted by the legislative policies of the House, Senate, and George H. W. Bush Administration. From then on, the principal role of the regulatory bureaucracy was to implement and enforce the provisions of FIRREA. With one exception, regulators had limited latitude with respect to the manner in which they dealt with individual thrifts.

Consequently, the criticism leveled at the "government" in the remainder of this Chapter is directed primarily at the Bush Administration and the United States Congress. The ultimate fate of hundreds of thrift institutions – including Empire – was settled once FIRREA became law and regulators were directed to take action inimical to the thrift industry.

However, there was one very significant exemption from the statutory constraints under which regulators labored. Provisions of FIRREA specifically empowered the FDIC's regulatory cadre to offset the especially Draconian impacts of the Act by providing "open bank assistance" to institutions in Empire's predicament. Alas, your author knows of no instance in which the FDIC productively intervened in this manner. The dismissal of Empire's Application for Substitution of Assistance was a harbinger of the regulators' unwillingness to use this kind of enabling provision to aid worthy thrift institutions.

## The taxpayers tab

Throughout the entire thrift imbroglio, much was made of the negative impact that its "resolution" had on taxpayers. It was variously reported that the entire nationwide effort cost in excess of $200 billion.

In its last public statement about Empire, the FDIC alleged that the bank's liquidation had cost the government $1.2 billion. While that might have been the feds' aggregate – self-inflicted – expenditure in the pursuit of a convenient wrap-up, the following pages reveal that the costs ascribed to Empire's resolution were, in fact, far less and, for the most part, unnecessary.

Even if, *hypothetically*, they were deemed legitimate, these alleged expenses were more than offset by the cumulative results of Empire's stewardship of the thirteen failing thrifts it assumed in the early 1980s. Over the six years prior to its liquidation, the bank had generated significant *positive* financial benefits for Uncle Sam that far surpassed the costs alleged by the FDIC.

Here are the details. When Empire assumed the thirteen failed savings and loan associations in its federally-assisted merger participations, it relieved the government of the necessity to use public funds to underwrite the liquidation of those institutions. As indicated earlier, the aggregate asset deficit of those acquired thrifts amounted to *at least* $926 million. (Note: This does *not* include the additional $300 million loan value deficiency that Empire discovered subsequent to the mergers, as described on page 176.)

Thanks to Empire's willingness to assume that obligation, the U.S. Treasury was relieved of the costs of immediately closing, selling, or re-capitalizing the failed S&Ls. Such action would have required a *cash* outlay by the government of more than $926 million *plus* an amount equal to the $129 million that Erie and the FSLIC contributed to the final acquisition transaction. (This $129 million contribution was needed to ensure the acquired institutions' attainment of the minimum levels of capital and of operating viability required by government regulations at that time.)

As a result, a total of $1.1 billion – *at least* – would have been required to "resolve" the crises of the thirteen thrifts. It would have been necessary for regulators to source these funds via U.S. Treasury borrowings since cash funding had not yet been provided for by tax revenues in the federal budget. Such massive borrowing would have created an interest cost (paid for by taxpayers) of $158.3 million *annually* until some point in the future when Congress finally got around to appropriating adequate resolution funds, and the U.S. Treasury debt could be supplanted by tax revenue.

During the seven-year period in which Empire actually carried the $1.1 billion deficit burden for the government, the Treasury's borrowing costs (i.e. interest) would have been – absent Empire's cooperation – more than $1.5 billion. Therefore, Empire's willingness to work with the government in the early 1980s enabled the government to avoid a direct, immediate cost that actually *exceeded* – by $300 million – the alleged $1.2 billion liquidation cost that it would later report. (The $1.5 billion cost is arrived at by applying the rate then paid on ten-year U.S. Treasury Notes to the amount of cash capital that the government would have needed in 1982 to liquidate or recapitalize the troubled S&Ls without Empire's help.)

This means that, when all was said and done and after all the exaggerated "worst case" impacts of Empire's liquidation had been incurred, the nation's taxpayers actually *benefited* – albeit by "merely" $400 million give or take – by virtue of the bank's merger transactions in the 1980s and its liquidation in 1990.

These true facts about Empire's positive financial contributions were never acknowledged by the government. As far as its ledgers were concerned, the government's seizure of Empire, the liquidation of its assets, and the write-off of its goodwill created a grand expense of $1.2 billion. This faulty interpretation of financial data led to the belief – widely trumpeted by the media – that Empire constituted "a big hit on taxpayers."

The government never commented on the salutary contributions to the public purse that were made by Empire during the seven-year period prior to its liquidation. Accordingly, taxpayers had no way of knowing that they would have been even better off in the long run if Empire had simply been allowed to continue its sweat-equity workout.

## The rest of the story: Responsibility for the "loss"

Once Empire had been seized by the regulators, the government's principal mission involved off-loading the bank's liabilities (principally deposit accounts) to other banking institutions; selling its assets; and, minimizing any losses entailed by doing so in a buyers' market.

The first public report concerning the liquidation of Empire was issued by the Federal Deposit Insurance Corp. in 1993. In it, the FDIC and the Resolution Trust Company indicated that they had disposed of 90% of the Big E's assets and collected ninety-three cents on every dollar of assets sold, suggesting a loss on assets of 7.04%. The last available report from the FDIC, which was compiled five years later, contended that the government incurred a total cost of $1.2 billion to effect the liquidation of the "failed" Empire.

Many uninformed observers reflexively attributed the alleged $1.2 billion loss to less-than-stellar operating performance by the Empire team. This, as the preceding page and the following paragraphs (which are based on the FDIC's own records) will demonstrate, was an unfair and inaccurate conclusion.

In fact, the costs comprising the $1.2 billion "hit" claimed by the FDIC were actually engendered by the government itself while it scurried to resolve a *potential, perceived* problem which it feared *might* be an embarrassment to Congress and its regulatory establishment.

The most revealing data that support this claim of government culpability can be found in an FDIC report entitled <u>Statement of Assets and Liabilities in Liquidation</u> (Statement) acquired by your author by virtue of his participation in a 1999 legal action in which the Resolution Trust Company was a defendant. The report was originally obtained through the <u>Freedom of Information Act</u> by a Buffalo law firm. It illustrates the course of Empire's FDIC liquidation from September 28, 1990 to December 31, 1998, and its findings constitute the basis for the calculations presented in the following paragraphs.

According to the Statement, the primary cost components of the $1.2 billion loss alleged by the FDIC consisted of the following items:

- o **Item One**: An $834.8 million *accumulated* asset deficit at the time the liquidation commenced. (Approximately $780 million of that deficit was the result of government actions between the time the bank was seized in January 1990 and September 1990, the point at which it was turned over to the RTC for liquidation. Most of the remainder was incurred in 1989 when the bank's affairs were being directed by government officials in accordance with its <u>Supervisory Agreement</u>.)
- o **Item Two**: A $117.7 million net loss on the RTC liquidation of loans and investments.
- o **Item Three**: $246 million of administrative expenses associated with the *process* of liquidation.
- o **Item Four**: $163 million of non-cash expenses classified as "adjustments" that were made subsequent to September 28, 1990.
- o **Item Five:** Premiums received in the course of business which accounted for *income* of $85.2 million.

The first four items will be analyzed in detail in the following pages since they constituted the negative items that contributed to the alleged net loss to the government. This examination will demonstrate that almost all of the real costs/losses incurred were actually attributable to policies and procedures that were implemented by the government – not the bank – prior to and during the bank's liquidation. As you will see, the fact that the bank had saved the Treasury $1.5 billion in the previous seven years didn't stop the government from embarking on a liquidation program that would *unnecessarily* wipe out at least 75% of those savings. Here's how it was "accomplished."

**Item One**

The FDIC Statement reveals that on September 28, 1990 the entire financial corpus (or corpse) of Empire that was carried on the FDIC's books consisted of assets with a *negative* value of $834.8 million. In the truest sense, this $834.8 million deficit represented the final, bottom-line outcome of all Empire's independent and government-mandated financial activities from September 1, 1854 to September 28, 1990, including the financial impacts suffered in the tumultuous and painful decade of the 1980s.

It should be emphasized, however, that the preponderance of this negative value was incurred *after* the bank was taken over in January 1990.

In its last independently-compiled quarterly SEC 10-Q Report on March 31, 1989, the bank reported $151 million of positive shareholder equity – after adjustment for doubtful loans. Therefore, in order to arrive at a negative $834 billion deficit, there had to have occurred a negative swing of $985 million in the bank's capital base in only eighteen months. During fifteen of those months the bank's financial affairs were being determinatively managed under a Supervisory Agreement (June-December 1989) and through a conservatorship (January-September 1990).

According to available data, the bank's net loss in 1989 amounted to $205 million. This loss was occasioned primarily because of asset sales that were conducted hurriedly at the behest of the Office of Thrift Supervision.

The OTC's overriding goal in 1989 was shrinkage of the bank to minimize any *possible future* loss to the government. Bargain sales of branches and other assets occurred at the direction of the government during that period.

(Since no official 1989 Annual Report was issued by Empire after the its seizure in January 1990, this $205 million loss number was derived by calculating the difference between the bank's $151.5 million positive net worth reported on March 31, 1989 and its negative net worth of $53.5 million at the end of 1989, as Reported by the United States General Accounting Office in 1991.)

An additional loss of $780 million was incurred in the first three months of 1990. Presumably, the largest component of that loss was the *total* write-off, by either the Office of Thrift Supervision (OTS) or the Resolution Trust Company (RTC), of the remaining $706 million of goodwill on Empire's books. (As earlier related, Empire vigorously resisted such action until the passage of FIRREA made it inevitable.)

(Technical note: The routine amortization of goodwill over time, in and of itself, did not constitute a cash loss to Empire as long as the bank remained in operation. The bank's contracts with the government had permitted the inclusion of the non-tangible value of all as-yet unamortized goodwill in its calculation of regulatory capital. When the bank's unamortized goodwill was summarily written off by the regulators after they took control of the bank, the $706 million diminishment of capital it occasioned permitted the seizure and liquidation of the bank under provisions of FIRREA and presented the government with a cash obligation.

The elimination of goodwill resulted in an "asset deficit" gap that had to be filled with real dollars, i.e. cash. That is to say, the government's pattern of actions ultimately resulted in an otherwise unnecessary $706 million cash cost to it and, by extension, to taxpayers. This number is included, as part of the "cost of liquidating Empire," in the FDIC's liquidation Statement.)

The bank's *non*-goodwill loss during 1989-90 was $279 million, most of which was caused by untimely government-directed sales of low-rate loans.

Also of consequence is the fact that the $834 million "asset deficit" reported by the FDIC *included* the goodwill amortization expense that Empire *did* incur during the seven years (1982-1989) when it dutifully carried the goodwill on its balance sheet. Those expenses, while not requiring an outlay of cash, constituted a direct hit of $220 million to Empire's cumulative bottom line and were, therefore, included in the final "asset deficit" that was ultimately reported by the FDIC in September 1990.

In addition, Empire incurred the substantial carry-cost entailed in *funding* the non-earning goodwill asset on its books for those seven years. When Empire acquired the troubled savings institutions, it accepted interest-bearing deposit liabilities as the necessary balance sheet offset to the assets it obtained. However, since $926 million of those acquired assets consisted of goodwill (i.e. non-earning intangible assets), Empire was burdened with tangible deposit-related interest costs that were greatly in excess of – and, therefore, not sufficiently supported by – tangible asset earnings. In other words, Empire had to pay annual cash interest on deposits that were equal in amount to the unamortized, non-earning goodwill remaining on its books.

This cost was substantial but, fortunately, it was somewhat mitigated in the years immediately following the mergers by virtue of the bank's ability to accrete income from the loan discount produced by the mergers, a legitimate accounting technique which was described earlier in this book.

It is clear, therefore, that the $834 million asset deficit component of the loss reported by the FDIC was created almost entirely by the amortization expenses and interest carry-costs associated with the S&L acquisitions that Empire facilitated for the government. Indeed, if Empire had been allowed to continue operations, the FDIC would not have been faced in 1990 – or subsequently – with an obligation to fund this kind of "asset deficit."

**Item two**

Another component of the loss reported in the FDIC's Statement was a $117.7 million net charge for losses incurred upon the liquidation of Empire's consumer loans, commercial loans, securities, real estate mortgages and other owned assets. This net charge represented the dollar difference between the losses incurred on the sale of those assets and the income earned by the FDIC on those "troubled" assets while they were awaiting disposition. The $117.7 million *net* asset-related loss acknowledged by the FDIC Statement turned out to be much smaller than many cynics assumed at the time of the government's seizure of Empire.

This observation is emphasized here because there was a common perception, fueled by media reports, that most of the touted $1.2 billion deficit was attributable to impaired loans and investments of greatly diminished value. The $117.7 million figure makes it abundantly clear that the government actually incurred a relatively "small" net loss by virtue of its liquidation of Empire's huge portfolios of loans and investments.

Most probably, the loss incurred on the assets sold by the FDIC would have been even less, had Empire's liquidation been scheduled and conducted differently. The government rushed to turn hard assets into cash and such haste proved costly. At the time of Empire's closure, the federal government was liquidating scores of institutions and selling tens of billions of dollars of assets. Given this glut of assets on the market, no savvy buyer was paying a reasonable price for the industry's entrails. Too often, the government was (once again) subsidizing investors' acquisitions of valuable, underpriced assets. This situation, of course, greatly inflated the loss reported on the sale of Empire's assets.

Actual transactions data were never reported by the FDIC, but the kind of negative impact that can result from an untimely liquidation – and from a sale of loans that takes place when interest rates are abnormally high – can be demonstrated by simulating a hypothetical liquidation sale. Let us assume, therefore, that Erie Savings Bank's $4.6 billion residential mortgage loan portfolio (which was subsumed by Empire in 1982) was sold in 1990 by the RTC at a price that would provide the buyer with the then-prevailing market yield, i.e. 13.54%. The yield actually being earned by Empire on those loans in 1990 was only 10.84%. (This below-average yield was attributable, in large part, to the lower-rate loans originated by the Erie County Savings Bank in the 1970s and early 1980s.)

In order to provide the buyer with a market rate of interest (i.e. 13.54%) on this bundle of loans, it can be reasonably postulated that the old $4.6 billion loan portfolio sold by Empire would warrant – in the then-current market – a price of only $3.5 billion. At this reduced value, the portfolio would throw off the kind of contemporary yield investors were demanding. Unfortunately, this essential discount would also create a $1.1 billion loss for the seller.

Of course, such a loss could have been totally avoided if the liquidation and sale had been deferred. (This example, once again, illustrates the government's folly in not allowing Empire to continue to operate in anticipation of lower interest rates.)

While interest rate data of record was used for the preceding illustrative analysis, no one really knows what kinds of prices the RTC was able to extract from buyers in the marketplaces that prevailed at that time. The example above is provided simply to illustrate that significant, unnecessary losses probably were incurred because of a rapid liquidation in a buyers' market where historically high interest rates prevailed.

To make matters worse, as realistic asset sales prices were understandably resisted by patient bidders who were keenly aware of the government's weak market position, the RTC decided to incentivize its selling process. In the course of liquidation, your author was told that one of Empire's former senior officers was retained by the RTC to develop an incentive program that rewarded contract liquidators not on the price they were able to achieve on the sale of an asset, but on how quickly that asset could be off-loaded... at any price.

The government's emphasis on the speed with which it disposed of assets – not the price that it was able to obtain for them – demonstrated that the primary goal set for federal liquidators was to get the "problem" behind them as quickly as possible, no matter the cost. To a well-financed, media-sensitive, bureaucratic government agency, money was apparently less important than time.

Another indicator of the costly consequences of such haste is the FDIC's reported loss of $83 million on Empire's "owned assets." At the close of business on December 31, 1988, Empire carried buildings and equipment on its books at a value – at cost – of $201 million; the depreciated value of these assets was $188 million. It is difficult to believe that the RTC's liquidation efforts garnered only $105 million for those properties.

At the time of its seizure, the bank also owned several dozen non-banking subsidiaries, almost all of them profitable. But included in the FDIC liquidation Statement was a $6.5 million net *loss* on "investment in subsidiaries." It is difficult to conceive how subsidiaries that had verifiable earnings of $33 million at the end of 1988 – and were showing a return on investment of 27% – had to be liquidated at a loss of over $6 million.

### Item three

Another very significant component of the total $1.2 billion loss reported in the FDIC Statement was occasioned by a $243.6 million liquidation *process* expense which included salaries, "indirect costs," travel, legal fees, and professional fees resulting from the administration of the liquidation. Shockingly, this expense – which resulted solely by virtue of an unnecessary liquidation – amounted to *twice* the net loss occurred on the sale of Empire's supposedly "troubled" assets. Absent the liquidation, this expense would never have been incurred by the government.

### Item four

Also included in the FDIC's $1.2 billion loss estimation was a nebulous item called "Non-cash Adjustments." This $163 million item was described as being "discovered liabilities" and was recorded as a "negative non-cash equity adjustment" which consisted of further "estimated" losses and the costs of "probable" litigation. Presumably, those not-yet-realized "potential" liabilities were to be converted to "actual" losses when certain events occurred. However, they were still carried on the FDIC estimate of total expenses/losses it reported in 1998... a full eight years after the liquidation process began. It is doubtful, therefore, that those expenses were ever realized.

Upon close examination of all of the above **Items**, it becomes apparent that the government *opted* to incur a loss of at least $1.2 billion in order to liquidate an operating institution whose only true, net loss exposure at the time was $117 million.

(It should be noted that your author recognizes that the use of words like "only" or "small" seems inappropriate and incongruous when discussing other peoples' money that is counted in millions. Be assured, I appreciate the significance of all of the big numbers cited in this book, and the terms "only," "small," and the like are used simply to portray relative or comparative dimensions; they are not employed as adjectives that describe significance.)

All of the costs cited in the above items were, in the final analysis, attributable to governmental actions in conjunction with liquidation... actions that would not have transpired if Empire had been allowed to continue to operate.

The preceding analyses of what *really* happened should encourage former Big E team members and shareholders to take great personal pride in in their valiant efforts to preserve and perpetuate a great and worthy institution.

Moreover, the accomplishments of the Big E team were attained despite protracted economic deterioration, a hurried liquidation, an imposition of severe regulatory mandates, the bank's assumption (over seven years) of $220 million of goodwill amortization, and the government's egregious disavowal of contracts that were critically important to Empire of America.

The vanquished Empire, *in reality*, had succeeded far beyond the expectations of the public, the press, and the government.

The government's single-minded desire to wipe-out any potential "embarrassment" or risks that *might* be attributed to its early-on deals with Empire – and to get the entire S&L "mess" behind it –caused it to unnecessarily incur hundreds of millions of dollars of loss and expense.

Of course, the FDIC never modified its assertion of a $1.2 billion "loss" resulting from the "failure" of Empire. While it continued to routinely refer to "Empire's failure," the *true* failure was a direct outgrowth of unwarranted intervention by the government.

In sum, the "rest of the story" presented in the foregoing analyses – even with the least favorable interpretation – strongly suggests that, from a cost point of view and when all things are considered, a *do nothing* approach which let Empire live would have been in the best interests of all.

Final score: Empire's team members *saved* taxpayers a total of $1.5 billion; the subsequent intervention by the government in Empire's affairs *cost* taxpayers $1.2 billion.

Go figure!

## Innocent victims

While the government never lamented any losses beyond those incurred by it, there were other victims of its financial follies.

- Empire's team members – many of whom were shareholders – lost income, suffered pension terminations, and incurred job-search and relocation angst and expense. It is reasonable to assume that some self-esteem – probably only a wee bit – was stolen from these proud warriors, too.
- Tens of millions of dollars were lost by Empire shareholders. From all appearances, they were considered mere collateral damage by a government fighting to reduce the risks that it had originally engendered.
- The bank's host communities – and the vendors, charitable organizations, and tax authorities within them – also lost "big time" as a consequence of the ill-conceived liquidation event. Banks like Empire and Goldome (a competing Buffalo savings bank that was seized shortly after Empire was confiscated) had been the promise of the future for Western New York. By the early 1980s, the region's steel, grain, power generation, and automobile industries were in decline and the only industries on an uptick locally were

computer technology and banking. Until January 1990, Buffalo had the opportunity to be a substantial home office – and back office – for the nation's banking industry. Ten years later, there was only one sizeable bank still headquartered in Buffalo.

The startling facts presented in the preceding paragraphs, I believe, validate my long-standing assertion that the liquidation of Empire was not only unnecessary... it made no financial – or practical – sense whatsoever. The calculations provided herein appear to put the lie to the government's portrayal of Empire as a hapless, hopeless institution that had created *potential* losses that could only be mitigated through a swift seizure and liquidation.

Indeed, your author's beliefs were confirmed in the early '90s, when interest rates began to decline and economic reality began to align with Empire's long-standing, post-merger projections. This turn of events strongly affirmed that the bank's workout would have, when all was said and done, gained the traction necessary to succeed... if only patience had supplanted panic.

(Since scant public data concerning Empire's liquidation is available, the information offered herein was culled from document searches, news reports, conversations with informed sources, and fragmentary government documents. The financial analyses are based on the data made available by the FDIC. It is possible – but not probable – that other, undisclosed transactions affected certain calculations and conclusions. For example, there has been no public report concerning the "premium" the government presumably received when it conveyed Empire deposits to commercial banks in 1990.)

*Chapter thirteen*

# VINDICATION

## The Supreme Court acts

Perhaps the most significant ex-post event that followed the seizure and dismemberment of Empire was the July 1996 decision of the Supreme Court which held that the federal government's actions – *and* the statutes that enabled them – in the matters that devastated Empire (and the plaintiff institutions in the case that resulted in this decision) *constituted a breach of contract.* This case appeared before the Court as a consequence of legal action taken by Glendale Federal Bank FSB, Winstar Corporation, and The Statesman Group, Inc., institutions that acquired failed thrifts in 1981, 1984, and 1988, respectively.

In essence, the Court held that, by seizing Empire and other institutions like it on the premise that goodwill and other financial assistance should no longer be considered in judging their viability, federal regulatory agencies, in effect, *breached the United States government's prior agreements with those institutions.* The Court recognized that those agreements were constructed as a means of inducing and enabling healthy institutions to acquire or otherwise assume the assets of failed thrifts in the early 1980s.

As was described in earlier Chapters, Empire had acquired thirteen failed thrifts along with goodwill in excess of $900 million. This goodwill, in combination with forbearances that the regulators contractually granted to Empire, became essential to the successful workout called for in the bank's Phoenix Plan. When these provisions of its contracts were no longer honored by the government, Empire became hopelessly insolvent and the disposition of its assets by the government to other financial institutions ensued.

With its 1996 decision, the Supreme Court acknowledged that the principal issue in this case was the enforceability of contracts between the federal government and participants in a regulated industry. The Court found that those contracts accorded their participants particular regulatory treatment in exchange for their assumption of liabilities which threatened to produce enormous claims against the Government as their insurer. Even though Congress subsequently changed the relevant law that had governed these contracts – and thereby barred the involved government apparatus from specifically honoring its agreements – the Supreme Court held that "the terms assigning the risk of regulatory change to the Government are enforceable, and that the Government is therefore liable in damages for breach."

The Court noted that "while the regulators had tried in the 1980s to mitigate the squeeze on the thrift industry generally through deregulation, the multitude of already failed savings and loans confronted FSLIC with deposit insurance liabilities that threatened to exhaust its insurance fund." According to the Court's decision, "Realizing that FSLIC lacked the funds to liquidate all of the failing thrifts, the Bank Board chose to avoid the insurance liability by encouraging healthy thrifts and outside investors to take over ailing institutions in a series of 'supervisory mergers.'"

"Such transactions, in which the acquiring parties assumed the obligations of thrifts with liabilities that far outstripped their assets, were not intrinsically attractive to healthy institutions; nor did FSLIC have sufficient cash to promote such acquisitions through direct subsidies alone, although cash contributions from FSLIC were often part of a transaction. Instead, the principal inducement for these supervisory mergers was an understanding that the acquisitions would be subject to a particular accounting treatment that would help the acquiring institutions meet their reserve capital requirements imposed by federal regulations."

The Court quoted M. Danny Wall, former Director of the Office of Thrift Supervision, who publicly acknowledged that acquirers of failing thrifts were allowed to use certain accounting methods "in lieu of [direct] federal financial assistance."

In its 1996 opinion, the Court further noted that "recognition of goodwill was essential to supervisory merger transactions of the type at issue in this case." Because FSLIC had insufficient funds to make up the difference between a failed thrift's liabilities and assets, the Bank Board had to offer a 'cash substitute' to induce a healthy thrift to assume a failed thrift's obligations."

The court cited former Bank Board Chairman Richard Pratt's previous testimony before Congress: "The Bank Board... did not have sufficient resources to close all insolvent institutions, [but] at the same time, it had to consolidate the industry, move weaker institutions into stronger hands, and do everything possible to minimize losses during the transition period. Goodwill was an indispensable tool in performing this task."

The Court further observed that "the impact of FIRREA's new capital requirements upon institutions that had acquired failed thrifts in exchange for supervisory goodwill was swift and severe. OTS promptly issued regulations implementing the new capital standards along with a bulletin noting that FIRREA 'eliminates [capital and accounting] forbearances' previously granted to certain thrifts. Office of Thrift Supervision (OTS) accordingly directed that '[all] savings associations presently operating with these forbearances ... should eliminate them in determining whether or not they comply with the new minimum regulatory capital standards.' *Ibid.* Despite the statute's limited exception intended to moderate transitional pains, many institutions immediately fell out of compliance with regulatory capital requirements, making them subject to seizure by thrift regulators."

## Background

After the passage of FIRREA, federal regulators seized and liquidated the Winstar and Statesman thrifts for failure to meet the new capital requirements. Although the Glendale thrift also fell out of regulatory capital compliance as a result of the new rules, it managed to avoid seizure through a massive private recapitalization.

Convinced that the Bank Board and FSLIC had promised them that the supervisory goodwill created in their merger transactions could be counted toward regulatory capital requirements, respondents each filed suit against the United States in the Court of Federal Claims, seeking monetary damages on both contractual and constitutional theories. That Court granted respondents' motions for partial summary judgment on contract liability, finding in each case that the Government had breached contractual obligations to permit respondents to count supervisory goodwill and capital credits toward their regulatory capital requirements.

In so holding, the Court of Federal Claims rejected two central defenses asserted by the Government. They were: 1) that the Government could not be held to a promise to refrain from exercising its regulatory authority in the future unless that promise was unmistakably clear in the contract; and 2) that the Government's alteration of the capital reserve requirements in FIRREA was a sovereign act that could not trigger contractual liability.

Not long after this decision, a divided panel of the Federal Circuit Court reversed it, holding that the parties did not allocate to the Government, in an unmistakably clear manner, the risk of a subsequent change in the regulatory capital requirements. The full Court, however, vacated this decision and agreed to rehear the case en banc. (In law, an "en banc" session is a session where a case is heard before all the judges of a court – in other words, before the entire bench – not just in front of panel selected from them.) After re-briefing and re-argument, the Court reversed the panel decision and affirmed the Court of Federal Claims' rulings on liability.

After much additional judicial consideration and many appeals by the federal government, the case was finally heard by the United States Supreme Court which rendered a decision in July 1996... more than six years after Empire's demise.

## The decision

The paragraphs below constitute a summary of the Court's ninety-six page decision which was abstracted and compiled by your author. It provides the findings in the matter of UNITED STATES, PETITIONER v. WINSTAR CORPORATION et al. ON WRIT OF CERTIORARI TO THE UNITED STATES COURT OF APPEALS FOR THE FEDERAL CIRCUIT [July 1, 1996]

Justice Souter announced the judgment of the Court and delivered an opinion, in which Justice Stevens and Justice Breyer join, and in which Justice O'Connor joins except as to Parts IV A and IV B.

The issue in this case is the enforceability of contracts between the Government and participants in a regulated industry, to accord them particular regulatory treatment in exchange for their assumption of liabilities that threatened to produce claims against the Government as insurer. Although Congress subsequently changed the relevant law, and thereby barred the Government from specifically honoring its agreements, we hold that the terms assigning the risk of regulatory change to the Government are enforceable, and that the Government is therefore liable in damages for breach.

As to each of the contracts before us, our agreement with the conclusions of the Court of Federal Claims and the Federal Circuit forecloses any defense of legal impossibility, for those courts found that the Bank Board resolutions, Forbearance Letters, and other documents setting forth the accounting treatment to be accorded supervisory goodwill generated by the transactions were not mere statements of then current regulatory policy, but in each instance were terms in an allocation of risk of regulatory change that was essential to the contract between the parties. Given that the parties went to considerable lengths in procuring necessary documents and drafting broad integration clauses to incorporate their terms into the contract itself, the Government's suggestion that the parties meant to say only that the regulatory treatment laid out in these documents would apply as an initial matter, subject to later change at the Government's election, is unconvincing. See *ibid.* It would, indeed, have been madness for respondents to have engaged in these transactions with no more protection than the Government's reading would have given them, for the very existence of their institutions would then have been in jeopardy from the moment their agreements were signed.

We affirm the Federal Circuit's ruling that the United States is liable to respondents for breach of contract. Because the Court of Federal Claims has not yet determined the appropriate measure or amount of damages in this case, we remand for further proceedings consistent with our opinion.

*It is so ordered.*

The 7-2 court ruling was a big victory for more than 120 institutions which, under agreements with the government, acquired ailing savings and loan associations only to see the government rescind the terms of the associated sale or merger contracts.

Unfortunately, Empire was not able to become a party to the case brought before the Supreme Court. When the action was initially commenced by Glendale Federal Bank, FSB, Winstar Corporation, and The Statesman Group, Empire no longer existed as an independent institution and, therefore, had no legal standing to pursue litigation against the federal government for damages. Even if Empire had survived long enough to bring an action, it would not have had sufficient financial resources to pursue it to conclusion. (In 1999, it was reported that Glendale had spent, over a period of ten years, approximately $100 million to gain $2 billion in recompense.)

After Empire's sudden seizure, its Board of Directors and officers had neither legal standing nor funds to bring an action on behalf of the bank. Of course, a suit could have been subsequently brought by individual Directors or shareholders but, as indicated above, the cost of *personally* prosecuting this kind of case would, most probably, have been beyond the means of anyone in Empire's camp.

Unfortunately, it was also impossible for a Director or shareholder to bring a follow-on action after the Glendale et. al. suit against the government had been decided by the Supreme Court. The statute of limitations that would have enabled such a proceeding had (conveniently for the government?) expired shortly before the Court's decision was handed down. Needless to say, other aggrieved parties were also foreclosed from suing the federal government after the Court's decision.

(The suspicion that the timing of the decision was concocted by the Supreme Court in concert with the Executive Branch or Congressional parties strains credulity, but the "coincidence" appears, to your author, to be significant enough to bear mention in these pages.)

In the end, Empire was left victorious but empty-handed. Nevertheless, as I had the opportunity to point out in a related newspaper interview, "This court decision vindicates the Buffalo ethic of working hard to make things turn out."

Later, in response to a follow-up article in the Buffalo News, I opined as follows:

"The Supreme Court decision finally and completely vindicated Empire of America's directors, managers, employees, professional advisors, and investors. While the government was found to be culpable, there never was any formal government finding of wrongdoing on the part of any Empire officer, employee, or Director despite numerous examinations and investigations.

"The demise of Empire was not occasioned by any capricious or deliberately inimical action on the part of any officer of Empire or by any representative of the government agencies that regulated it. The unfortunate chain of events that controlled Empire's fate emanated solely from poorly-crafted, ill-timed, panic-driven legislation that was roundly criticized by many knowledgeable authorities, including Congressman John LaFalce, a ranking member of the House Banking Committee. The <u>Financial Institutions Reform, Recovery and Enforcement Act of 1989</u> (FIRREA) was signed by President Bush on August 7, 1989.

"Empire of America had no legal basis for a cause of action against the government until a regulatory agency actually took, or threatened to take, adverse action against it. At the time of its seizure on January 24, 1990, Empire operated in accordance with contracts with agencies of the United States Government that guaranteed that adverse action would not be taken if the bank remained in compliance with their provisions. The bank's Board of Directors had a meeting scheduled for January 25, 1990 to discuss its options with respect to the management of its goodwill in light of the recently passed legislation. The government was aware of this meeting and precluded it by its surprise takeover of Empire the day before. The timing left the bank no opportunity to pursue legal action.

"The Court's decision finally established the government's responsibility for our unnecessary financial loss but it did not provide financial satisfaction for the former shareholders, employees or community beneficiaries of Empire."

Case closed! *Sort of.*

## The feds flip-flop

Ultimately, 120 savings institutions were entitled to damages as a consequence of the Supreme Court decision. It was estimated that, if all prevailed, the federal government would be on the hook for as much as $50 billion. The plaintiffs included heavyweights like Dime Bancorp, Long Island Bancorp, and California Federal Bank. Another was Glendale Federal Bank, an original plaintiff in the Supreme Court action. Glendale was seeking $2 billion in aggregate damages for the illegal impacts it suffered because of the enactment and implementation of FIRREA.

All of these victorious plaintiffs *sloooowly* learned that there is a big difference between winning and collecting, especially when Uncle Sam is the deadbeat. The defense had access to ample funds and was willing to use them mercilessly.

Glendale's claim was a good case in point. It lingered for three years until the U.S. Court of Federal Claims awarded it $909 million, which was less than half of what it sought.

As might be expected, the Justice Department quickly petitioned the United States Court of Appeals, Federal Circuit, in Washington DC. In February 2001, that Court returned the case to the Federal Claims Court for recalculation of damages.

This time around, the feds claimed that Glendale was only entitled to damages as a consequence of its "reliance" on government agreements, but was due nothing for its "restitution" claims. In essence, the court decided that, because interest rates overall declined since the breach of contract occurred in 1989, the "magic" wrought by a recovering economy during the 1989-2000 period "erased" the very *real* income and balance sheet damages incurred by Glendale in 1989 and 1990! Amazingly, lower interest rates made Glendale's injuries vanish... at least in the eyes of the government. Following this logic, the Court allowed a revised award of only $381 million.

This decision reflected a giant flip-flop in governmental thinking. In 1989, when Empire requested "open assistance" to buy time until interest rates declined, the FDIC decided that this did not constitute a "least cost solution." In the Glendale decision, the federal court acknowledged that, when it came to decimated balance sheet values, a decline in rates was *the* no-cost solution.

It took twelve years for the federal establishment to flip-flop and, in effect, "concede" that Empire's plan for an extended workout was, in reality, a prudent course of action. Unfortunately, we were denied an opportunity to enjoy the "magic."

(The Glendale case went back to the Supreme Court once again in 2005 but the Court failed to increase the $381 million award. Your author was unable find any public record of when – or if – "the check was in the mail.")

*Chapter fourteen*

## STRICTLY PERSONAL

### The Big E Team

There are no bounds to the appreciation I have for the work of my team members at Empire who formulated the strategy and implemented the critical tactics that enabled the bank to prevail time and time again during many challenging years.

Hopefully, the able, fearless, and noble efforts of the bank's team members during that time have been appropriately recounted and acclaimed in the pages of this book. Suffice to say, to describe their struggles as a seven-year-long Super Bowl game would be an understatement. I was truly privileged to witness their talent, dedication, selflessness, hard work, and unique personal contributions, which went far above and beyond those which any enterprise might ever hope to assemble.

They were stalwart and proud of the institutional custody they were given; they were ever-determined to preserve and perpetuate the ideals and goals of a most worthy institution.

While, at best, their glasses were only half full, they saw them as brimming. At all times, they could see – *taste* – a better future. Their time and energies were generously and selflessly dedicated to achieving it.

Their commitment to hard work – and play – afforded them unmatched, if not appropriately recognized, success.

Not one essential coach or key player left the team during the endless procession of tough games. As was fitting, our team members went on to other challenging and rewarding careers.

At organized gatherings and chance encounters over the years, I have often found one or more of these champions still chuckling at the memories, bristling at the misfortunes, savoring the accomplishments, and loving each other as only winning players can.

This book is dedicated to them. In fact, it is intended to be a *first* edition since I expect I will be receiving numerous corrections, modifications, criticisms, and additions to this story from them. I fully intend to publish a second edition that includes them all. This was a story that was lived by all; it is best told by all.

## Trustees and Directors

The Empire of America Board of Directors, which consisted primarily of former Trustees of the old Erie County Savings Bank, was totally immersed in the formulation and oversight of the policies designed to accomplish Empire's turnaround.

For over 130 years, a Board of Trustees set policy for the bank and oversaw its operations, providing both guidance and a sounding board for management. When Empire became a public company in 1986, the members of its Board of Trustees became Directors and took on the added, extremely important, responsibility of representing shareholder interests. Their advice and consent was especially critical during the turmoil of the bank's final years.

Through the Board of Directors' monthly meetings, Executive Committee meetings, and frequent assemblies of an array of functional committees of Directors, the members of our Board remained always vigilant with respect to Empire's evolving circumstances; they were intimately involved in all major efforts to enhance those conditions. Frequent informational mailings, in-depth reports at Board meetings by managers at all levels of the bank, special Board meetings, and comprehensive financial statements relating to each principal area of the bank and the bank as a whole, kept our Directors informed of the progress and problems of the bank, and gave them the basis for taking informed action.

Each Director gave willingly and generously of his or her time and talent.

The annual plans of the bank were carefully reviewed – and modified by Directors where appropriate – prior to their approval by the full Board and their implementation by management. These plans included considerable factual and financial detail that was assiduously discussed and deliberated with the members of Empire's management team.

Director participation in bank affairs was exemplary and their questions and concerns always received immediate response from the officers of the bank who were most familiar with the issues at hand. Directors had unrestrained access to any officer or employee of the bank and to the professional firms which served Empire. When a Director had a question, he or she asked it… and got an answer.

Members of the Board invested significantly in the stock of the bank at the time it was initially offered, thereby evidencing their confidence in the institution and signifying their willingness to see the bank's metamorphosis through to a successful conclusion.

Their confidence in the Big E is evidenced by a courageous and selfless act on their part as the bank was entering its most troubling period. In 1988, our Directors decided that, as representatives of our shareholders, they could not condone the exorbitant expense of "directors' and officers' liability insurance", i.e. D&O insurance.

This type of insurance policy, which was first marketed in the 1930s by Lloyd's of London, provides the officers and directors of public companies a measure of indemnification against financial claims that arise from litigation relating to their official acts. The chaos that prevailed in the thrift industry during this period provided a fertile field for recrimination and litigation. In many cases, lawsuits and regulatory enforcement actions levied heavy fines and penalties on thrift institution managers and Directors.

As might be expected, the enormous travails of the thrift industry caused the premium costs of such policies to escalate dramatically during the 1980s. Since our Board members were confident that neither they nor any of our management team members acted improperly, they concluded that the expense of this type of protection could no longer be justified.

Their selfless action in this regard was one of my most gratifying experiences during my service at the bank. I was awed by the fact that these individuals were willing to expose themselves personally in the pursuit of shareholder welfare. To me it was also a singular demonstration of confidence in the Empire team.

I have never before, nor since, had the opportunity to serve such an able, well-informed, well-intentioned, and industrious panel of policy formulators and decision makers.

All were true Gentlemen... except one.

She was a phenomenal Lady.


## Shareholders

Shareholders who tapped their purses to help Empire achieve its vision deserve especial recognition. They extended their financial and moral support in a difficult time for the thrift industry. Of course, the primary motivation of most was a healthy return on their investment. But, many also harbored a desire to see a local, revered, and well-serving institution thrive.

Their number was unusually large for a public company like Empire. Their individual investments, on average, were much less than those associated with typical public offerings. But those financial commitments were extremely important to our worthy mission. The personal investment losses they ultimately incurred were painful and, even more regrettably, unnecessary.

To this day, I appreciate more than I can express the personal and monetary support that our shareholders contributed to Empire's fight for survival and success.

**Regulators**

The nation's regulatory establishment played a determinative role in both the evolution and devolution of Empire.

Our regulators inherited, during the 1980s, the unenviable task of converting a legacy of poor legislation and inadequate public policy into – what everyone hoped would be – effective and judicious supervision of a critical industry.

The field personnel who manned the regulatory apparatus were, in my experience, sincere, hard-working professionals, dedicated to efficient execution of their responsibilities in accordance with prevailing policy. Certainly, the integrity of our regulators was never in question. The capable staff of the Federal Home Loan Bank – New York, as an example, was attuned to our situation and always responsive. Nevertheless, regulators were continuously inhibited by the conflicting agendas of members of Congress and the directors and staffs of the Federal Home Loan Bank Board, the FSLIC and FDIC. Acquisitive commercial bankers also contributed to the consternation.

The over-arching problem was that governmental policies frequently shifted or were subjected to varying interpretations, and this often put the implementers within our regulatory agencies into difficult circumstances. Unfortunately, in their desire to "do the right thing," they frequently issued conflicting or confusing guidance or direction. This also caused them to, all too often, remain non-committal or totally mum on important issues about which we needed input. Their reticence probably was due to the fact that they could not get firm direction themselves.

Of course, the representatives of the regulatory establishment and Empire's team members were driven by different motivations, and that sometimes put them at odds. The careers of the regulators depended upon supporting the risk-averse dogmata of *insurers* like the FSLIC and FDIC. The Big E's team members, on the other hand, were charged with the responsibility of accepting risks to achieve results that benefited shareholders and customers.

Our team members – and probably our regulators – were frequently frustrated by an elaborate bureaucracy which caused delays and deferred decisions. Not only were the regulations themselves complex but, given their origins, they were too often contradictory. Congress and the Administration were constantly critiquing and "second guessing" the regulators. Accordingly, every regulator's actions and pronouncements had to be carefully crafted to both implement the specific terminology of the regulation or statute *and* convey the prevailing intent of the policy-makers (who often behaved like proverbial "Monday morning quarterbacks").

In sum, most of the pejorative criticism of regulators that is levied in these pages is directed primarily to the Pooh-Bahs in Congress and to the regulatory *agencies* that existed to implement their will. As far as individual regulators "on the line" were concerned, there were simply too few of them… and, for too long, they were intimidated – some say harnessed – by Congressional meddlers; by the trade associations that represented the thrift industry; and, by financial institutions that competitors of thrifts.

Given the prevailing circumstances, recruitment and retention of experienced, motivated personnel was difficult. Too many of the field examiners and agency representatives had insufficient familiarity with the extremely sophisticated, sometimes esoteric lending, money management, and pricing tactics that had emerged, of necessity, within the industry.

Also, as the ranks of the regulators grew to match the burgeoning crisis in the industry, there was an influx of personnel who had less expertise and seasoning than the relatively small cadre of veterans that served the industry during the early years of the crisis.

Our regulators were caught up in the same vortex of anxiety-induced change as Empire. It triggered confusion and consternation that were compounded by the panicked top-level policy-makers who had, for too long, ignored the problem and avoided facing the music.

In the interests of market order and self-preservation, therefore, the regulators on the front line had no choice but to implement policies and procedures that were in opposition to the contracts and understandings that Empire had struggled to honor and to implement fruitfully.

The confusion and panic that mushroomed as the crisis worsened served to instigate even more ill-founded legislation, regulation, and enforcement, much of it designed to transfer the problem to somebody else's watch or to immerse it in bluster that produced "actions" that looked respectable to the public but were too weak, misguided, or self-serving to do any real good. The aura of misinformation and fear that the federal government created was not unlike that which was generated during the (Senator Joseph) "McCarthy era" of the 1950s when many innocent, law-abiding folks were deleteriously tarred with the same brush… a brush that was being simultaneously exploited to paint a picture of a righteous government.

## Our "representatives"

At the peak of the S&L crisis, many of our "comrades" in Congress were scurrying to blur lines of responsibility and to create, for themselves, images of virtuous statesmen who were working feverishly to stem a "growing crisis." Often, their self-righteousness morphed into desperate attempts at self-preservation and demands for aggressive regulatory intervention.

What pains me to this day is the meager support that Empire received from our solons at all levels in the markets we served. As cited earlier, Rep. John LaFalce, ranking Member of the House Financial Services Committee, promptly came to our aid and Rep. Henry Nowak offered the help he could. But most of our governmental representatives appeared detached and offered, at best, a few terse expressions of angst over Empire's plight.

As the '80s unfolded, it was apparent to the Big E team that, with the exception of Empire's Representatives in Erie County, most Congresspersons were doing little to gain a *true* appreciation of what was unfolding in the thrift industry. Apart from an inquiry in Texas, I am not aware of one instance in which members of Empire's management team anywhere in the country were approached by a federal or state legislator – or legislative staff member – and asked to explain the genesis or depth of our plight… or to suggest remedies for it. There were no inquiries about even the most basic of our problems or initiatives.

Most communication was a result of implorations initiated by us. Even when we (infrequently) received responses, they were often naïve and feeble. Typically, no tangible – or even moral – support was forthcoming.

This, perhaps, was to be expected since, for years, members of Congress habitually declined to entertain proposals for constructive action proffered by the thrift industry. It can be fairly assumed that part of this reluctance was due to pressure from special interest groups and a dread of appearing allied with "greedy, unworthy S&L moguls."

Further, there was little meaningful support or intervention forthcoming from local politicians and elected officials in our various markets. (Understandably, Buffalo's mayor was piqued by our decision to build a new national headquarters complex in Amherst, New York. He carried this grudge despite the fact that we did commit to keeping our Western York operations headquartered in the city at their then current employment levels.) I found the apathetic attitude of local officials disheartening because the communities and constituents they served were being directly harmed by Empire's diminishment.

Even on the rare occasions when it was successfully elicited, the support from our "representatives" was scant and guarded. One U.S. Senator from New York, with whom we had arranged a visit to seek support, had us wait in his anteroom while his staff checked our banks' – and their executives' – past histories of political contributions to his cause. Other political figures seemed oblivious to our plight as they continued to importune us to buy tickets or make donations in support of their personal interests.

Ironically, politicians, who today will go to the mat to create ten jobs, were uncommonly silent as thousands of positions were being lost. Part of this reluctance on the part of our supposed political "allies" was probably due to the trumpeted transgressions of the notorious "Keating Five," a group of US Senators – including John McCain – who fashioned a grand but flawed and futile bailout of a large savings and loan association that had dug itself into a deep hole. This peccadillo garnered a lot of negative – almost manic – press coverage and demonstrated to other potentially supportive political figures that the S&L debacle was a "tar baby" that they would do well to avoid.

Many of these recalcitrants had been our cheerleaders back in the "good old bad days" when the federal government had not yet mustered the funds to accomplish a resolution of troubled S&Ls by itself. But later, after Empire had made so much progress on its own, few political figures would even try to understand what we desperately needed in order to complete our mission. To your author, their disassociation appeared to be a result of convoluted reasoning. After all, for them, Empire's success would have been a big "win" that preserved jobs, tax revenue, and the viability of many vendors in the precincts they served. Conversely, the failure of Empire would have an extremely detrimental economic effect on their constituent communities.

As FIRREA loomed and continued to gain traction, concerns about its probable impact prompted Western New York Congressmen John LaFalce, Henry Nowak, and Bill Paxton to vote for legislation which would provide the kinds of capital standards that would allow banks like Empire to continue to operate notwithstanding the new statute. But their legitimate protestations were shrugged by their colleagues and belittled by the press.

To be sure, the plight of the thrift industry had presented Congress with an extremely complex bundle of conundrums. But, ironically, most of them had been occasioned by prior ham-handed federal laws and regulations that weren't really crafted to resolve issues but, rather, to curry favor with constituents and counter the implorations of lobbyists, the emotional pleas of self-appointed public advocates, and the criticism of the press.

In addition, politicians had historically been prone to accept faulty or unfounded criticisms as legitimate grievances. Unfortunately, that kind of uninformed input really didn't help our "representatives" to forge substantive policies that would lead to meaningful problem resolution in the thrift industry.

Our solons were under pressure from another front, too. For decades, legislators and regulators who had *any* dominion whatsoever over the thrift industry were constantly hectored by commercial bankers and their representatives seeking an edge in the financial marketplace. Indeed, from the time of the commercial banks' first "assault" on Erie in 1859 to the thrift industry's collapse in the 1990s, commercial bank interests took advantage of every opportunity to hobble or entirely extinguish thrift industry influence in their marketplaces. Their vehement opposition in 1974 to the authorization of checking accounts for savings banks was just one example.

Throughout the twentieth century, commercial banks worked diligently on both state and federal levels to eliminate competition from savings banks and savings and loan associations. By the late '80s, it was "carpe diem time" and they unabashedly pressed Congress and its regulatory apparatus to convey chunks of the industry to them or, at least, rid the marketplace of their irritating presence. In the final analysis, uber-aggressive lobbying by commercial bankers had much to do with the irresponsible diminution or eventual downfall of many worthy, long-serving American savings institutions.

What was especially distressing was the fact that most federal legislators didn't even appear to fully understand what they had wrought with the passage of FIRREA. Ironically, much of their perplexity was a result of iterations of poor legislation, regulation, re-regulation and second-guessing that they had fostered over previous years. Clarity was never a guiding principle in Congress. I can remember attending (as an observer, not a participant) Congressional mark-up sessions where bills concerning the savings industry were being drafted and re-drafted by Congresspersons and their aides. On numerous occasions I heard responsible, but harried, legislators raise questions about obscure or incomprehensible provisions being added to a putative bill, only to be hushed by equally harried but less responsible colleagues and staffers who wanted to move ahead in order to quickly quiet the din of dissatisfied constituents, lobbyists, and the press ... no matter how counterproductive the actual outcomes of their drafting efforts might be.

By the late 1980s, wariness, confusion – and, all too often, ignorance – were driving the mechanics of government at a critical time. It was apparent that, in the face of a rapidly-deteriorating financial environment, most political figures harbored an overpowering fear about re-election. None wanted to risk "death by electorate" for attempting to extinguish the flames of the thrift crisis when they could get along by simply by "fighting" the fire.

As a consequence, in just twenty-years, almost all of the thrift institutions in Western New York disappeared; thousands of jobs were lost: and community contributions and tax revenues were significantly diminished. The same outcome was suffered in our fourteen markets across the nation. And, there was nary a "peep" from our elected officials.

In mid-1989, the die was cast. In the opinions of many Members of Congress, their FIRREA "accomplishment" was THE "final solution" and the less they became involved in the thrift crisis thereafter, the better.

Later that year, the National Thrift & Mortgage News presented an insightful take on the matter. The newspaper opined that "Empire of America made only one substantial business mistake. It did business with the federal government."

In his book Why Government Fails So Often, Yale professor Peter Schuck observes: "the relationship between government's growing ambition and its endemic failure is rooted in an inescapable structural condition: officials' meager tools and limited understanding of the opaque, complex social world that they aim to manipulate." In reviewing the book for the <u>Wall Street Journal</u>, Yuval Eleven, the editor of <u>National Affairs</u>, expands on that criticism by stating: "Most initiatives – whether of the left, right, or center – are likely to fail, and politicians should contend with this fact by crafting policies as simple and incremental as possible. As Alexander Hamilton put it in <u>Federalist 70</u>, 'a government ill executed, whatever it may be in theory, must be in practice, a bad government.'"

**The press**

A large segment of the working press struggled valiantly to make sense of the thrift industry imbroglio and to convey an understanding of it to their clienteles. However, as the thrift meltdown threatened their incumbencies, too many career-minded members of the House and Senate and high-level bureaucrats in Washington spent a lot of time rallying the press to their "points of view." The most nefarious among them simply wanted to spin the story in a way that provided plenty of CYA opportunities.

As a consequence, numerous influential newshounds and commentators – most of whom were denizens of our nation's capital – complied with these entreaties and became "co-contributors" to the unnecessary trauma suffered by many savings institutions and their employees, communities, and investors. It appeared that those in this minority of the "fourth estate" didn't expend adequate effort to understand the realities evolving in the thrift industry. A great deal of their output was unnecessarily inflammatory, and a lot was outright wrong.

As a result, an enormous sense of futility engulfed those on the firing line in the savings industry who had to get up and do something practical and effective every day to protect their institutions.

As a former newspaper columnist with the <u>Buffalo News</u> and the daily trade paper <u>American Banker</u> – and as a radio commentator for more than a decade – I understood the problems the press encountered in providing clued-up coverage. They were under great pressure on many fronts. The "thrift crisis" was possibly the biggest "scandal" of the 1980s and publishers didn't want to spare the ink. Readers wanted "villains" identified in two paragraphs.

As far as journeyman reporters were concerned, so much was happening so rapidly and so unpredictably that it was extremely difficult to distill and present the savings industry news of the day in a manner that could diffuse, to any significant degree, the unwarranted prevailing hysteria.

In addition, too many of the responsible and intelligent journalists who were covering the story simply didn't have the experience, time, or resources necessary to enable them to adequately dissect and understand the complex issues – and the reactions to them – that were unfolding in the financial world. Too few reporters had first-hand familiarity with the way laws and regulations were cooked-up and served in Washington. Moreover, most had an insufficient understanding of either the history or present-day workings of savings institutions.

Both publishers and their publics were placing a premium on investigative reporting, and this emphasis prompted some over-worked print and broadcast reporters to create tenuous local "story-hooks" that mirrored the negative copy that was being generated on a national level.

Concurrently, many beleaguered, often naïve, managers of savings institutions became unintentional "co-conspirators." Most of them had never before been exposed to public scrutiny and they were disadvantaged by their inability to articulate their circumstances, the causes of them, and the potential cures for them. Too often, in their panic and bewilderment, they offered up patently specious defenses.

To complicate matters, some of the big-money gunslingers who had recently acquired stakes in the thrift industry were posturing to take advantage of a confused regulatory structure for the sake of short-term return on investment. Their self-serving exploitations contributed even further to the diminished image of the industry and prompted even more deleterious press coverage.

Unfortunately, a few prominent savings industry executives abetted this image with their braggadocio, false protestations, and penchants for opulent lifestyles.

All the while, readers, listeners, and viewers were clamoring for answers. They wanted simple explanations... and someone to blame. A blatant "bloodlust" emerged in many quarters of an otherwise fairly rational society. Much of this was probably triggered by a long-standing envy or downright dislike for the rich S&L "kingpins" who often had appeared to be depriving them of their due when it came to savings account interest, mortgage loans, or toaster count (yes, "premiums" were still being offered to savers who opened new accounts). Many otherwise good people actually appeared to be getting satisfaction from the travails of highfalutin' bankers, who, they probably believed, were vastly – and unjustifiably – more fortunate than they.

*Schadenfreude*, the Germanic self-serving mindset of finding solace in others' misfortune, enjoyed wide acceptance in this country in the twentieth century. It became even more prominent in the wake of the thrift industry collapse. This trait is the opposite of compassion, i.e. the feeling of sorrow for those less fortunate than you. In the context of schadenfreude, it is *happiness* that is derived from the misfortunes experienced by others. This indulgence typically derives from jealousy or a lack of self-esteem. No matter, because it contributed to an attitude that was duly-reported by columnists and pundits in their stream of stories about the industry.

Back in my early radio days, Paul Harvey, a distinguished news commentator and sometimes mentor to your author, sagely responded to my questions: "Why is so much of the daily news negative? Why don't more journalists focus on the positives?"

Mr. Harvey advised me in his singular, dulcet tone, "Young man, you have to realize that the fire that burns some, warms many." I guess it's the same reason that so many of us read the obituaries every day.

The devolution of the thrift industry attracted a torrent of press coverage and public attention. A frightening sense of alarm and anxiety enveloped the nation.

Its effects were acutely felt in the halls of Empire of America.

## Crony capitalists

Fragile by Design: The Political Origins of Banking Crises & Scarce Credit, a book by Charles W. Calomiris and Stephen H. Haber, documents the history of bank crises. In 2014, it was reviewed in Barron's Financial Magazine by Gene Epstein who observed:

> "Government has been known to distort normal market incentives of profit and loss in a whole range of different industries. But since banks, to steal a phrase from the notorious Willie Sutton, are where the money is, it is hardly surprising that politicians have had more involvement in this industry than in any others, as the authors amply demonstrate.

> "Their (the authors') approach runs counter to the conventional view that would have us assume that government's role in banking crises is at worst a sin of omission, but never of commission. According to this view, the banks get themselves into trouble through the irrational pursuit of profit, while government stands idly by, because either its leaders are ineffectual or they've been corrupted by the bankers. The possibility that government might have taken a proactive role in causing the problem, in a full-blown version of

crony capitalism, is not even considered, but gets strong confirmation in Fragile by Design."

Hints of crony capitalism attended the "bargain sale" of Empire to a number of larger banks across the nation, including Bank One, Barnett Bank, California Federal Bank, Comerica Bank, Key Bank, and Manufacturers & Traders Trust Co, (M&T Bank).

Some of the commercial banks that eagerly gobbled up our bank – and its very valuable market share – were the beneficiaries of what could easily be described as "sweetheart deals" designed for "cronies."

Of course, cronies are not always bad bankers. But, according to feedback received by your author, a few of these covetous banks had continually pressured regulators and legislators during the '80s to "do something" about Empire. They obviously saw grabbing market share as a "capitalistic" opportunity worth exploiting. Indeed, some of them repeated this gambit again with Goldome, another Buffalo savings bank.

As noted in earlier pages, the commercial bank industry lobbied relentlessly – for generations – for laws and regulations that would enfeeble savings institutions. They long coveted the relatively inexpensive (in their view) deposit funds that savings banks and savings and loan associations were able to accumulate.

For reasons that are difficult to comprehend, a vast segment of commercial bankers felt that savings institutions had been unfairly advantaged and did not "deserve" their enormous deposit accumulations and the depositor loyalty that facilitated them.

By and large, the commercial banks' persistent entreaties to hobble – perhaps to entirely extinguish – savings institutions were increasingly embraced by both federal and state regulators. The government alleged that intervention in this regard was warranted primarily to "preserve" the traditional role of thrifts in housing finance. The thrift industry debacle of the 1980s gave the appeals of commercial bankers' a patina of legitimacy and gave the government an excuse to move aggressively with respect to confiscation of individual savings institutions

M&T Bank, a Buffalo commercial bank, was the lead institution in the Empire and Goldome takeovers in Western New York. M&T controlled less than 20% of the region's deposit market prior to its acquisition of Empire of America. With its bargain acquisition of a huge chunk of Empire and a quick follow-on takeover of Goldome, M&T came to dominate more than one-third of the Buffalo area marketplace. With these and subsequent mergers, M&T doubled its size in the early '90s. (By 2014, M&T Bank had captured a 45.9% share of the Buffalo region's total deposit market.)

It's not surprising then that in 1991 – shortly after Empire's liquidation – Warren Buffet's Berkshire Corp. scooped up 40,000 shares of preferred stock in the holding company that owned M&T Bank. At the time, Mr. Buffett said he would convert the preferred shares to common shares which had risen significantly in price. By the end of 1992, the value of Berkshire's preferred stock investment had jumped 45% or $28 million (not counting dividends earned). Apparently, the entrails of the supposedly "valueless" Buffalo institutions liquidated by the government at enormous public cost did have great value to other advantaged investors.

The breakup and acquisition of Empire might have been on Mr. Buffett's radar for some time. Who knows? In my various meetings with him, he often asked questions that suggested a sincere skepticism with respect to the traditional savings institution business model. Perhaps I should have paid more attention to his widely circulated quote: "When management with a reputation for brilliance tackles a business with a reputation for bad economics, it is the reputation of the business that remains intact."

It's pretty apparent that, amidst the panic of the thrift "crisis," quite a few government-supervised liquidations were engineered to the benefit of the government's "cronies" in the commercial banking industry.

I have occasionally asked myself, "Could it be that the advantageous tipping point that Empire and Goldome provided M&T Bank in the early '90s triggered Berkshire's original stock purchase and its additional equity purchases in 1999 and 2000?

By 2014, Mr. Buffett's enterprise held approximately 6% of M&T's stock with a value of almost $700 million. If Empire did, in fact, trigger a tipping point, I took some consolation in seeing somebody, for once, take advantage of the government!

I had lunch with Warren six months before I left Empire. He wanted to know about our industry's plans for dealing with its implosion.

I should've asked him about his plans.

## Me

Needless to say, for me, the demise of Empire was a bitter pill to swallow. Banking had been an integral part of my life for fifty years. For almost half that time, I had dedicated myself to the welfare of the Big E, its customers, employees, and shareholders.

The personal disappointment and sense of loss I felt in the face of Empire's disintegration was almost overwhelming. In my mind, I knew I did all I could; in my heart, I felt I should have done more. But, when the federal government finally seized control of the Big E, I had to accept the fact that there was nothing further that I could do to enhance Empire of America's saga of success.

For years to come, this heartache would continue, often exacerbated by continuing inquiries and investigations into my personal life that were conducted to determine if there was any culpability on my part for Empire's downfall. During this frenetic period of industry devolvement, the federal government was seeking whatever funds it could in order to offset the enormous costs of its new FIRREA initiative. This included monies that could be derived as a consequence of legal action against former officers and employees of – and investors in – "failed" savings institutions. During the course of federal enquiries to this end, many well-meaning managers of thrifts had been ruined professionally and financially. Some even perished as a consequence.

Given the post-takeover scrutiny that was being afforded Empire, it was a foregone conclusion that I would eventually be a "target" of governmental probes. It became time to heed the 18th century observation of Voltaire: "It is dangerous to be right when the government is wrong."

After soliciting some advice from others in the industry who had suffered such attention, I came to the conclusion that legal representation was in order. I retained Buffalo counsel and one of our first orders of business was to visit with seasoned attorneys in several Washington law firms that specialized in defending "targets" in the thrift industry. By that point in time, such representation had become a big business in the legal community.

The attorneys we called on gave us very little hope for prevailing in (much less affording) a defense against the kinds of formal civil charges that were levied with increased frequency in the industry. (I never considered the possibility of criminal charges since my personal experiences and the results of past bank audits, examinations, and inquiries had never hinted at that kind of impropriety.) However, even the simple negligence charges that were then being widely leveled by the government against thrift officials were enough to bankrupt a person both financially and reputationally.

The Washington experts advised me to "negotiate" the best deal I could when the regulators came to my door. Experience had demonstrated, they said, that going to the mat with the government in court was folly. They opined that, on average, alleged thrift "perpetrators" were pre-negotiating settlements in amounts that averaged approximately 40% of their personal net worth. They claimed that this was a bargain in contrast to protracted judicial proceedings. Of course, the ultimate cost would depend on the government's abilities to assemble – perhaps create – grievances of consequence.

Given my familiarity with Empire's performance and my confidence in the integrity and ability of all the team members who served it, I concluded that my exposure was limited and wouldn't require rote acquiescence to a "settlement."

From time to time during the following months, I received disturbing feedback from colleagues still in government employ at Empire concerning the tenor of the regulatory inquiries that were being conducted. While not rising to the level of a "witch hunt," their investigations seemed to be vigorous, thorough, unrelenting and, in my opinion, structured to find almost *any* possible grounds for legal prosecution.

After two years had passed, attorneys for the Resolution Trust Corporation contacted me requesting any bank documents I possessed and all of my personal financial records for several years. They also indicated that I would be summoned to provide a deposition with respect to my role in Empire's affairs both before and during its rapid devolution. They indicated that a number of our Directors would also be "interviewed" and that financial records would be requested of them.

It took almost a month of dedicated effort to compile and present my records according to the attorneys' specifications.

My proposed deposition was even more problematical. A deposition is the out-of-court oral testimony of a witness that is reduced to writing for later use in court or for discovery purposes. Deposition testimony is taken orally, with an attorney asking questions and the deponent (the individual being questioned) answering while a court reporter or audio recorder (or sometimes both) records the testimony. Deposition testimony is generally taken under oath, and false comments in a deposition are considered perjurious.

The nature of this kind of inquiry troubled me since the information I could provide would be greatly constrained by the specific, and probably very narrow, questions asked by the examining attorney representing the government. This, I felt, would not allow me to present the "big picture" concerning the rise and fall of Empire. I believed that I would need an opportunity to illustrate *all* of the diligent work done by the Empire team and to fully describe the distressing conditions in which it labored. A comprehensive representation of circumstances, I believed, would be necessary to ensure that the government had a full understanding of any actions they might be questioning.

Accordingly, my attorney negotiated for an "interview session" wherein I could describe facts and circumstances that went beyond the specific questions asked of me. My responses would remain on point but would allow for enlightening elaboration. Of course, any testimony provided under such a framework could still be subject to a charge of perjury should it be found to be untruthful.

The examining attorney agreed, and the deposition date was set.

Since I could not take any formal documentation or records to the interview session, I spent several weeks contemplating and refreshing my mind about the circumstances of actions and events that I believed to be relevant.

Despite the personal risks entailed, this approach to the deposition provided me with an opportunity to expose the real causes of Empire's demise to the investigating attorneys to and introduce them to the challenges that they would face should they continue to pursue action against me or other officials of the bank.

I had a powerful story to tell, much of which has been recounted in the preceding pages of this book. I believed that the *complete* story of Empire's struggles constituted a potent defense, if not vindication.

Several years passed after the deposition and I had received no communications from the government. During that time, the statute of limitations had been extended to ensure that the government had ample opportunity to pursue legal action despite the slow pace of its proceedings.

Then I received a request for another interview by an attorney who had been retained by the Resolution Trust Corporation

(RTC) to make a final determination concerning any potential culpability on my part. This was not to be a formal deposition and, once again, it afforded me an opportunity to explain, in detail, Empire's posture and my responsibilities with respect to it. This interrogator seemed to really want to know what happened... and why.

Another year passed without a reply so I took it upon myself to personally call the attorney who had interviewed me to determine if the government planned follow-on action. He indicated that, in his opinion, it was improbable that the RTC would initiate further formal proceedings. I never received an official confirmation of this conclusion, but the absence of inquiries in the following years affirmed it to my satisfaction.

Needless to say, those years were a time of consternation and anxiety. They took a toll on my family, health, relationships, friendships, finances, and reputation.

My life circumstances were in constant doubt; my convictions were not.

Years later, a federal Commission subsequently investigated the reasons for the thrift debacle and determined that the vast majority of thrifts were honest and well-meaning in their attempts at self-resolution. As far as thrift managers were concerned, there were, as history substantiated, far fewer villains and "crooks" than originally believed. Nevertheless, many thrift officers were convicted, fined – and even imprisoned – as a consequence of protracted investigations following the industry's collapse.

Fortunately, to my knowledge, not one Empire team member was found blameworthy of any type of negligence or transgression as result of the comprehensive investigations that followed the bank seizure. It is what I expected; but it still gives me great satisfaction.

## Other bankers

The tribulations presented in earlier paragraphs constitute, in a manner, a warning to any bankers and shareholders who might be contemplating alliances or agreements with the government. To those souls, I offer the admonitions listed below.

- An innocent "date" with Uncle Sam doesn't preclude regulatory date rape. *Your* deal is not always *their* deal. Before signing on the dotted line, make sure you contemplate all of the alternative scenarios that might emerge down the line; craft appropriate contingency plans; and, prepare for vastly different tomorrows. On the banks of the Potomac, there is a history of changing the rules in midstream. In the wake of a "re-interpreted" deal, what is a prudent banking practice today could easily become a transgression tomorrow.

- Don't stumble. While the government's side of the deal will always be in flux, you will be expected to perform as per original agreement no matter how your circumstances might change. If you embarrass the other party to the deal, your side of the deal sandwich – and your institution – could quickly become toast.

- Your deal isn't the last one that will be made. New and different government "arrangements" with other institutions and investors could dramatically alter your relative prospects.

- Foul winds create fair-weather friends. Keep in mind that, while most of the *individual*, on-the-line regulators you consort with will, in all probability, be good, well-intentioned folk, they do not formulate, nor can they mitigate, the truly damaging policies that can afflict you. It is the convoluted, ever-changing, partisan, pandering, commonly-inapplicable policies that are forged by *groups* of powerful, insufficiently informed, and easily influenced people (THINK House, Senate, agencies, commissions, boards, "czarist" task forces, etc.) that will ruin your days. To make matters worse, policies tend to mutate as they move through Byzantine bureaucracies.

- Don't count on good ol' American "fairness" as a guiding principle. As I related in earlier pages, during the last months of my efforts to save our shop from the ravages of rapidly-evolving legislation, a senior government representative asked me a question for which I had no ready answer, to wit: "Where, Mr. Willax, is it written that things have to be fair?" I should have been more nimble on that occasion and cited a very relevant Calvin and Hobbes comic strip which offered a similar but more complete colloquy: *"The world isn't fair, Calvin."*
*"I know, Dad, but why isn't it ever unfair in my favor?"*

So, fellow bankers, if you hear the siren song *"C'mon down!"* from inside the beltway, be advised that the price might not be right.

In the parlance of Schwartzenegger-of-yore, *"Caveat emptor, baby!"*

## EPILOGUE

### A dark night turns bright

On the dark night of the day designated for the transfer of Empire's treasures to its eager acquirers, I drove to a parking lot across the street from our Transit Road branch in Amherst, New York. Through the large windows, in a setting illuminated by bright lights, I could see Empire team members, their successors, and their regulatory overseers scurrying to complete their parts of a transition that I worked so hard to forestall.

I remembered that this was the first branch that had been opened during my tenure with the Big E and I recalled the life-changing events at Empire that had occurred since then.

There were many past successes, but they were not being celebrated this evening. There was little to relish about today. There was no tomorrow to contemplate.

I was sad.

I was angry.

But, as I thought about the many Empire team members whose lives were changing, my concentration turned to the future. I began to look past their silhouettes and focused on the bright lights that enveloped them. I recalled, once again, how the true success of Empire was due to the spirits of these team members. It struck me that these spirits were not being extinguished. They were moving on... to new challenges, satisfactions, and rewards. The energies and abilities of those spirits would contribute to the welfare of other people, other institutions, and other communities.

Their collective spirit would be individualized and go on to do great things in many places.

I was proud.

I was gratified.

I moved on.

"Forsan et haec olim meminisse iuvabit" exclaims Vergil in the <u>Aeneid</u>, as he comments on the human spirit in the face of hardship. *"Someday, perhaps, the memory of even these things will be pleasant."*

## Déjà vu

The following is an excerpt from a <u>Wall Street Journal</u> editorial entitled "No Good Rescue Goes Unpunished," that was published on August 8, 2014:

> The U.S. Department of Justice aims to extract as much as $17 billion from Bank of America for the crime of taking problems off Washington's hands in 2008.
> Regulators were high-fiving when the bank bought Countrywide Financial and then Merrill Lynch during the crisis. But now Washington seems intent on making bank shareholders pay again for the problems that caused these firms to need a rescue in the first place. Come the next crisis, CEOs will know to run in the other direction when the government offers a deal on a failing firm. And when private capital flees, guess whose money will be used to prop up the banking system.
> In some earlier post-crisis settlements, the feds at least pretended that the cases were about making mortgage investors or borrowers whole. But the pending Bank of America settlement appears to consist largely of a penalty for alleged mortgage sins committed by the two failing companies the feds wanted the bank to buy, and in one case pressured it to buy.

In December 2013, more than thirty years after Empire's first deal with the federal government, the Reuters News Service reported the following:

> JPMorgan Chase & Co. sued the Federal Deposit Insurance Corporation in federal court on Tuesday, saying the agency owes it more than $1 billion in compensation for not assuming legal claims arising from

its acquisition of Washington Mutual's assets after its 2008 implosion.

JPMorgan bought Washington Mutual's banking operations in an FDIC-arranged deal at the height of the financial crisis, a little more than a week after Merrill Lynch agreed to sell itself to Bank of America Corp and Lehman Brothers filed for bankruptcy.

Under the terms of the deal, an FDIC receivership "broadly agreed to indemnify JPMC both for liabilities JPMC did not assume and for numerous other matters," the bank claimed in the 24-page lawsuit, filed in U.S. District Court for the District of Columbia.

"They are promises that the FDIC made to JPMC to induce JPMC to enter into the agreement when WMB failed in September 2008, in the largest bank failure in this nation's history," the lawsuit states.

The bank accused the FDIC of breach of contract and breach of the covenant of good faith and fair dealing, while seeking declaratory judgments that the agency is obligated to compensate the bank.

The lawsuit states that JPMorgan seeks to recover "substantially in excess of a billion dollars of indemnification," and that $2.75 billion of assets it says remain in the Washington Mutual receivership "should be sufficient" to satisfy its claims.

The bank claims it is entitled to compensation from settlement amounts it paid to Fannie Mae and Freddie Mac stemming from bad loans they bought from Washington Mutual, numerous lawsuits that allege that Washington Mutual misled investors in residential mortgage-backed securities, and claims by various state taxing authorities seeking to recover Washington Mutual tax obligations, among others.

JPMorgan, which had agreed to maintain Washington Mutual's documents, is also seeking compensation for costs incurred producing "many millions of pages" of documents in these and other cases, the lawsuit said.

In the oft-quoted words of baseball great Yogi Berra, it is *"Déjà vu all over again."*

# ACKNOWLEDGEMENTS

There are too few remaining pages to express adequate appreciation to the many people whose efforts enabled me to create this chronicle. However, some deserve special mention:

- My fellow team members at the Big E who worked to create the contributions, satisfactions, and excitement recounted in the previous pages.
- My dear wife, Shelley, who provided the understanding, support, encouragement – *and proofreading* – that enabled me to relate this saga.
- Thousands of shareholders who saw promise in Empire and made the commitment to help realize it.
- My many friends and colleagues who were there when I needed them. (You know who you are!)
- Dr. David Mason, whose book, <u>From Building and Loans to Bailouts,</u> contributed greatly to the historical overview of the thrift industry.
- Tom Hoffman, Pete King, Joe Mendelson, and Tom Bennett who collaborated with me on the compilation of <u>It Happened Here</u> and <u>One Hundred Twenty-five Years.</u>
- Bill Schreiber, the big E's unofficial historian for decades.
- The bank's many fact finders and number crunchers who helped me compile annual reports since 1967.
- Noah Webster for his dictionary; Peter Roget for his thesaurus; Winston Churchill for his opinion; George Bailey for his example.
- The staff of the FDIC for its scant but revealing records.
- My personal "rabbis" who helped me live the dreams and survive the nightmares recounted in this story: Dan Brown; Nancy Churchill; Mabel Elias; Doug Faucette; Leonard Graziplene; Maury Janeczko; Gerry Lippes; Austin Murphy; Beverly Polito; Dan Stoll; Sue Wardynski; Howard Yood; and Moot Sprague et. al.
- The makers of Motrin and Bombay Saphire.

## ABOUT THE AUTHOR

Paul Willax is an experienced, award-winning journalist who has "walked the walk" in businesses both large and small. His banking career began while in college when he was employed as a relief teller in a large commercial bank where his father had worked as a branch manager for fifty years. In his subsequent banking career, he rose through the ranks to become Chairman and Chief Executive Officer of the sixth-largest federal savings bank in the nation. In 1985, the bank was voted one of the twelve most innovative financial service companies in the world.

He is an experienced entrepreneur, business owner, corporate executive, and educator. During the past four decades, Paul has produced seventeen books and thousands of articles, columns, and media presentations for business owners, managers, and money-minders around the world. As an award-winning newspaper and broadcast journalist, a Distinguished Professor of Entrepreneurship, a member of MENSA, and a radio and television personality, he has inspired and enabled countless individuals with his insight and advice.

He's "gone for the gold" in everything he's done..... advancing from bank teller to CEO… from owner of the 75-year old Kazoo Co. – a business with less than $1 million in sales – to co-founder of a company that grew from scratch to over $40 billion in sales… from teaching assistant to Professor of Management… from student reporter to newspaper owner and award-winning, nationally-syndicated journalist… from ham radio operator to prize-winning broadcast reporter… from door-to-door salesman to top man in over two dozen successful corporations… from bookworm to author of acclaimed books… from Private to Major General in the military.

Dr. Willax has owned and operated successful businesses in a wide variety of industries beyond banking and financial services, including retail, automotive, publishing, broadcasting, computer technology, real estate, business brokerage, and audio and video production. He has been included on Forbes listing of "The Eight Hundred Most Powerful People in Corporate America."

**E-mail Paul at: *Willax@BrainFoodToGo.com***